Mental Health Public Policy in Global Context

Timothy Philip Fadgen

Mental Health Public Policy in Global Context

A Comparative Study of Policy Transfer in Samoa and Tonga

Springer

Timothy Philip Fadgen
University of Auckland
Auckland, New Zealand

ISBN 978-981-15-6478-9 ISBN 978-981-15-6479-6 (eBook)
https://doi.org/10.1007/978-981-15-6479-6

This Springer imprint is published by the registered company Springer Nature Singapore Pte Ltd.
The registered company address is: 152 Beach Road, #21-01/04 Gateway East, Singapore 189721, Singapore

Contents

List of Common Abbreviations

ABS	Australian Bureau of Statistics
ADB	Asian Development Bank
AGS	Archives of German Samoa
AusAID	Australian Agency for International Development
CRC	Convention on the Rights of the Child
CRPD-OP	Convention on the Rights of Persons with Disabilities & Optional Protocol
DALY	Disability Adjusted Life Year
DSM	Diagnostic and Statistical Manual of Mental Disorders
IBHR	International Bill of Human Rights
IGO	Intergovernmental Organisation
IO	International Organisation
JICA	Japan International Cooperation Agency
LAMIC	Low and Middle Income Country
LDC	Less Developed Countries
NCD	Non-communicable Disease
NGO	Non-governmental Organisation
NZAID	New Zealand Agency for International Development
PICs	Pacific Island Countries
PIMHnet	Pacific Island Mental Health Network
SBS	Samoa Bureau of Statistics
SLARD-MHB	Samoa Legislative Assembly Record of Debate on Metal Health Bill
SMoH	Samoa Ministry of Health
SNHS	Samoa National Health Service
SNZ	Statistics New Zealand
SPDR	Samoa Parliamentary Debate Record
SUNGO	Samoa Umbrella of Non-Government Organisations
TMoH	Tonga Ministry of Health
TTMH	Tupua Tamasese Meaole Hospital
UN	United Nations

UNDP	United Nations Development Program
UNFPA	United Nations Population Fund
UNICEF	United Nations International Children's Fund
USAID	United States Agency for International Development
VHPF	Victorian Health Promotion Foundation
WB	World Bank
WHO	World Health Organization
WHO-WPR	World Health Organization, Western Pacific Region
WTO	World Trade Organization

Chapter 1
Introduction

I will begin by telling you about two formative experiences that served as the catalyst for this book. Both occurred in 2008, when I was a young Assistant Attorney General in American Samoa. The first experience was not such a happy memory for a young lawyer: being called out in open court for your client's situation. I had recently been standing before a judge in an old United States Navy administration building serving as the primary territorial courthouse – an elegant old building that would later be damaged in the 2009 tsunami. My task that day was relatively straight-forward: to inform the court that the government was in the process of studying where to house individuals with mental illness then being detained in the Territorial Correctional Facility. With a dismissive wave of the hand the judge informed me that my oratorical skills might be put to better use at the Fono (the territorial legislature) than the courtroom. The only issue in the case, as far as the court was concerned, was whether the government's executive branch was developing a mental health policy to better deal with inmates with a mental disorder. The defendant then before the court, the reason for my presence on that day, had been held at the prison instead of in a hospital or similar facility to receive mental health treatment. While I assured the judge that a policy was, in fact, under development, the issue from the government's perspective was (in addition to the lamentable absence of a mental health policy) that there was simply no suitable place in the territory for an aggressive individual with a mental disorder to be treated. This was, of course, as I was curtly reminded, "our" problem to solve and I was promptly dispatched to continue work on the matter.

The second experience happened as a result of the first. I went to meet with the only psychiatrist then serving the American Samoa public, some 55,000 people, to discuss our predicament. The psychiatrist was not Samoan and had recently joined the staff at the Territorial hospital, the Lyndon Baines Johnson Tropical Medical Center. He oversaw a very small office that consisted of himself and a Samoan psychiatric nurse. The doctor spoke Fijian and English whilst the nurse and patients spoke Samoan and English. Upon my arrival for our meeting, I was asked to sit in a small threadbare waiting area adjacent to the doctor's consultation room. He was

T. P. Fadgen, *Mental Health Public Policy in Global Context*,
https://doi.org/10.1007/978-981-15-6479-6_1

just finishing with a patient and would be with me soon, I was told. As I sat there, I could hear the voices of the ongoing office visit through the paper-thin walls. The patient would discuss her symptoms, in Samoan. Then, the voice of the psychiatric nurse would be heard, translating into English the patient's words for the doctor, who would then reflect on the patient's comments and respond in English with his words translated to Samoan by the nurse. This exchange continued for some time in this manner. I reflected on just how complicated mental health treatment and policy development would be with such an apparent disconnect between medical and mental health expertise and cultural and linguistic contexts. And that included my experience in courtrooms and institutions for clients whose mental health struggles had brought them into jails and prisons rather than treatment programs. It seemed we were all approaching these issues, often with good intentions, but from very different points of views and patients, clients and their families would suffer many of the same delays and limitations I subsequently observed in the course of the policy research.

These experiences and the circumstances surrounding them served as the catalyst to this book. I came to the Pacific Islands as an attorney who had worked for several years on mental health and disability matters and was thus assigned to handle mental health issues. The process that ensued raised several troubling issues for me concerning the policy development process in American Samoa and, by extension, in other developing contexts. Firstly, there was no process in place for developing the needed policy; I was basically given *carte blanche* to develop a policy and had I elected to simply copy one *in toto* from elsewhere, this likely would have been accepted. This would have been, of course, an undesirable way to form public policy. A palagi lawyer, only a year in the territory, single-handedly crafting a far-reaching public policy about the government's approach to mental health for its people. Instead of this, I saw my role as a messenger and organizer, of sorts, to assemble the relevant governmental and nongovernmental stakeholders and arrange meetings to identify the goals and objectives for the policy. Given the judicially instigated need for this policy, the process focused on determining which department would ultimately bear responsibility for the care and custody of individuals subject to civil commitment orders. These orders are the primary judicial vehicle through which an individual posing a likelihood of harm to himself, herself or others lands in the care and custody of the state for detention and treatment.

During this process I instigated a review of other mental health policies throughout the world and found that neighbouring Samoa had adopted a mental health policy and law change only a few years prior. Inquiries were subsequently made to the World Health Organization (WHO) office in Apia, Samoa. It was at this juncture that I became aware of a rather large gulf between common understandings of mental health and existing law and policy models in Samoa that might well explain the seemingly general reluctance for policy actors to engage on this topic. However, by this time my plans to take up my doctoral study at the University of Auckland in New Zealand could no longer wait and once the mental health policy team was assembled, I departed the territory and the project was assigned to another assistant attorney general. I would later return to the study of mental health policy development in the Pacific first in my doctoral study at the University of Auckland, New Zealand and later for this book.

A few additional preliminary points are in order to properly introduce this research topic. In some ways, the motivation for this book is born of experience: as mentioned, my work as an attorney on mental health issues in the United States, American Samoa and later Samoa as a Fulbright fellow, introduced to me first-hand the many challenges involved in the movement and translation of public policies and laws across contexts. Others, notably Ethan Watters's influential book *Crazy Like Us* (2010), published near the beginning of the underlying research for this book, have clearly addressed the influence the United States has had over the global zeitgeist of mental disorders like eating disorders, to name just one of his examples. Building on my own experience on these matters in the Pacific, this book has a narrower mandate: it will engage in a comparative examination of mental health policy development in two independent Pacific Island nations: Samoa and Tonga. In order to allow for a cleaner, cross-national comparison of mental health laws and policies, American Samoa, a United States Territory, was not included in this study. The basis for this decision and justification of the case selection is discussed later in this chapter.

Such a broad consideration of governmental practice, including what might best be described as nonspecific government action, suggests arriving first at a definition of 'policy'. This book adopts Anderson's definition of policy 'as 'a purposive course of action followed by an actor or set of actors in dealing with a problem or matter of concern' (1984, p. 3). Anderson's definition permits the inclusion of a wide range of responses, formal and informal, to a perceived or actual issue thought to be within a government's capacity to manage. Given the policy contexts I expected to confront in my selected case studies of Samoa and Tonga, such as low coordination between frontline mental health practitioners and the central health bureaucracy, the selection of a broad-based, inclusive understanding of policy would permit the consideration of a wider range of government activities within the mental health realm. 'Mental health', as discussed in the next chapter, implicates a wide swath of often overlapping policy areas. The construction of the modern mental health system as promulgated by WHO, for instance, includes 'all the activities whose primary purpose is to promote, restore or maintain mental health' (Chisholm 2006, p. 2). Hence, a system can involve both nongovernmental as well as governmental activities such as laws, policies, programmes, as well as practices engaged in by government actors, whether or not in furtherance of a formal governmental policy or position.

Diane Stone and Stella Ladi (2015) have convincingly laid out the case for how public policy and administration scholarship has taken on a more global perspective in recent decades. Part of this stems from the fact that as our sophistication in problem identification has developed, there has been an increasing recognition of the cross-national character of many policy problems as well as responses to them. This has opened-up a new line of inquiry for policy scholars. They observe that other scholars are examining agenda-setting processes and monitoring and evaluation systems as part of the broadening of the 'policy cycle' to these new and emerging cross-national policy problems (2015, p. 11). Stone and Ladi's most prescient insight is their observation that "the practice of transnational administration and Global Public Policy often focuses on the outcomes and outputs of an international organisation but less on how its processes, that is, the internal rules, procedures and processes, along with civil servant expertise, organisational cultures and other stakeholders, shapes outputs" (2015, p. 12). In other words, as critics of the policy transfer framework have argued, there is often too great an emphasis on the positivist pursuit of identifying, categorising and describing attributes of the policy transfer process and insufficient emphasis placed on the normative development of the policy process itself and the interactions and historical influences that contribute to success or failure. This book is an attempt to focus on policy transfer as process and is not intended to evaluate the implementation of these policies in either Samoa or Tonga. These questions are left for others, specifically those in the policy arena in both countries; in other words, those best suited to understand the details of policy success or failure.

Samoa and Tonga were two nations whose policy and law contexts were and in many ways continue to be influenced by foreign powers. First, by colonial powers including Germany, Great Britain and later New Zealand in Samoa and Great Britain's indirect influence over Tonga all initially formally enabled by the Treaty of Berlin in 1890. Later, as will be explored throughout this book, both nations continued to experience external influence over its domestic policymaking process well into the twenty-first century with later modes of influence being exerted through international and regional organisations in addition to bilateral relationships and international development agendas. All of which implicate an additional body of research known as policy transfer. First identified in the 1990s by British political scientists, David Marsh and R.A.W. Rhodes, policy transfer study was proposed as way to systematize and organise the movement of public policies from place to place. As Chap. 3 explores in depth, policy transfer scholarship has evolved tremendously in the decades since to not only perform the positivist function of systematically organising actors, instruments and ideas of public policy to allow for analysis and comparison but to consider structuralist and post-structuralist concerns about how policies are mediated and translated in the transfer (and policy adoption) process.

At the same time, maintaining such a broad definition of public policy within comparative context runs the risk of lacking sufficient precision upon which to analyse the policy transfers here under examination. For instance, a mental health system might be argued to necessitate an equitable and just economic system in order to ensure mental wellbeing, though few would presently argue a state's responsibility extends to such a responsibility. Chisholm's definition succeeds however in avoiding the traditional medical-centred focus of mental health by recognising that mental health is something that should not be limited to only government involvement in medicine or therapy provision. Mental health might be promoted, restored or maintained through a myriad of governmental methods, such as adopting laws that promote a human rights ethos, balancing individual rights against community interests in ensuring public safety, and protecting the individual from self-harm. The mental health policy context is further developed in Chap. 2.

1.1 Situating the Book

This book is an examination of the historical processes that established mental health policies in Samoa and Tonga. My analysis of the mental health policy transfers in Samoa and Tonga is focused by three empirical enquiries. Firstly, I am interested in how international mental health best practices are localised or adapted, if at all, into indigenous policy contexts. In order to answer this empirical enquiry, this book will provide an in-depth examination of the international mental health policy artefacts, consisting mostly of international policy documents and agreements, to construct a global mental health policy context. I then review the policy instruments developed in Samoa and Tonga and compare them with international models to consider the extent of localisation of international best practices in this policy area. Related to this first question is a second concerning the conditions leading to successful policy transfer in Samoa and a rather incomplete transfer in Tonga. Thirdly, I am interested in the specific roles played by various policy actors in the transfer process and to understand their individual construction on mental health policy within their respective contexts. To this end, I ask what effect these individuals had on the mental health policy transfers into each of the examined cases.

This book provides an account of how key international mental health policy actors influenced the construction of mental health policy regimes in Samoa and Tonga that would not only reflect their impressions of mental health best practices but also a version particularly tailored to their construction of each nation's unique national context. This study is both important and timely to the current international policy context for several reasons. Firstly, mental health policy is a policy area that in recent decades has undergone a period of rapid proliferation throughout the developing world generally and in the Pacific in particular and no previous study has considered the forces behind this process or examined the process of policy transfer in this policy area. Secondly, this book contributes to a recently expanding body of policy transfer literature applied to non-Western nation-states. I argue, following Dolowitz and Marsh (1996), that policy transfer with its emphasis on 'small-N' case study research methods is not only well suited to the developing state context, which often lacks reliable data needed in larger quantitative studies, but also particularly useful to the mental health policy context. Scholars have referred to mental health 'exceptionalism' due to its implication of a number of overlapping policy areas and the high degree of community stigma attached to the policy area (see e.g. Rochefort 1997). This stigma will be seen to be a concern within Samoa and Tonga.

Thirdly, this book expands the policy transfer framework by incorporating the dimension of 'localisation' to consider the success or failure of policy transfer. I argue that policy transfer scholarship has been primarily interested in the movement of policies between advanced, industrial nations and has not fully considered the effects of different actors on different types of 'policy'. Studies have been made on law transfer and actors typically engaged in this type of policy transfer in developing nations but these have not clearly articulated the roles of key policy actors on the transfer of lower levels of policy transfer, including practice-level change. In this book I examine whether policy transfer scholarship is useful to tell us about the transfer of informal practices as well as formal transfer of legislation and policy. The concept of 'localisation', which is introduced in Chap. 3, offers some theoretical basis for assessing the contributions of such actors and for understanding under which circumstances transfers might be successful. This book tests several of these assertions to assess whether they apply to the mental health policy transfers in Samoa and Tonga over the past decade. Fourthly, this book provides an empirical application of historical institutionalism to two developing, non-Western nation states. I argue mental health policies are part of historical state health institutions. The dominant historical institutionalism perspective argues such institutions tend to require a 'punctuating' event to bring about change. I intend to examine these assertions in Samoa and Tonga and to see whether this type of change took place in these instances or whether instead change was more incremental in nature. Moreover, given the broad construction of policy adopted above, I ask whether change to different policy tiers can be understood as the result of both a punctuating event and incremental change, depending on the type of policy.

1.2 Why Samoa and Tonga?

Samoa and Tonga are two relatively small, upper-middle income countries with nearly homogenous Polynesian populations located in the Southern Pacific Ocean. Both countries have large, public health systems and similar population structures. Moreover, whilst Tonga is a Constitutional Monarchy, Samoa is a parliamentary republic, both with relatively stable party politics. This section will briefly consider these and several other variables relevant to a nation's mental health profile, discussed in greater detail in Chap. 2, but will include such key variables as: urbanisation, population and lifestyle attributes. Population statistics for Samoa and Tonga are maintained, to varying degrees by each government as well as several international agencies. The purpose of this section is to establish the similarities between these cases and to highlight several key variables relevant to each country's mental health profile to lay the foundation for comparison later in the book (Map 1.1).

1.2.1 Population Snapshot

Samoa is a collection of two major islands, Savaii and the more populous Upolu, home of the nation's capital Apia, as well as numerous smaller islands with a land area of approximately 1130 square miles. Samoa is roughly midway between New Zealand to its southwest and Hawai'i to its northeast. Tonga, often referred to as the 'Friendly Islands' due to the warm reception Captain Cook experienced when he arrived on Tongatapu in 1777, is located 1770 kilometres northeast of New Zealand,

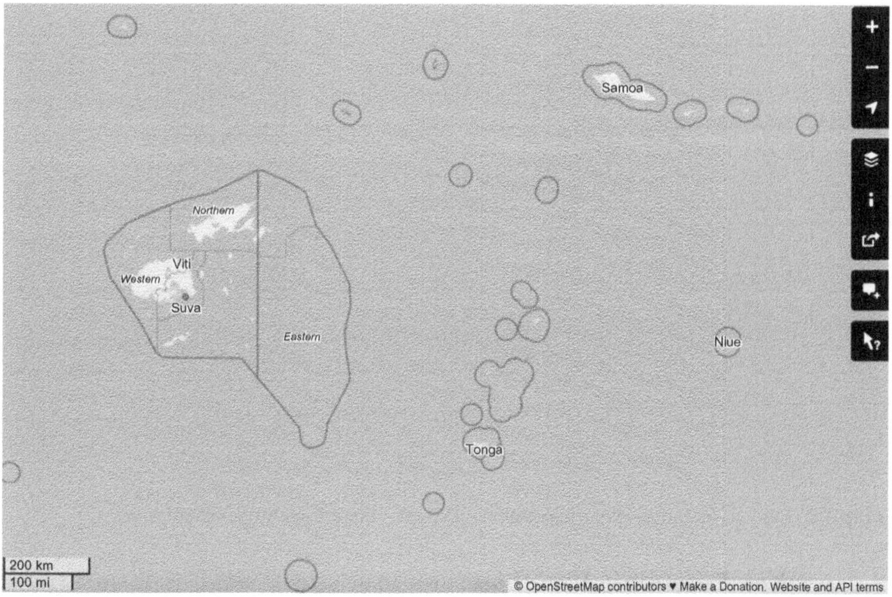

Map 1.1 Samoa and Kingdom of Tonga in relation to Fiji and Niue. (Source: https://www.openstreetmap.org/)

676 kilometres southeast of Fiji, 805 kilometres south of Samoa, and 5058 kilometres southwest of Hawai'i. The oral histories of Samoa and Tonga suggest the two peoples have had considerable contact with each other since at least the twelfth century (Lawson 1996). Tonga is an archipelago, the largest island of which is Tongatapu, a mere 256 square kilometres. The population is spread over 36 of Tonga's 160 islands which are divided between three groups: Tongatapu (the southern region and home of the nation's capital, Nuku'alofa); Ha 'apai (the central region); and Vava'u (the northern region).

Samoa's population of roughly 202,506 (Samoa Bureau of Statistics [SBS] 2020) is concentrated on two main islands and several smaller ones have a combined surface area of 2831 square miles. Over 76% of the population resides on the main island of Upolu with a further 52% of that population residing in the nation's capital city, Apia including the long stretch of 'suburbs' between the capitol and the airport (Samoa Bureau of Statistics [SBS] 2020). Samoa's population density is calculated at 71.5%, which includes an urban population of 18% (World Bank 2020). Tonga neighbours Samoa geographically and ethnically with a nearly homogenous Polynesian population of about 100,651 (Tonga Department of Statistics 2017). Nearly 23% of the population live in an urban area and is concentrated in Nuku'alofa (World Bank 2020). From 1996–2020, Samoa and Tonga's overall populations remained steady or tracked only slightly upwards due to a continuous, high net emigration. This trend has improved the ability of both nations' health systems to provide for its remaining population (Maps 1.2 and 1.3).

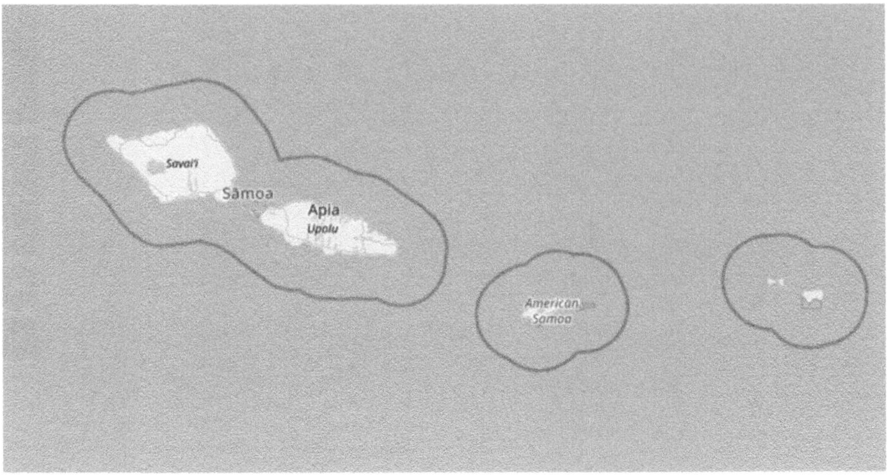

Map 1.2 Samoa, including American Samoa. (Source: https://www.openstreetmap.org/)

1.2.2 Key Economic Variables

The state of both national economies is a critical factor in constructing a national mental health profile. Samoa has a gross domestic product (GDP) of about US$4316 (World Bank 2020) per capita whilst Tonga has GDP per capita of US$4364 (World Bank 2020). The labour market in Tonga is still largely agriculture-based, though declining as an overall percentage of the labour force – 31.8% in 2003 – whereas industry comprised about 30.6% and services 37.6% (Tonga Statistics Department [TSD] 2012). Annual public expenditure on health amounts to only 4.2% of GDP (UNDP 2011) compared to 6.8% of GDP expended in Tonga (Somanathan 2010). The economy relies mostly on agriculture, tourism and significant remittances from the diaspora, not uncommon in the region. Samoa trades most heavily with Australia and New Zealand (UN 2011). While GDP is low compared to more developed countries, overall experiences associated with poverty, such as hunger, are relatively non-existent in Samoa and Tonga owing to the abundance of local food and the strong traditional governance structures which are described below.

1.2.3 Key Health Indicators

Several important health variables have become stabilized and have improved in recent decades, particularly from 2000–2018. Samoa has seen declining under-5 mortality rates (from 18 to 13.6 per 1000); increasing lifespan (from 69 to 73 years) and decreasing levels of infectious diseases and occurrence of epidemics (but increases in 'life-style' diseases), as well as steady birth rates, longer life

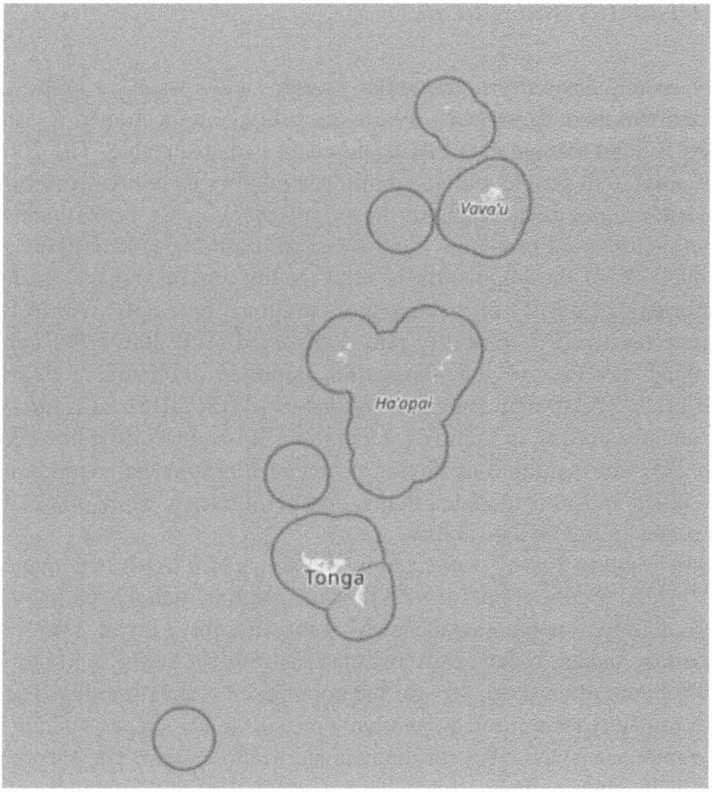

Map 1.3 Kingdom of Tonga. (Source: https://www.openstreetmap.org/)

expectancy (74.9/68.5 years for women/men 2005–2010) (UN 2011) and fewer people succumbing to epidemics (in 2006 the leading causes of death were diabetes hypertension [26%] and heart problems [14%]) and other infectious diseases. An ageing population, due to this epidemiological transition, gives rise to lifestyle diseases and mental conditions such as dementia which are associated with living longer lives. In addition, Samoa is also at high risk of recurring natural disasters. Tonga also witnessed increasingly positive health outcomes. Infectious diseases have largely been controlled. From 2000–2018 Tonga's infant mortality rates declined from 15 to 13.4 per 1000 live births (World Bank 2020). Tongans have a life expectancy of 71 years, up from 70 in 2000. Like Samoa, Tonga remained particularly vulnerable to natural disasters having implications for health and development. These are all circumstances increasing the long-term mental health burden in both countries.

1.2.4 Disability and Suicide

Disability, mental disability in particular, remains a key issue for both Samoa and Tonga's national medical services. While disability data for Samoa is collected by the Samoa Bureau of Statistics [SBS], this data is questionable. The 2006 census identified only 2096 people with disabilities, a number including deaf, blind, hearing and vision impairments, mental illness, speech/language impairments, autism, 'behavioural/emotional problems', and physical disabilities. This figure translates to little over 1% of the population in total having any disability – including the rather amorphous category of 'behavioural/emotional problems'. World Bank estimates suggest a 10–12% disability rate is expected (WB 2007). For comparison, New Zealand has 17% of the population identified as having a disability and Australia 17.7% (Australian Bureau of Statistics [ABS] 2018). This might suggest possible under-reporting in Samoa's population. It is noteworthy, however, that of the total, 28% are identified as having a mental illness or behavioural/emotional problem. When autism is included in this number it rises to nearly 40% of the total reported population with a disability.

A 2006 Disability Survey conducted by the Tonga Red Cross in conjunction with the New Zealand Aid Programme (NZAID) and other international partners identified only 2.8% of Tonga's population as having some disability (Taylor 2007, p. 8). This, as was seen in Samoa, is far below international estimates which would suggest a more likely figure of closer to 10% of the population with a disability. The low percentage of officially recognised population with a disability suggests a high degree of possible unmet needs and costs for the national health system. The survey cites two factors as likely contributing to this under-reporting. First, mild impairments, such as slight mobility difficulties, were excluded. Second, stigma associated with disability in Tonga likely contributed to under-self-identification. Only 5% of the total population identifying as having a disability designated mental illness as the cause of disability. The report went on to observe that individuals with mental illness were amongst the most likely to suffer social isolation as measured by non-involvement in village or church social activities (Taylor 2007, p. 44).

Related to the issue of disability, particularly mental health concerns, and of continued concern over the same period, has been the incidence of suicide (see e.g. Bourke 2001; Bowles 1995; Macpherson and Macpherson 1987; Zinn 1995; and Eddleston and Phillips 2004). According to the Samoa Ministry of Health (SMoH) statistics for the period 1999–2004, there were 163 suicide attempts with 76 resulting in death and, of these, 38 were due to the victim ingesting Paraquat, a restricted, highly toxic herbicide used in farming. These figures yield a yearly average of 33 attempts and 15.2 deaths – a rate of more than 47%. These suicides mostly involved males less than 29 years of age. In response to this rash of suicides the Samoan government moved through legislation to restrict the sale of Paraquat in the country (see e.g. *Samoa Observer* 2001). Accurate suicide statistics are similarly difficult to locate for Tonga. There is a very strong social stigma associated with suicide and this likely influences both the accuracy of existing data as well as the availability of such information outside of the nation's urban areas. The most recent study of suicide in Tonga was brief and written in 1998. Vivili et al. (1999) observed an average of three suicides per annum from 1982–1997 (1998, p. 211). Males were the most likely to commit suicide and over 90% of those committing suicide were under the age of 14. This study observed a possible link between suicide in Tonga and the spread of mass media and technology. Unfortunately data concerning how prolific information technology is in Tonga is non-existent and hence this claim is difficult to quantify.

1.2.5 Cultural Beliefs

As discussed later in this book, both nations have substantially similar ethnographic makeup centred on shared cultural beliefs and views towards mental health, such as substantially similar folk-level belief in supernatural origins for many common mental disorders such as schizophrenia. In addition, both nations came into contact with European knowledge on mental health and the role of the state in managing mental health in the eighteenth and nineteenth centuries, with most policymaking done during the twentieth century. These facts suggest both a common indigenous cultural context for mental health as well as confrontation of similar European motifs from at least the early twentieth century, with the United Kingdom's influence felt in Tonga and that of the former British colony New Zealand in Samoa following annexation from Germany. These experiences created similar legal contexts for mental health policy, as was explored above and will be discussed below. These data suggest Samoa and Tonga are substantially similar cases on several grounds.

1.2.6 Government

Samoa and Tonga are also most similar systems in terms of their institutional composition, with come important caveats. Firstly, whilst Tonga is a constitutional monarchy and Samoa a parliamentary democracy, both states have, in practice, endured long periods of essentially single-party rule. This stability, punctuated by episodes of political upheaval, has resulted in similar institutional change patterns. In Samoa, upheaval occurred during the late 1980s resulting in universal suffrage, whilst eligibility restrictions for seats in parliament restricting candidacy to *matai* (chiefly) titleholders persisted. In Tonga, by contrast, constitutional reforms have been episodic but did not lead to diminished monarchical authority until 2010. Until this time there had been a gradual increase in the role of non-nobles in managing government affairs. This transition very much remains a work in progress in Tonga. The judiciary in both countries is founded on the British model of judicial independence yet subservience to the legislative branch. As such, in both countries the judiciary has not been the vehicle for change as in other strong judiciary leaning systems, such as the US context suggested in Chap. 2.

1.2.7 Health Systems

Health ministries in both countries have also tended to follow similar trajectories. Both systems have their origins in interactions with European powers. Samoa's first hospital and health system was a German colonial introduction continued by New Zealand and independent Samoa's government. Similarly, British missionary and governmental intervention heavily influenced Tonga's health system. Both health systems maintained links with European and international partners throughout the course of the twentieth century and continue to do so in the twenty-first. Policy and law have persisted in being heavily influenced by cosmopolitan legal regimes. The study of these cases seeks to address Marsh and Sharman's (2009) critique of policy transfer scholarship being overly European and North American in case selection. In addition, the small-N sample and relative unreliability of certain key mental health data (e.g. disability, mental disorder prevalence and suicide data) in both countries suggest the policy transfer research approach is appropriate in this study (Dolowitz and Marsh 1996). As one species of this analysis, the mental health policies at study in this book tend to confirm this general point, as will be discussed below.

In addition, Samoa and Tonga both have universal public health services, though there has been some movement in recent years as part of health sector reforms to a shift for fee-for service model. Mental health services in Samoa are managed by the Samoa National Health Service (SNHS) with policy coordination originating with SMoH. These functions, both previously handled by the SMoH, were separated by the structural reforms undertaken in 2006. SMoH maintains regulatory oversight of the health sector as well as other related responsibilities whilst the newly established SNHS is the government division providing health care services and accounts for over 80% of the public sector health budget, management of which has shifted to the Ministry of Finance. Tonga's health system is administered by the Ministry of Health (MoH). Health services operate through a diffuse network consisting of 4 hospitals, 14 health centres, and 34 reproductive health clinics. Overall, physical health system inputs in Tonga, measured in terms of doctors as well as hospital beds per capita, are high compared to its regional peers (Somanathan 2010). The private sector is a relatively minor actor in Tonga and consists of non-governmental organisations (NGOs) and some government doctors maintaining private practices (Somanathan 2010). In short, while the NGO sector role is increasing, most of Tonga's medical service remains a government responsibility.

1.2.8 Section Summary

This brief profile of Samoa and Tonga is suggestive of two nations sharing many attributes. Both nations are lower- to middle-income and have undergone the epidemiologic transition marked by the control of infectious disease and the onset of NCDs, which as discussed in Chap. 2, such rise of NCDs is strongly associated with mental illness. Moreover, with a population increasingly living longer, age-related mental diseases such as dementia become more common. These neurological disorders are often treated through national health systems. Urbanisation and the social disruption caused through out-migration are further social factors contributing to mental illness and its resulting strain on the health system.

1.3 The Pacific Research Context

In her seminal book *Decolonizing Methodologies* (2012), Linda Tuhiwai Smith argues that the process of research inherently involves biases between subject and object. Research on indigenous cultures, no matter how benevolent the intent, involves an aspect of taking from those cultures. Moreover, Tuhiwai-Smith argues that the process of research has developed within a historical context of oppression and inequality whereby indigenous peoples are not looked to as providers of insight in their own right; they are rather looked at through the interpretive and cognitive processes of Western methodologies. These insights informed the underlying research for this book. At various points, primarily in the latter chapters of this book, reference is made to the many government, nongovernment – both local and international, officials and experts interviewed as part of the research for this book. Open-ended questions designed to elicit a narrative from the individual respondents and which sought their individual understandings of 'mental health' were developed in order to focus respondents on the topic of mental health policy but not to influence their subjective responses. From these individual responses, patterns or themes were identified to help construct 'mental health' as understood by the policy actors in each nation, which could then be compared and contrasted with other policy artefacts, such as official policy and law documents as well as ostensibly foundational sources from international documentary sources.

Kabini Sanga (2004) argues that Pacific research must be performed within its own 'philosophical orientation' in order to contain the dual qualities of 'confidence and credibility'. Sanga argues that the Pacific notion of time is an integral aspect of relationships, along with 'space, the self and self-image and attitudes towards others' (2004, p. 43). In terms of ontology, the author argues that the indigenous Pacific research assumption is that social phenomena are 'intangible, soft and internal to people's cognition'. Pacific epistemology 'assumes that knowledge is relativist and inseparable from the context of social realities of Pacific peoples' (2004, pp. 44–45). Finally, Sanga (2004) notes an 'axiological' dimension to Pacific research, whereby the Pacific attitude is that it is 'value-bound' and subject to researcher influence and potential bias. In terms of methodology, indigenous Pacific research methods should be designed to understand the individual and collective contexts examined through actively seeking out insider participation in the research project. Such inclusion will permit a more fully developed context (Sanga 2004). In addition, Sanga considered previous research that had emphasised the need for Samoan-based research to take into account the dynamic between respondent and researcher. The process should be more interactive in the sense that respondents can contribute information outside of the questions' scope.

These insights informed the research methodology of this book. Insiders are not the only ones critical to this perspective; so are those other stakeholders that might seem peripheral from an official standpoint, e.g. those community members that inform the process but are not, at least in the policymaking process, necessarily insiders per se. Furthermore, informed by Sanga's insights, the technique selected in this book involved semi-structured interviews containing several open-ended questions, including a final question to all participants asking them to suggest (and answer) any questions they feel should've been asked by the interviewer but were not.

In terms of data gathering, Tipene Filipo urged a culturally appropriate research approach when seeking input from Pacific peoples (2004, p. 180). He employs in the Samoan context the concept of *fa'a'aloalo* (respect) in respondent interaction in an effort to establish rapport with participants. There is also the need to demonstrate a cultural sensitivity to such relationships as those one has with one's elders ('showing humility and respect in terms of rank') and the related cultural practice of *tautua* (service) to demonstrate thankfulness and appreciation (Filipo 2004, p. 180). These principles, and their Tongan analogues, informed the field research in this book. Seating oneself before speaking and allowing respondents, particularly elders, to fully explain themselves with little interruption, at times resulted in longer sessions, but was abided in order to demonstrate *fa'a'aloalo*. In addition, respondents often asked for copies of laws or policies that he or she did not have, but were interested in obtaining, and I was more than happy to oblige as a reflection of *tautua*. In addition, the practice of *meaalofa*, or the giving of small gifts by the investigator to the interviewee following a session was followed (Phillips 2004).

Baba et al.'s (2004) work on research methods involving specifically Pacific and indigenous peoples also informs the present study. Mahina's (2004) chapter on 'Issues and Challenges in Pacific Research' highlights the pitfalls for both 'insider researchers' – those coming from and studying within a culture who are equipped with standard research training – and 'outsider researchers' – those who have endured a process of Western education and acculturation 'when learning about cultures other than their own' (2004, p. 191). While I had worked as a legal practitioner in a Pacific culture prior to taking up my doctoral research, I am an 'outsider' to the cultures studied but not necessarily to the predominant mental health policies and framings at the heart of this research. In order to better manage the risks associated with the 'cultural relativism-ethnocentrism dialectics' the above studies suggest might be embedded within such research, particularly in light of my cultural outsider status, great care was taken with the research design and process. In order to limit the possibility of these elements tainting the research process, I carefully crafted the interview questions to avoid any preconceived notions about the respective cultures or cultural framings of mental health and relied solely on the international literature to frame the substantive questions concerning mental health and the policy process generally. The open-endedness of the questions tended to elicit responses that provided rich detail about each culture's indigenous perspective on mental health and its cultural milieu.

In sum, in following a qualitative, historical research approach within two Pacific cultural contexts great care has been taken in both the research design and subsequent data analysis not to implicate judgment on the traditional mental health discourses other than to examine the constructions of mental health by policy actors in both nation-states and their understandings of their respective population's understandings of 'mental health' and 'mental illness'. No judgment on the appropriateness of the construction of both mental health and mental illness as a category of the human experience within its cultural context has been made. The focus is on process; the respective roles played by indigenous and international actors in the creation of the mental health systems in both Samoa and Tonga since contact with European nations. With this context in mind, we shall next examine the research approach informed by this context.

1.4 Book Outline

This book is divided into two parts. Part I consists of Chaps. 1, 2, 3 and 4 and establishes the theoretical foundation for the cases studies and analysis presented in Part II (Chaps. 5, 6, 7, and 8). Following this introduction, Chap. 2 presents an overview of the historical development and current context of mental health policy in what I label here as the "policy core": the regions of North America and Western Europe. Bound up in this discussion is a consideration of the scholarship surrounding mental health as policy problem in these core countries and the reasons for policy changes over time. Mental health will be seen to be reliant on the social context containing a cultural component which situates it within the constellation of domestic policy problems and institutions. Given the underlying ideological assumptions in core countries, particularly those concerning the welfare state and the state's traditional role in ensuring public safety in an environment conducive to maintaining mental health, the state's enduring centrality in mental health policy is explored.

Chapter 2 begins our look at mental health as a comprehensive policy area implicating numerous state institutions from hospitals, prisons and social welfare apparatus. Given this comprehensive policy milieu, I propose to use 'mental health policy' as a form of metapolicy framework. This rubric draws together various strands of policy constructions (e.g. human rights; state police powers; medical; social welfare; state versus private sector care provision) into one mediated construct packaged and promoted as 'best practice'. Given these overlapping institutional arrangements including the affected epistemic and professional networks working within these formal institutions, an outline of institutional theory with particular focus on historical institutionalism is presented. Insights from historical institutionalism will be seen to include the enduring legacies of institutional creation and their stubborn nature even in the face of change. The mental hygiene movement, which developed in Western Europe and North America in the early years of the twentieth century, would have profound institutional impacts upon recently colonised nations and those reaching independence in the mid-twentieth century. Its underlying ideology of profound belief in state control over the mentally ill became core to the mental health institutions established in these nations, including Samoa and Tonga, which shaped official institutional responses to mental disorder into the twenty-first century.

Building on the insights offered by historical institutionalism and mental health policy scholarship, I argue that in order to effectively study mental health policies in borrowing or transferee nations, one must examine how policies move from place to place within their specific historical contexts. Institutions established in non-originating cultures as part of decolonisation or other related event must be examined with reference to that context. Similarly, such transfers of policy easily lend themselves to historical analysis since the existence of the state as well as an implicated policy can be fixed in time.

Chapter 3 introduces the policy transfer framework as a tool to study the movement of mental health policies to Samoa and Tonga. This chapter sets out to accomplish two broad objectives in relation to situating the book within policy transfer scholarship. Firstly, I review the policy transfer literature with a particular focus on gaps in the current literature, such as the European and North American focus of the literature and its emergent application to examine localisation processes in non-Western nation-states as well as in considering the mental health policy domain. Secondly, I present Dolwoitz and Marsh's (1996) policy transfer framework which is then applied in the remaining chapters of this book. In essence, the utility of the policy transfer framework is in its ability to comprehensively account for a number of variables influencing policy transfer analysis. By providing a template to guide research on any issue of transplanted public policy it ensures an intellectual consistency and rigour across cases. At the same time, by not being overly descriptive of a wide range of sub-variables it also allows significant flexibility for case-by-case differences that add to the body of knowledge in this growing area of scholarship.

From this analysis, I propose to determine whether the existing literature is adequate for fully explaining the policy transfer process or whether further inquiry or theoretical development is required. From these broad aims, several specific questions emerge. Following Dolowitz and Marsh (2000), I am primarily interested in identifying the scope for the transfer event or events and asking whether different policy actors become engaged in the transfer process at different process points. As such, the next step in analysing the transfer process is to identify the relevant actors and texts forming the international mental health policy context. I identify who is involved in mental health policy development and proliferation and how they are involved in the policy transfer process. I am also interested in investigating whether these different transfer agents engage in different types of transfer (e.g. statutes, written policies, practices engaged in by policy actors), what these processes look like, and what influences them. In order to examine these overarching research questions, I examine how mental health policy has developed in Samoa and Tonga over time. I also explore whether mental health policy and practice is similar or different in Samoa and Tonga and what might account for the similarities or differences.

Chapter 4 serves as a transition between the Part I of this book which discusses the substantive context for mental health policy and Part II which explores the movement of mental health from the global policy context to that of Samoa and Tonga. The elevation of mental health to the international health agenda was brought about by the recognition of the enormous costs mental disorders imposed upon national health systems. This recognition emerged out of a neoliberal fiscal policy emphasis within health policy and planning advanced by World Bank. This neoliberal emphasis found a ready partner in the form of human rights discourses for the mentally ill advanced, for example, in United Nations agencies. The convergence of these two constructions advanced the mental health agenda where a human rights framing alone had failed to effectively influence policy and law prior to neoliberal health system reform being firmly entrenched in the international policy agenda. This is established by the fact that in both Samoa and Tonga local commentators from the 1960s onwards have recognised the human rights implications of the treatment of the mentally ill yet these attitudes failed to materialise into either policy or law innovations in either nation.

Organisational overlap between World Bank and WHO in promoting global mental health policy is also explored in Chap. 4. World Bank, through working with development partners, will be seen to have been critical in shifting the focusing from the Organisation of Economic Co-Operation and Development (OECD) to the developing nation's policy context. Over the course of the 1990s and early 2000s World Bank was actively engaged in producing reports and promoting programmes designed to facilitate health sector reform in developing states. WHO will be seen to have long been engaged in global health matters and to that end has been involved in mental health policy and service best practice proliferation for many decades. There has therefore been convergence of these two groups with World Bank's emphasis on economic and fiscal matters related to controlling health costs and encouraging government efficiency and WHO's health-services focus on mental health, particularly its adoption of the increasingly human rights-oriented mental health framework steadily developed in international instruments since the 1970s.

The activities of these two large IOs will be seen to provide the impetus for regional efforts in the Pacific to reform health care and, by implication, mental health systems through policy innovation. Regional development partners have also been involved in these efforts. The Australian Agency for International Development (AusAID) and the New Zealand Aid Programme (NZAID) have long had a presence in Pacific Island Countries (PICs), maintain diplomatic missions in these countries, and have historically had large populations of Samoans and Tongans residing in their respective nation-states. As will be seen, AusAID's involvement in mental health reforms in both Samoa and Tonga was clearly more significant than the formal involvement by any of the other international actors. At the same time, the Pacific Islands Mental Health Network (PIMHnet) was formed through efforts by the WHO and NZAID to promote mental health through policy-sharing and best practices promotion. In addition, two largescale regional analyses on mental health needs, the Pacific Regional Strategy for Mental Health and the Situational Analysis of Mental Health Needs and Resources in Pacific Island Countries were completed to identify the Pacific mental health context. These two studies forcefully argued for the need for updated policies by noting that most regional states either lacked a policy or law altogether or had antiquated laws and policies.

The presentation of a looming global mental health crisis and its particulars in the Pacific region, together with the identification of seriously deficient legal and policy structures necessary to effectively equip the state to manage the crisis when it arrives, will be argued to constitute critical calls to action for regional government leaders. Amongst the nations selected to pilot a mental health policy and plan by these studies were Samoa and Tonga. Besides this fact, however, the existence of numerous international instruments and other documents meant to underline the importance of mental health as a policy issue and to advance the particular framing of state responsibilities regarding mental health in human rights terms, raises the inevitable question about how much these factored in to the indigenous policymaking process. For instance, did policymakers and other stakeholders refer to or rely upon these documents in making policy decisions? Through interviews I inquire whether policy actors raise primarily cost justifications for developing a mental health policy or law or whether they frame mental health policy decisions in human rights terms. I also wish to glean whether policy decisions were thought of in terms of their ‘fit’ or appropriateness in the local context. These matters are taken up in the remaining chapters of the book.

Chapters 5 and 6 constitute the comparative case studies of Samoa and Tonga. One of the key aspects of Samoa’s mental health policy transfers is that it succeeded in transferring a law and written government policy, something which Tonga did not. As a result, the Samoan policy experience provides considerable documentary material to analyse and several more policy actors and stakeholders to consider than Tonga’s policy process. In Chap. 5, I address Samoa’s key cultural and historical institutional variables and introduce the reader to the mental health context. I then take up the mental health policy transfer process including law, policy and informal practice level changes. I use the establishment of Samoa’s mental health policy through the policy transfer framework as set forth earlier in the book and explore critical historical events in its establishment. In achieving this reconstruction of Samoa’s mental health policy context, I examine several critical dimensions.

Specifically, I outline Samoa’s and Tonga’s key governmental and health system institutions and provide a historical overview to the mental health policy setting. This section includes consideration of each nation’s indigenous governance institutions. In addition, European institutional influences including the introduction of state structures, law and regulation – both of which contribute significantly to the contemporary mental health policy context by introducing official attitudes and indigenous constructions of mental health and hospital, prison and public health ordinances, including the government’s right to confine individuals under the guise of quarantine regulations – are considered.

With these institutional and attitudinal aspects of each nation’s development over the early twentieth century in place, I next consider the specific mental health policy context. Mental health policy transfer in its earliest forms in Samoa and Tonga will be seen to involve essentially ‘hard’ policy in the form of cosmopolitan laws transferred to each country. These laws will be seen to continue an essentially ‘mental hygiene ethos’ empowering the state to confine individuals but with little consideration of individual rights or natural justice. Domestic mental health policy remains essentially silent in terms of ‘hard’ policy. The issue re-emerged on the public agenda in the early 2000s with international focus on mental health and the targeting pilot project, described in Chap. 4, emphasising policy changes in Samoa and Tonga. The 2000–2006 policy changes in Samoa and Tonga were rapid and significant. During that short span of time, both countries developed, vetted and implemented new Mental Health Acts. I explore these policy artefacts, supporting material, and the perspectives of key policy actors engaged in the policy development process, including local and foreign policy actors. The emphasis on ‘hard’ policy transfer, however, belies the other half of the mental health policy transfer experience in Samoa and Tonga.

The decades between these ‘hard’ transfers of the 1940s in Tonga and 1960s in Samoa and the present would witness significant ‘soft’ policy changes that are not reflected in any formal government policy yet instituted many community-based mental health care principles, such as the shift in primary locus of care from the mental hospital or unit to the family home and village. These changes occurred on the practice level and involve an individual actor engaged in mental health service delivery. In this context I also draw attention to the importance of professional networks in proliferating best practices on this informal policy level and for providing a possible forum for policies and practice to be repatriated, albeit with the latest iterations bearing the imprimatur of the transferee nations as well as those of the country of inception. I consider the substantive points made in this and the following chapter in my analytical discussion in Chap. 7.

Fundamentally, these chapters present an overview of both the historical and contemporary contexts for mental health policy transfer from the international level to Samoa and Tonga. While I am primarily interested in identifying the relevant actors, texts and themes active in each of these transfers in constructing the respective mental health systems, I am also interested in capturing the essential aspects of the policy transfer contexts for analysis. Specifically, I am enquiring about the amount of indigenous influence over the process of mental health policy adoption as well as whether or not and to what extent the adopted policies and laws actually reflect the indigenous context they were meant to operate within. In both cases, I review the substance of transferred policies over time while providing context from available records of debate or other textual sources to consider the process of transfer, including the motivations, if any, for policy adoption. In addition, I assess the content of adopted policies in both countries compared with the proffered policies or constructions of the problems from the local policy actors’ points of view. In Chap. 8, I offer some reflections on the policy transfer histories provided by the comparative case studies based on the framework utilised in this book, such as whether successive mental health policy transplantations have better enabled Samoan and Tongan policymakers to react to novel policy problems within the mental health sphere.

This book's central research questions concern the process of mental health policy transfers and localisation from the international level to the collectivist, PICs of Samoa and Tonga. These transfers occurred within the context of foreign policy actors actively engaged in the domestic policy process, and an explanation of them requires a theoretical and methodological approach that takes into account the international mental health policy environment while maintaining significant attention to the dimension of domestic policy constructs and indigenous constructions of mental health in developing national policy. Therefore, I propose to delineate mental health as a discrete policy area and situate it within its policy context within the core countries of North America and Western Europe. Once mental health policy and its associated institutions are defined, and institutional theory is defined in order to understand the nature of state institutions associated with mental health, I propose to establish the criteria for studying its movement from the core countries to Samoa and Tonga. The policy transfer framework developed by Dolowitz and Marsh (2000) will be used to accomplish this task. In addition, because mental health will be seen to constitute a unique policy area in regard to its implication of often deeply held cultural beliefs, a culturally sensitive research methodology will be offered. Because institutions and individual actors were deeply involved in the mental health policies of Samoa and Tonga, a consideration of the structural and agentic contexts must be fully explored. I aim to present a more holistic appraisal of the mental health policy process in Samoa and Tonga and such an approach requires consideration of both the actual policy process (considering policy artefacts such as policy instruments and statutory frameworks) as well as consideration of the subjective understandings of the policy problem (mental health) and the process bringing about change. With the demise of colonialism, policy transfers within the mental health realm will be observed to involve the intervention of IOs. Next, in Chap. 2, I situate the analysis on the area of mental health policy by establishing the necessary historical context for the current construction of mental health as policy area.

1.5 Summary

The case studies presented in this book present several key insights for the study of policy change. Firstly, the systematic approach of the policy transfer, localisation and translation frameworks are useful for the study of public policy development in developing countries since many public policies will have defined historical inflection points and involve different constellations of policy actors from metropolitan and local contexts. Secondly, historical institutionalism is a useful theoretical lens through which to organise the study of policy change in developing countries since, again, institutions and formal policy changes are likely to offer discrete snapshots for examination and policy epochs are marked by relatively long periods of policy stability and acute episodic policy change. To date, change has been most often due to colonisation, decolonisation and reform agendas undertaken by international actors.

Beyond lending support to these policy transfer and historical institutionalism, the examination of mental health policy change in Samoa and Tonga presented in this book will propose three important insights about the policy process. Firstly, while it is useful to examine discrete policy transfer episodes as done in this book, policy transfers should not be viewed as only occurring at these moments in time or due solely to these exogenous shocks. In both cases examined here, practitioners began informal practice shifts in the years between formal policy changes to laws and formal government policies or strategies. These earlier discursive and practice-level changes are essential to successful formal policy transfer as these activities serve to spread ideas about mental health policies that would later find a place in law and policy reforms that were made possible at the latest critical juncture provided by international organisations and neoliberal health sector policy reforms. Future studies should bear this in mind and not only focus on the specific tangible, visible outputs of an apparent policy change, but to dig deeper to understand from the actors involved or texts, the larger historical context within which these actors have operated.

Secondly, understanding how and by whom constructs of the policy context are made is an important and often overlooked element of policy transfer scholarship. This research revealed that views of 'context' were starkly different depending on whether the policy actor was a foreign consultant or a domestic policy actor. Foreign consultants tended to view local contexts narrowly and used it to reduce or eliminate policy content of those policies and laws transferred from abroad. Local actors, in contrast, took an expansive view of the policy need and tended to view foreign laws and policies as inadequate to that need. Local policy actors felt that the proffered policies did not contain sufficient content important to the local context such as the central role of family and community in mental health treatment and care. This insight underscores the importance of examining perspectives on policy drafts and versions from a range of actors involved in a particular policy formation process.

Finally, given the predominantly European colonial and neo-colonial attributes of governmental and medical institutions, indigenous policy actors who find windows of opportunity within which to advocate for a greater indigenous voice for cultural principles within policies present a novel form of policy entrepreneur that this research identifies as 'culture entrepreneurs'.[1] These actors, behaving much like policy entrepreneurs in the policy literature, rely upon policy windows to open to permit the inclusion of cultural norms and principles into the formal practice and substance of public policy.

[1] This concept is not to be confused with 'cultural entrepreneurs' who Gehman & Soublière (2017) use in the management literature to identify those actors engaged in the entrepreneurial applications of culture in business and social pursuits.

References

Anderson, J. (1984). *Public policy-making*. New York, Holt/Rinehart and Winston.

Australian Bureau of Statistics. (2018). *Disability, Ageing & Carers, Australia: Summary of findings, 2018* [online], Canberra, Available from: https://www.abs.gov.au/ausstats/abs@.nsf/mf/4430.0. Accessed 21 Apr 2020

Baba, T., Mahina, O., Williams, N., & Nabobo-Baba, U. (Eds.). (2004). *Researching the pacific & indigenous peoples*. Auckland: University of Auckland.

Bourke, T. (2001). Suicide in Samoa. *Pacific Health Dialogue, 8*, 1.

Bowles, J. (1995). Suicide in Western Samoa: An example of a suicide prevention program in a developing country. In D. RFW, W. Gulbinat, I. Kienhorst, & D. de Leo (Eds.), *Preventive strategies on suicide*. Leiden: EJ Brill.

Chisholm, D. (2006). *Dollars, DALYs & Decisions: Economic aspects of the mental health system*. Geneva: World Health Organization.

Dolowitz, D., & Marsh, D. (1996). Who learns what from whom: A review of the policy transfer literature. *Political Studies, XLIV*, 343–357.

Dolowitz, D., & Marsh, D. (2000). Learning from abroad: The role of policy transfer in contemporary policy-making. *Governance: An International Journal of Policy & Administration, 13*(1), 5–24.

Eddleston, M., & Phillips, M. (2004). Self-Poisoning with pesticides. *British Medical Journal, 328*(7430), 42–44.

Filipo, T. (2004). In search of a culturally appropriate approach to research: A Samoan case. In Baba et al. (Eds.), *Researching the Pacific & Indigenous peoples*. Auckland: University of Auckland.

Gehman, J., & Soublière, J. F. (2017). Cultural entrepreneurship: From making culture to cultural making. *Innovations, 19*(1), 61–73.

Lawson, S. (1996). Tradition versus democracy in the South Pacific. In *Fiji, Tonga & Western Samoa*. Melbourne: Cambridge University Press.

Macpherson, C., & Macpherson, L. (1987). Toward an explanation of recent trends in suicide in Western Samoa. *Man: New Series, 22*(2), 276.

Māhina, O. (2004). Issues & challenges in Pacific research. In T. Baba et al. (Eds.), *Researching the Pacific & indigenous peoples*. Auckland: University of Auckland.

Marsh, D., & Sharman, J. (2009). Policy diffusion & policy transfer. *Policy Studies, 30*(3), 269–288.

Observer, S. (2001). Samoa studies use of paraquat in suicides, report on seminar in Apia 'Can Samoa afford paraquat? *Samoa Observer*, 26 June 2001.

Philips, S. (2004). The organization of ideological diversity in discourse: Modern & neotraditional visions of the Tongan State. *American Ethnologist, 31*(2), 231–250.

Rochefort, D. (1997). *From poorhouses to homelessness: policy analysis & mental health care*. Westport: Auburn House.

Samoa Bureau of Statistics. (2020). *Samoa Census, Apia: Government of Samoa*. https://www.sbs.gov.ws/population

Sanga, K. (2004). Making philosophical sense of indigenous Pacific research. In T. Baba et al. (Eds.), *Researching the Pacific & indigenous peoples*. Auckland: University of Auckland.

Smith, L. (2012). *Decolonizing methodologies: Research & indigenous peoples*. New York: Zed Books.

Somanathan, A. (2010). *Financing options for the health sector in Tonga, East Asia & Pacific Region (EASHD)*. Jakarta: World Bank.

Stone, D., & Ladi, S. (2015). Global public policy and transnational administration. *Public Administration, 93*(4), 839–855.

Taylor, D. (2007). Tonga national disability identification survey, Nuku 'alofa: 'Ofa Tui 'Amanaki Centre.

Tonga Department of Statistics. (2012). Tonga Statistics, Nuku'alofa.

United Nations Development Programme. (2011). International Human Development Indicators.

Vivili, P. S., Finau, S. A., & Finau, E. (1999). Suicide in Tonga, 1982–1997. *Pacific Health Dialog, 6*(2), 211–212.

Watters, E. (2010). *Crazy like us: The globalization of the American psyche*. New York: Simon and Schuster.

World Bank. (2007). *Social analysis and disability: A guidance note*. Washington, DC: World Bank.

World Bank. (2020). World Development Indicators. https://databank.worldbank.org/source/world-development-indicators#

Zinn, C. (1995). South Pacific leads the world in rates of youth suicides. *British Medical Journal, 311*, 830.

Chapter 2
What Constitutes a Mental Health Policy?

In this chapter, I will provide the substantive context for mental health policy as outlined in Chap. 1 and will situate it within historical context. I argue here that the mental health policies now permeating the globe are the product of a long-standing policy development process which has the nation-state as central mediator of mental illness and its treatment. Further, that this cultural vetting has taken place primarily in the nation-states of North America and Western Europe, regions that I will refer to collectively as constituting the mental health 'policy core'.

This chapter proceeds by first establishing what I mean to discuss under the rubric of 'mental health'. Mental health, as a policy concept, needs to be understood within its global formulation in international texts and promoted by international organisations (IOs), as well as within the particular cultural assumptions bound up with mental health, including those used by medical and legal practitioners. Mental health will therefore be seen to encompass more than merely mental disorder; it will be seen as an expansive construction of a right common to human beings as individuals, involving the inherent conflict this liberal construction has with collectivist and traditional cultural constructions of mental health and illness. With the concept of mental health situated, I next present the notion of a 'mental health system'. A mental health system will be seen to encapsulate, in the context of this book, any state activities implicating mental health such as state health care, welfare and criminal justice systems. This broad construction also envisions public-private collaboration on certain aspects of mental health service delivery including the important shift of the locus of mental health care from the institution to the community care model (see e.g. Morrissey and Goldman 1984; Susser 1965). Once this generic mental health construct has been assembled, I ask whether the political science concept of institutionalism, specifically historical institutionalism, applies to this context and argue that it does. Mental health systems contain a myriad of elements (laws, formal policies, rules, norms) that are historically situated. They are also deeply embedded within the state apparatus and can both constrain and be influenced by the actions of individuals. I consider several aspects of this rich research including Tuohy's (1999) consideration of the theory in the broader health care context.

T. P. Fadgen, *Mental Health Public Policy in Global Context*,
https://doi.org/10.1007/978-981-15-6479-6_2

With this preliminary construction of the mental health context and the theoretical conception of it within historical institutionalism, I next consider the historical development of mental health policy in the policy core regions of North America and Western Europe. I argue that the mental health best practices construct is one founded on two pillars of Western thought. First, mental health, as an area of policy, and the provision of mental health care, has long been an important area of state responsibility. As an area of public expenditure, it has contracted and expanded over time along with dominant fiscal attitudes. At the same time, mental health 'exceptionalism' will be explored. Given mental health policy's common focus on individuals who might be dangerous (or are often thought to be) and the deep stigma suffered by these individuals across cultures, the state has a special responsibility to protect the public from risk of harm and to protect the rights of individuals suffering from a mental disorder. These dual concerns have given rise to a human rights-based framing of mental health within the core countries which will be seen later in this book to have set the framing of mental health as global policy issue. With the core region mental health policy posture firmly established, I introduce the topic of global mental health as a precursor to considering policy transfer in later chapters.

2.1 What Is Mental Health?

The World Health Organization (WHO) definition of mental health provides a useful starting point for examining the particular framing of mental health as a global policy agenda item. WHO defines mental health in various publications as a 'state of wellbeing in which every individual realizes his or her own potential, can cope with the normal stresses of life, can work productively and fruitfully, and is able to make a contribution to her or his community' (WHO 2007). Mental health is framed as something larger than mental disorder, something that includes all the basic human rights expectations inherent in the individual. Mental disorders, in contrast, are commonly understood to constitute a combination of abnormal thoughts, emotions, behaviour and relationships with others (see e.g. WHO 2003). Mental disorders are understood by how they inhibit the individual from the ideal state of mental health and are marked by various diagnoses assigned to constellations of individual symptoms embodied in behaviours deviating from the social norm. They include both psychological and behavioural conditions such as schizophrenia, bipolar disorder, and depression and extend to addictive conditions such as those involving drugs, alcohol or gambling. Hence, mental health is more than the mere absence of an active mental disorder, it might be better viewed as the ideal state of individual existence.

This view also maintains that the state should affirmatively contribute to this positive state of mental health. This role can be constructed in terms of both positive obligations on members of the political community as well as limitations on its power. Positive responsibilities related to mental health are those steps that a state can take to promote and nurture the ability of individuals to manage his or her own stress, live to their potential, and contribute to their community. These rights might extend to such varied things as access to public accommodations to ensure that social participation can occur or work protections to ensure non-discrimination against an individual based on his or her mental condition. In contrast, limitations on state authority over the individual with mental illness are understood as legal protections to ensure an individual suffering under the symptoms of a mental disorder is treated with dignity and with respect to natural justice principles and typically involve rigid procedural safeguards such as mandatory rights of judicial review of any detention longer than several days for a mental condition.

These measures have been linked to the economic arguments in favour of full participation in the labour force and the economic impacts of nonparticipation. Murray and Lopez (1996) observed the international efforts to coordinate global public health intervention efforts through the World Bank initiated (later joined by WHO) Global Burden of Disease (GBD) study (Lopez et al. 2006). The results of these efforts were published in World Bank's World Development Reports for 1993 and 1994 and indicated that depression and other 'nonfatal health outcomes', such as neuropsychiatric conditions, bipolar disorder and schizophrenia have significantly adverse impacts on Disability Adjusted Life Years (DALYs), thus constituting an acute challenge to a national economy (see eg WHO 2012; Barendregt 2003). Moreover, the GBD projected conditions, such as depression, would rise in global prevalence between 1990 and 2019 (Rehm and Shield 2019). These demands on national health systems, and by extension the global economy, required concerted policy interventions. World Bank and WHO's collaboration, which led to the GBD study, has been heralded as an exemplar to ensure effective policy interventions in the public health context. Given the recognition of the global health importance of sound mental health strategies, a significant concern for mental health policy intervention is whether culture is an important consideration in mental health policy.

2.2 "Institutionalising" Mental Health Systems: The Government Context

Mental health policy implicates numerous governmental institutions such as legal and bureaucratic structures, including hospitals, prisons and police, as well as social services and guidelines for medical professionals in managing individuals with mental illness who pose risks to themselves or to the community. At the same time, mental health policies exist within a normative context about defining behaviours as being abnormal and hence requiring state intervention for protection and treatment. In this regard, mental health implicates numerous 'old' institutions, such as formal government structures (e.g. legislatures and courts), legal institutions (laws) (Steinmo et al. 1992, pp. 24, see also March and Olsen 1984 and Thelen 1999), and manifest political organisations [and] aggregations of norms, values, rules and practices that shape or constrain political behaviour [and] describe how individuals who are assumed to be autonomous actors in dominant theoretical perspective… have their behaviour shaped and constrained. (Peters and Pierre 1998, p. 565). Other scholars such as Hall and Taylor (1996) have argued that institutions are formal rules, compliance procedures and standard operating procedures that structure relationships between people in various societal units. Ikenberry (1988) extends this to include the nexus of government institutions within a society's normative order. Hence many formal state institutions are implicated by such constructions.

Mental health care has traditionally utilised coercive tools of the state to detain, confine and treat individuals with mental illness who prove unmanageable (or merely a nuisance) in the community. Prior to the rise of the welfare state, state interventions were custodial in nature and tended to involve varying degrees (and quality) of actual treatment. Most of the time individuals were simply detained in prisons or specialised hospitals, often indefinitely. Once welfare state institutions had broadened the menu of possible mental health interventions, other community-based interventions were included. This shift in the locus of care was assisted by the emergence of human rights-based arguments founded upon both moral and legal grounds for individuals who have committed no criminal offence, suggesting the proper place of care was in the community setting. Prisons and compulsory hospitalisations were maintained for only the most serious of cases.

The persistence of these institutions in the face of changing attitudes and data questioning their efficacy suggests a body of scholarship prominent among political scientists known as historical institutionalism. One of the early proponents of this perspective, Theda Skocpol, observes that the decisions made to establish particular institutions (or not) have enduring legacies (Skocpol 1992). This phenomenon has been described as the institution, in essence, persisting (institutional stability or 'equilibrium') until a sufficient force (described as 'punctuation') is brought to bear on it forcing change: this phenomenon is called 'path dependence'. Hence, historical institutionalism might be seen as 'an attempt to illuminate how political struggles are mediated by the institutional setting in which they take place' (Steinmo et al. 1992).

Krasner in his oft-cited *Review: Approaches to the State: Alternate Conceptions and Historical Dynamics* (1984), extends the historical institutionalism-related notion of path dependence from its narrow confines of impacting future decisions of an isolated domestic institution to its broader implications for policy developments in other developing and developed nations (See also Steinmo, et al. 1992 and Cortell and Peterson 1999). Krasner notes that once 'functions … are viewed as proper and legitimate for the state are influenced by general international norms and practices', these entrenched policies and practices become identified as 'best practices', and thus play an agenda-setting role in developing nations (Krasner 1984, p. 241). The effect is that 'these characteristics come to be associated with the essential nature of the "modern" state and cannot be ignored even by states with very different needs' (1984, p. 241). As an example of this, Krasner mentions that fact that regardless of the resources needed for proper implementation, most countries have some manner of social security system and have identified education as a state responsibility. These are innovations made at the more developed nation level yet persist in policy-making decision in developing nations.

In the particular context of the decolonisation following World War II, Krasner (1984) observes that despite colonies lacking in several key capabilities of the modern nation-state, an aggressive decolonisation policy was pursued because, as he notes, '[t]he triumph of the national state in Europe became a triumph of the national state around the globe'(1984, p. 242). These regions became a part of the historical process of state creation and the idea of a sovereign nation was transferred from developed nation to developing nation, making that option (independence and statehood) the only acceptable, legitimate offer.

James Mahoney and Kathleen Thelen (2010) are among those scholars attempting to move historical institutionalism beyond the narrow confines of punctuated equilibrium in understanding institutional change. The authors observe that previous research on path dependence argues that 'path-dependent lock-in ... is exceedingly rare in actual institutional practice' (Mahoney and Thelen 2010, p. 3). Instead, the authors suggest that 'problems of rule interpretation and enforcement open up space for actors to implement existing rules in new ways' (2010, p. 4). This observation permits greater consideration of individual agency in the study of institutional change. Tulia Falleti provides a useful example of this in her study of the evolution of health care reforms in Brazil. Falleti finds that the traditional historical institutionalism analysis with its emphasis on such punctuated equilibria as economic crises or other critical junctures risks missing the layering or gradualist reforms of the Brazilian health system. She begins with a 'crucial opening' that began a gradual process resulting in significant national health care reforms that played on the military regime's efforts to consolidate authoritarian rule beginning in the 1970s. Her findings suggest the presence of three components in Brazil leading to change: subversive actors; infiltration by these actors into the apparatus of government and expansion beginning in one health care sector; and these actors then spreading throughout the remaining government health structures.

Falleti's focus de-emphasises the critical juncture preoccupation in historical institutionalism in favour of a gradualist approach to change. A more intensive case study approach to research is likely to yield more accurate insight into institutional change. In order to do historical analysis, one must rely on the historical record in toto and not on a particular selective reading of it to fit an existing model, in the historical institutionalism case punctuated equilibrium in order to explain change. Given the influence, however, of the underlying motivations for health sector reform in Brazil, the overarching ideological context of health systems, and sound public management principles, a question might be posed about what fore-shadowed the crucial opening, thereby making any institutional change possible.

This ideational component of the institutionalist literature concerns the central influence of ideas on the path dependency model, and this offers a possible answer to the above question. Peters et al. (2005) identify a politics of path dependency influenced by economic and political factors that require the 'articulation and insertion' of 'ideas and belief systems' into the domestic political discourse (2005, p. 1296). A proper appraisal of institutional change involves both consideration of the 'larger social, economic and political context' as well as the ideas responsible for change (2005, p. 1297). Here, ideas take the place of specific agent action as a variable. Ideas, however, are multifaceted and identifying which ideas contributed to institutional change requires identification of agency within a discrete policy area in order to offer a complete account of such change.

In their study, Peters et al. note the influence of monetarism as an 'idea' that shifted the notion of government primarily serving in a spending and regulatory capacity to a more market-based role. This shift constituted a primary, organic contextual shift on the nature and role of government in the modern liberal state. Similar to Pierson's (2000a, b) earlier observation of the influence of ideological shifts on welfare and public education which saw them become public concerns as opposed to private ones, functions traditionally thought to be within government capacity are increasingly being privatised. These various discourses, ideas and ideologies then frame the policy orientations of IOs, the options available to less developed nations, and the worldviews and analytical orientations of experts provided to assist developing countries with 'modernising' or 'bringing into line' their domestic policies with the prevailing ones of a particular time.

In an analogue to the mental health context, Hansen and King (2001) address the divergence in eugenics policy outcomes in the United States and United Kingdom, employing an ideational analysis. The authors are broadly concerned with how ideas come to exercise a causal influence on policy and find that simply demonstrating prominent ideas are widely known does not answer the enquiry. They argue that ideas are more likely to be translated into policy where there is 'a synergy between ideas and interests, when actors possess enthusiasm and appropriate institutional position, and when the timing' of the policy adoption coincides with a particular context that reinforces the proffered policy idea (2001, p. 239).

Like mental health policy, eugenics was an 'international movement articulating genetic hypotheses, social theory and policy prescriptions' which implicated many policy areas and sought to define the state's role acting in the furtherance of a science-based social goal (Hansen and King 2001, p. 238). Hansen and King maintain that ideologies or 'programmatic beliefs' must first be identified. Programmatic beliefs are understood here as 'abstract, integrated, systemic patterns of belief with aims directly relevant to particular courses of policy' (Hansen and King 2001, p. 242). Following this, an 'observable correlation' between the idea and policy option, selected or not, must be demonstrable. As a final step, the authors argue that one must define the manner in which the studied ideas have actually influenced the political process in order to rule out epiphenomenal occurrences (2001, p. 242).

Their explanation for US adoption of eugenics and the United Kingdom's failure to adopt similar measures is best explained by how well the proffered ideas associated with eugenics 'mapped onto policymakers' strategic political interests' (Hansen and King 2001, p. 243). In the United States, eugenics coincided with a larger movement against the growing influence of undesired migrants flocking to America due to permissive immigration standards and demand for cheap labour. Political actors were able to take advantage of the ideas of eugenics to further their political objectives designed to preserve the social elites thought to be the engines of American economic prosperity and power. The United Kingdom lacked similar internal constructs with which the eugenics movement could merge; the movement ended up not being enacted due to the ghastly enactment of eugenics-inspired laws in Nazi Germany. This raises the notion of timing in Hansen and King's analysis. In this regard, they observe that when eugenics ideas and policies were 'associated with fiscal prudence and national greatness' there was widespread political support (2001, p. 262). Once eugenics became synonymous with Nazi overreach, the policies (and idea) quickly fell out of favour.

In addition to exercising requisite enthusiasm for a particular policy, and as observed above, professional associations play a key role in forming and proliferating ideas and institutional practices. These profession-based practices both influence and are influenced by institutional arrangements. Besides professional education and licensing requirements, continuing education requirements for professionals, conferences, publications and networks serve an important function in maintaining unity on current best practices within a particular profession or community. Scholarly literature on institutionalism has observed the importance of such networks as 'epistemic communities' or 'policy networks'. These entities are institutions in the sense used in this book in that they create 'substantial stability in their interactions and due to patterns of expected and predictable and common shared behaviours and values' (Peters 2005, pp. 118–119). Peters follows the policy community literature in finding that 'common scientific or professional understandings and training as a basis for (recognisable continuity) tends to rely on the presence of individual entrepreneurs (or key actors) for formation' (1999, p. 120). Medical communities, in particular, as science actors, develop particular discourses and modes of interacting with each other and the public.

Medical and legal professionals in core countries have common educational and licensing requirements. Often, as will be discussed further below, professionals in developing countries are trained in metropolitan or regional educational institutions heavily influenced by the professional practices in the core countries (see e.g. Acharyya 1996). For instance, from the beginning of European engagement in both Samoa and Tonga and until today, most attorneys and judges have been trained in New Zealand or Australian law schools. Similarly, most doctors and other health professionals have been trained either in Australia, New Zealand or Fiji (See e.g. Brown and Connell 2004). The centralized educational system for these actors, who later go on to influence policy in their respective fields, serves to standardize knowledge and analytical approaches. In addition, prospects for maintaining currency in the profession are nurtured at the professional education level and social networks are created. These professional and social networks, as well as increasing opportunities for exchange within global regions, create opportunities for exchange of best practices and serve to reinforce the normative contexts within the professions. Hence, the identity and influence of such organisations over the domestic policy development process must be taken into account in examining the mental health institutional context.

In many ways, Carolyn Hughes Tuohy's (1999) study of the general health sector as institution brings many of these various institutional strands together. As she observes, from the 1950s onwards a prevailing institutional norm developed encouraging increased access to health services whilst seeking to control the costs of care (1999, p. 18). By the 1990s health care reforms were atop the policy and political agendas of most advanced industrial countries (1999, p. 3). Tuohy links these health sector reforms to overall neoliberal notions of limited state involvement in what would otherwise be a competitive market. The Organisation for Economic Cooperation and Development (OECD) further advanced these health care reforms by publishing many reports between 1992 and 1995 considering health care reforms throughout OECD countries and establishing a best practices model for adopting nations to rely upon in embarking upon their own reform endeavour. These OECD publications and policy ideas would inform World Bank efforts in promoting reform of the developing world's health systems.

In Tuohy's construction of health care, it is an institution that once established tends to develop a particular 'logic' governing both actor behaviour and the trajectory of potential change (1999, p. 7). Given the complexity of health systems, systemic change occurs rarely and when it does it is highly influenced by prevailing ideas of best practices during what Tuohy calls a 'policy episode' (1999, p. 11). These episodes must themselves be significant in order to alter the inertial forces of entrenched institutional interests. A policy episode requires two central factors to make systemic change possible. Firstly, a political system must provide a 'consolidated base of authority for political action' (Tuohy1999, p. 11). Strong party control in the unitary, Westminster-style parliamentary system will typically suffice, but is not itself a prerequisite in this regard. Secondly, health care policy reforms, in particular, require high priority amongst key policy actors.

Importantly, Tuohy's construction of the health care institution isolates it from the broader health policy ideas context in regard to health service delivery (1999, p. 12). Ideas about practice can persist for many years, even decades, before being formally adopted. Yet, eventual health reform itself will be highly influenced by such ideas. Success is likely to arise where there is convergence between the 'strategy of a proposed change' and the 'internal logic of the system' (1999, p. 13). System logics represent the institutional legacies of past events. Between times of acute change, they are shaped by the key actors' behaviour, which is itself shaped by the institutional context as well as other overlapping institutions. Similarly, Rochefort (1997) observes that mental health policy developments in core countries, tend to coincide with changes to the larger health systems within which they were historically located. The health system changes emerged from within each nation-state but have occurred for different reasons over time, such as fiscal demands on the public health system.

The policy context itself is guided by WHO's further construction of a 'mental health system' as constituting all the activities whose primary purpose is to promote, restore or maintain mental health (WHO 2005). Similarly, Rochefort defines the system broadly to include 'all government activities, specifically concerned with the prevention and treatment of mental disorders as well as with the living situations of mentally ill persons' (1997, p. 5). In fact, the mental health systems in the core regions typically include public and private mental hospitals, special mental health services for war veterans as well as community-based services such as residential treatment centres, outpatient clinics and multi-sectoral mental health agencies (Rochefort 1997). Hence, the context itself often includes myriad policy interventions, such as income support, housing support, and subsidized medical care. Therefore, in order to effectively study the mental health policy universe, it is necessary to review artefacts of it, such as the record of law and written policies, as well as the words of actors involved in all aspects of this diverse context.

Government policies concerning poverty, urbanisation, unemployment, education and criminal justice are all viewed as forming part of the mental health policy mosaic. Poverty, including homelessness, is one of the strongest factors affecting mental health because the poor suffer environmental and psychological adversity that increases vulnerability to mental disorders (Patel and Prince 2001). Urbanisation leads to increased risk of mental disorders because of its disruption of family life, reduction in family supports, and increases the risks of homelessness, poverty and exposure to psychological distress (WHO 2003). Related are nations prone to natural disasters such as cyclones or tsunamis, as Samoa and Tonga are (see e.g. Steinglass and Gerrity 2006; Marmot 2005; Kokaiet al. 2004). These frequent disruptions to social life and the uncertainty they create is a risk factor for mental health conditions related to the events and their aftermath (WHO 2003). Unemployment has a two-way association with mental disorders, those having employment but suffering from mental disorders, in particular where there is no existing antidiscrimination law present, risk being discharged from employment for either direct discrimination related to their condition or for performance-related issues when there is an exacerbation of an existing mental health condition (WHO 2003). Primary public education systems that provide early detection of mental disorders can be one of the most useful means of preventing the long-term debilitating effects of disorders. Finally, the criminal justice system and people with mental disorders often intersect. Hence, prisoners tend to be more likely than the general population to suffer from a mental disorder. As such, policy interventions might include mental health treatment and care in prison to more effectively manage the nation's overall mental health profile. Yet, these institutional variables, which might be somewhat predictable given the general policy mandates of modern nation-states, do not paint an entire portrait of a nation's mental health profile. Indeed, mental health policies depend not only upon the state's actual or aspired to capacity to control those deemed to be at risk but also revolve around the social and medical constructions of mental illness and deviant behaviours. And to understand these, we must explore the question of culture and cultural constructions of mental illness and wellnesses.

2.3 De-institutionalising Diagnostic Regimes: The Cultural Context

Given the prominence of behavioural factors in mental disorder diagnosis, including for the identification of symptoms of nonconforming social behaviours, implicates intimate knowledge of conforming behaviours and the diagnostic skill to differentiate between the two. This fact brings questions of culture or rather cultural competence to the fore. In Marsella and White's (1982) seminal *Cultural Conceptions of Mental Health and Therapy*, the general theme is that 'illness experiences are an interpretive enterprise' subject to the 'construct(ion) of social situations according to the premises of cultural theories about illness and social behaviour generally' (1982, p. 3). The studies included in their collection reveal mental illness as a 'domain of behavioural and medical experiences of practice specific culturally and historical traditions which regard certain forms of behavioural dysfunction as essentially psychological and medical in nature' (Marsella and White 1982, p. 5).

Hence, local understandings of behaviour likely to trigger such an analysis are symbolically represented in words categorising the origin of the behaviour and whether the individual should bear individual responsibility for the conduct or whether the behaviour is the result of phenomena outside of the individual's control. Diagnostic process and condition identification are done, at least in the first instance, according to cultural knowledge about illness and mental disorder (Marsella and White 1982, p. 10). When considered in this light, otherwise 'neutral' observations have led to'[d]iagnoses of idiocy, insanity, and dementia involved overt behavioural criteria that largely excluded the subjective, experiential symptoms of the afflicted individual', and these come to have particular currency for diagnostic and treatment purposes (Nadesan 2008, p. 141). This can be particularly problematic for diagnosis-making in a culture not well understood by the practitioner whose training of symptom recognition was vetted in a foreign, individualist culture.

What is often overlooked in the mental health context, is that within the Western mental health paradigm are embedded concepts of the 'egocentric person' (Marsella and White 1982, p. 20). These individualist constructions are often at odds with some of the collectivist interpretive frames employed in mental disorder recognition in nations such as Samoa and Tonga, where 'personhood' notions will be seen to involve 'a greater blending of agency and responsibility between both self and other' (Marsella and White 1982, p. 11). Mental health policies are inextricably linked with notions of self that are vetted in the cultures of origin and implicate notions of 'acceptable' social behaviours and personal responsibility originating in the culture developing the implicated norms – norms that often confront persistent (and often nonconforming) indigenous beliefs in the supernatural.

As Robert Evan Kendell pointed out, even in European nations – members of the mental health policy core – the notion that a mental illness was caused by 'divine intervention, evil spirits, fevers, heredity, unbridled passions, strong liquor, the influence of the moon, and blows to the head' (1996, p. 17) persisted for many centuries. Similarly, early healers with titles such as 'priest, shaman, physician, apothecary' used 'ceremonies, spells, potions, medications' to remedy the malady (Kendell 1996, p. 17). While most of these beliefs are no longer widely held in the policy core regions, they still hold currency in many cultures. These same actors and types of curative measures will be seen as still possessing significant purchase in both Samoa and Tonga.

Significantly, however, as will be discussed below, in Western Europe and North America advances in medical science led to a decline in the prevalence of these traditional healing methods in favour of scientific methods and techniques (Kendell 1996, p. 18). The first of these movements spawned by these advances became known as 'moral treatment' and was inspired by the innovations of Francis Willis in England and Philippe Pinel in France. Policymakers and the public began to favour these more morally based and humane treatment regimes over the status quo represented by confinement in the madhouse (1996, p. 19). It was also during these years, according to Kendell, that the terms 'lunacy' and 'madness' gave way to 'mental disease', transferring the category of mental existence from the spiritual to the scientific and thus physical realm.

Bass et al. (2007) note much of the global mental health literature works off of a common assumption of the universality of mental illness descriptions and symptomology across cultures. They note, however, that an 'uncritical application of standard diagnostic criteria such as the (Diagnostic and Statistical Manual of Mental Disorders, version 4 (DSM-IV[1])) cross culturally might yield misleading or erroneous results where such criteria are applied locally and appropriately' (2007, p. 918). They do not argue for relativism, however – only that such broad assumptions should be more thoroughly vetted before serving as the basis for interventions worldwide.

Thomas Scheff also argues that concepts of mental illness in general are not 'neutral, value-free scientifically precise terms but are, for the most part, the leading edge of an ideology embedded in the historical and cultural present of the white middleclass of Western societies' (1996, p. 65). The peril is, in his view, that utilisation of the medical model of disease suggests a cultural value neutrality or universality of the human condition that when used in the particular identification and management of mental illnesses is inherently problematic, particularly in light of that fact that 'symptoms are themselves offenses against implicit understanding of particular cultures' (Scheff 1996, p. 65). In other words, dissent exists within the notions of the universality of mental health diagnostic categories established within particular social contexts. One response to such criticism is to craft policies that address institutional and broad social values such as consideration of human rights protection within the liberal state. This approach requires a consideration of which state institutions are implicated in a mental health system.

[1] The DSM is now in its 5th edition, the DSM-5.

2.4 Mental Health Policy Development at the 'Policy Core': North America and Western Europe

Michel Foucault is often cited in studies examining mental health due to his significant research on the development of madness as a category of 'other' in Western thought. Foucault argued that as notorious infectious diseases of the fifteenth century (plague and leprosy) began to fade from prominence, madness came to be seen as the primary threat to social welfare. By the seventeenth century, vagabonds, particularly mentally ill vagabonds, were regarded with increasing intolerance by industrialized Europe society and as a consequence institutions emerge. (Foucault 2008, p. 140). Similarly, as infectious diseases have slowly been eradicated or effectively managed, particularly in the Pacific – a phenomenon known within the public health literature as the 'epidemiological transition' (see e.g. Omran 1971 and Kessler and Ustin 2008) – there has been an increased international emphasis on both lifestyle diseases and, by extension, mental health (Allen and Laycock 2000). In addition, public health systems and public health care systems are inextricably linked to the welfare state.

As an outgrowth of the institutional predecessors of public health concerns related to infectious disease and as part of the general welfare state structure, the formation of mental health structures in Europe and North America implicated the relationship between the welfare state and the medical profession. Medical professional practices, often effectuated through scientific discourses sought state sanction over control and treatment for the mentally ill. The medical profession introduced, and perpetuates, the notion that 'there are discrete, separately identifiable mental illnesses with distinct symptoms, syndromes and causes, as well as typical modes of onset course and prognosis' (Busfield 1996, p. 132). As mental disorders became associated with bizarre and often criminal behaviours, the medical profession and in particular the speciality of psychiatry became entrenched as the arbiter of mental health and illness and veritable quasi-judicial arm of the state in making preliminary determinations to confine and treat. In essence, the psychiatrist, empowered to provide the tribunal with expert testimony as to the individual's mental state, is then also empowered to treat the individual and ultimately determine whether or not he or she may return to society.

This institutional alliance between psychiatry and the state's bureaucratic structures has its origins in the nineteenth century and endures, albeit in a slightly less central role, in contemporary mental health processes (Busfield 1996, p. 134). In exchange for the powers to confine, treat, and thus control a certain class of individuals, the psychiatrist concedes the state's authority to license and regulate the profession. In terms of market regulator, this 'exchange' by psychiatrists also served to eliminate any possible threat to the supremacy or primacy of the psychiatrist in this system and to bar other actors from engaging in what was now the authorised official practice of medicine. Traditional and spiritual healers were now at risk of civil or criminal sanction for engaging in certain activities with an individual suspected of being mentally ill. This divide between sanctioned and non-sanctioned care providers will be seen to be critical to the current mental health policy context in Samoa and Tonga where, despite state regulation over mental health, the majority of the population persists in engaging these traditional and unofficial (and thus unregulated) medical or quasi-medical actors.

The official state role in the mental health policy context is often explained in terms of 'governmentality' and the role of 'biopower' in society. The governmentality literature is itself an outgrowth of Foucauldian thought (see e.g. Foucault 1965, 2006, 1980). Foucault's purpose was to explore how population health was related to the 'the economic and political security of the state', which, in turn, would cause policies and practices of control, through disciplinary regimes or governmentalities on populations (Nadesan 2008, p. 93).The nexus between governmentality and mental health policy is perhaps best exemplified under the rubric of government surveillance, or monitoring and control, of disease. The possibilities for government surveillance were opened by calls for regulation of public sanitation (once its connection to disease was demonstrated in the eighteenth century) and regulation of public spaces occurring in industrial democracies during the nineteenth century. Incidentally, these government forays into public health coincided with the age of colonialism and were consequently exported in law, policy and practice to territorial possessions with significant institutional ramifications. As Pierson in summarising Tilly (1984) has suggested in the institutionalism context, 'when things happen matters for how they happen' (2000b, p. 73; emphasis in original).

Parallels between public health policy and mental health policy transfer can be seen in the framing of public health as individual health. The purpose is to justify the standardisation and bureaucratisation of public health practice (Nadesan 2008, p. 100).This public health bureaucratisation is itself unremarkable. The state sought to regulate and manage these public concerns through surveillance, the creation of statistics about the prevalence of disease, and by using its coercive police powers to control individual conduct (2008, p. 55). In the mental health context, state officials exercised these police powers or their authorised agents (police, medical officers/ psychiatrists and court officials) to identify, label, confine and treat individuals deemed to be ill. Since there has long been an association of mental disorder with socially undesirable behaviours, governments have sought to 'integrate surveillance within a disciplinary framework to be applied [...] to the... population' (2008, p. 139). While surveillance might not have diminished, how one is subjected to it has and is now thought of as proper only when it is as minimally invasive as possible when balanced against the public interest in community safety. I now discuss how mental health policy came to this point.

David Rochefort's (1988) seminal study of mental health policy in North America finds several peaks and valleys in the pattern of mental health policy development due to issue attention caused by the prevalence, or perceived prevalence, of mental health problems (e.g. crime, homelessness/vagrancy, drug abuse). From this he notes peaks of progressivity in the 1960s community treatment movement; the early decades of the twentieth century and the mental hygiene movement; and the moral treatment of the late nineteenth century. He finds in each period times where 'warehousing' significant populations in state facilities occurred. The widespread confinement inevitably led to professional and public backlash and resulting paradigmatic shift.

Rochefort's findings are consistent with those of other policy scholars in noting that mental health policy has tended to follow cyclical patterns. These patterns tend to track along with public perception of the efficacy of medical (and by implication legal) interventions meant to control and ameliorate the mental disorder. When the perception is that an approach is failing, a competing formulation of best practices will gain ascendancy and replace the ineffective practice. Rochefort (1988) refers to this as 'policy succession'. Under this formulation, mental health policy in core countries is presently operating under the community treatment paradigm that succeeded the mental hygiene movement of the early twentieth century.

Furthermore, Rochefort (1988) considers other factors relevant to the mental health policy cycle. These factors include prevailing professional discourses of the time as well as public opinion: notions of unenlightened and hostile views towards individuals with mental ill health can lead to citizen activism to confine and take an unsympathetic view of these individuals. On the other hand, positive attitudes towards individuals with mental illness, such as the public perception of injustices in state confinement practices, can lead to their advocates enjoying 'active, informed citizen support at the community level' (1988, p. 142). The approach implicates the 'community' as the ideal service delivery context. Over time, this natural state for maintaining good mental health has, however, been disrupted by social factors such as urbanisation, industrialisation and economic pressures to engage in the wage labour force. These factors have led to the collapse of the family unit as a viable treatment option for an affected family member. As such, state policy is designed to replicate this community setting. It seems implicit, however, that efforts to implement similar policies in societies lacking this degree of community degeneration is intended to stave off the possibility of these anachronistic and inhumane practices from ever taking shape.

Rochefort observes profound changes occurring on several different policy fronts at once in arriving at the latest manifestation of the mental health policy paradigm, the aforementioned community mental health movement. The changes have a social philosophical aspect and, identifying the 'sources, prerequisites and repercussions of the policy episode composes a vast standing case study of the dynamics of policy innovation, generating important propositions for assessment and other policy areas' (Rochefort 1997, p. 13). Ultimately, however, Rochefort is unable to point to a single motif or policymaking development that explains community treatment ascendancy. Instead, mental health issues have been advanced at different times by the broad currents of general health system reforms. At other times, mental health care was less a function of general health care trends, but instead was restricted to its own context, shaped by ideologies, professional practices, research, and political energies from within the domain.

These policy debates tended to take place within what Rochefort (1997) refers to as the context of mental health 'exceptionalism'. Since, unlike many other policy areas, mental disorders tend to be accompanied by a debilitating social stigma (see e.g. Golberstein et al. 2008), populations tend to maintain both unsophisticated and even hostile views towards those with such conditions. Given these various complicating conditions for mental health policy development, one might expect to find a rich policy literature devoted to studying how policies are developed and changed, particularly given the political marginalisation that logically accompanies social stigmatisation. However, as Rochefort (1997) notes, only a very small number of scholars (see e.g. Goodwin 1997, Good 1997; Mechanic 1969, 1998 and Rogers and Pilgrim 1996) have examined mental health policy in-depth and fewer 'relate mental health policy development to the theoretical issues in the policy research field' (1997, p. 13). Moreover, few tend to study policy development in non-Western cultures at all (McKenzie et al. 2004; Lurie 2005; Lebra 1976).

The professional, political and ideological context within which mental health policies tend to be debated has often coincided with myriad social movements in the core countries. Simon Goodwin (1997) argues that social movements around mental health treatment, including those advocating civil rights and anti-institutionalisation, were each formed around a common conceptual core privileging the 'social rather than medical origins' of mental illness, whilst emphasising poor mental health as the result of 'unequal power relationships in society' (1997, p. 37). It is perhaps no coincidence that many of these points of view and resulting changes coincided with the American civil rights movements and the subsequent establishment of these rights through American adversarial legal process (see e.g. Kagan 1991) and a similar rise in other broad-based social movements in Western Europe. The view that community care would be more beneficial, however, had been recognised in England earlier than the dates of these social movements might lead one to believe, and was primarily motivated by a fiscal recognition that the current trajectory of institutional care was simply unsustainable.

This is not to say, however, that change was primarily an economic decision. As Goodwin (1997) notes, paradigm shifts in mental health treatment were also based on a careful assessment of the therapeutic benefits of community-based care. The diminishing therapeutic benefit to the biomedical institutional model suffered from the bureaucratic tendency to send more and more individuals to a space not designed to accommodate such large numbers. The more or less 'sympathetic' nature of the mentally ill created a public distaste for tales of woe emerging from these specialised hospitals. These factors all contributed to the ascendancy of the community care model. While hospital directors initially resisted such calls for fundamental reform, opting instead to demand greater resources to regain the level of service provision they intended to provide, the movement to the community had begun, regardless of whether or not the community was ready for it.

Similarly, Gerald Grob (2008) notes the ideological component to such community care efforts, particularly in a neoliberal age insisting upon individual responsibility and the appropriate state role in the mental health regime. Grob argues that the fiscal crises currently facing many nations, particularly the United States and the United Kingdom (which divide society into deserving and undeserving poor), pose a dilemma for mental health advocates (2008, p. 89). In sum, interpreting community-based psychiatry from a governmentality perspective suggests that 'the home and personal relationships were constituted as a primary context for expert surveillance and professional and philanthropic intervention' (Nadesan 2008, p. 152). Hence, as large, centralised mental hospitals and asylums gave way to community centres and outpatient care, so too did the accompanying legal regimes and institutions premised on custodial treatment. Laws with stigma-inducing language were replaced, for instance, by person-first language emphasising the primacy of the individual over diagnostic label. Additional procedural safeguards were implemented to curtail the authority of psychiatrists to detain people indefinitely based on their mental health status. Accompanying these shifts were changes in professional attitudes, perpetuated by shifts in the professional perspectives and training on appropriate mental health treatment towards patients and patient rights, with a greater sensitivity to informed consent in both treatment regime and setting.

In sum, the community treatment model set about creating a set of institutions meant to approximate the traditional community institutions, primarily the family home, displaced by urbanisation and economic development in the core countries of Western Europe and North America. An important question to consider is whether these same institutions are appropriate for contexts within which strong family structures and community governance institutions persist. As will be seen later in this book, policy transfer and localisation suggest that policy success is more likely where transferred policies are nimble and do not cause a direct confrontation with existing institutions or deep societal norms. Therefore, it is necessary to examine existing institutions and the particular form that transferred policies take in addressing the perceived community mental health needs.

2.5 Mental Health as Human Right

The foregoing discussion about the development of mental health policies in the core regions of Western Europe and North America and the eventual ascendancy of the community treatment paradigm implicates several contextual factors. Firstly, the economic or rather fiscal realities of warehousing individuals, often numbering in the thousands to tens of thousands, in what the public perceived to be expensive, ineffectual and often cruel public facilities, led to a search for a more cost-effective manner of treating the mentally ill. A solution promising greater efficacy at a lower cost was offered in the community treatment model that conveniently tracked along with government downsizing efforts during the 1960s onwards. Secondly, the notion of human rights as civil rights became a prominent issue throughout the core regions during these years. Philip Fennell (1999) argues that rights, in the context of individuals suffering from mental illness, contain both a positive and negative dimension. Negative rights include the freedom from arbitrary detention or interference with one's person whilst positive rights pertain to a reasonable expectation to a certain amount of standard of care (1999, p. 103). As public perception of the institutional inefficacy together with the presence of a viable alternative treatment paradigm in community care, the individual being treated in the community and not the institution became seen as a human right.

Mario Maj's (2011) presentation of the World Psychiatric Association's view on the universal rights of individuals seeking mental health treatment serves as an illustration of just how entrenched this human rights framing of the community treatment paradigm has become. He notes four critical rights, starting with the requirement that individuals in need of mental health treatment have access to a knowledgeable health professional within their own country. Related to this is that this medical professional be up to date with the latest best practices and professional knowledge appropriate to the needs of the individual and be able to offer such care in a humane manner and setting. On this basis, Maj notes the need, particularly within the disability context, for the individual to be engaged in the planning of any treatment or services he or she might receive, including equal access to insurance and health access. These rights must increasingly be accessed in an environment of relative scarcity in a key resource: professionally trained psychiatrists. This fact requires psychiatry to operate much like other health areas in devolving responsibility over the specialty to 'adequately trained non-specialist providers, including medical and nursing professional in the delivery of mental health care'; he refers to this phenomenon as 'task-sharing' (Maj 2011, p. 1535). Task-sharing is particularly critical in developing nations (and rural areas within developed nations) with very low psychiatrist/psychologist (or other paraprofessionals) to individual ratios such as Samoa and Tonga.

Given a prevailing combination of arcane laws permitting essentially arbitrary and indefinite detention (and seclusion) of individuals with mental illness, as well other legal barriers to equality and justice in the developing world, Drew et al. (2011) argue law and policy reform should be prioritised. Their logic is that 'well formulated policies and laws can promote the development of accessible services in the community, stimulate advocacy and education campaigns, and establish legal and oversight mechanisms to prevent human ights violations' (2011, p. 1671).The authors note that laws and policies might be the first essential step, but permanent standing bodies and institutions in each nation must be erected to ensure the laws are enforced, policies pursued, and individual rights secured. International treaties, notably the United Nations (UN) Convention on the Rights of Persons with Disabilities, require bodies such as community visitors or ombudsman offices; and in several regions (Europe, Africa and the Americas but not yet for the Asia-Pacific region) human rights tribunals offer the possibility of relief to aggrieved claimants. These changes are presented as providing essential protection for individuals subject to compulsory mental health treatment.

Finally, Drew et al. (2011) discuss the close association of social stigma (often involving social ostracism) with human rights violations (including such things as abuse, discrimination, stigma, exclusion and financial and employment disadvantages) involving individuals with mental illness in low and middle-income countries. The authors urge that nations adopt and apply the UN Convention on the Rights of Persons with Disabilities as the framework to remedy these violations. Strategies to accompany this normative framework would include 'changing negative and incorrect beliefs, providing services in the community and empowering people with mental and psychological disabilities, reforming law and policy and establishing legal and oversight mechanisms' including such efforts as 'mental health literacy, empowerment, service user organisation, complaint mechanism, rehabilitation, and advocacy' (2011, p. 1664). These measures would require significant government stewardship of public education efforts needed to overcome these endemic belief structures.

In sum, there is a clear perception born of the experiences in the policy core that the myriad difficulties confronting individuals with mental illness in developing countries are best served by adopting a human rights frame to justify policy interventions in these nations. Mental health, as a species of the broader disability context, involves social stigma, which typically leads to isolation in social and economic interactions. This isolation serves to deprive individuals of their full rights as citizens and must therefore find protection in law. Since legal frameworks in the developing world are argued to be inadequate in this regard, it follows that this reform must take precedence. Once enshrined, individuals will be afforded access to judicial remedies to assert rights and discriminatory conduct that is presently tolerated will become disfavoured.

Framing mental health in this way also promotes moral pressure to ensure government buy-in. The international community might perceive a nation that disregards international human rights norms, such as those concerning disability and mental health, as failing to fully embrace the role of good global citizen. The mere adoption of a human rights frame, however, fails to explain recent widespread mental health policy changes in the Pacific. As will be discussed in Chap. 5, disability discrimination framed as a human right, including individuals with mental conditions, has existed in international documents since at least the 1970s – yet state statutory regimes designed to ensure human rights protections for individuals with mental illness, particularly in the Pacific region, did not reflect these values until the first decade of the twenty-first century. As was seen in the policy core, these rights-based frames alone were insufficient to see policy change. Instead, such changes needed to be accompanied by fiscal or economic arguments to warrant state intervention and to mobilise the international community to seek policy change.

2.6 The Global Mental Health Context

With this general framing of state mental health policy context writ large in mind, Jacob et al. (2007) canvassed the global mental health situation. According to their statistics, the median estimated neuropsychiatric burden for all countries was 2964 Disability Adjusted Life Years (DALYs) per 100,000 people. The research found that developing regions tended to allocate far fewer resources to the mental health system than those nations located in the core regions of North America and Western Europe, but the core had the highest prevalence of mental disorders. In fact, the authors observed that over 30% of countries worldwide reported no mental health care budget at all (2007, p. 1062). An area of particular concern is that between 20–30% of developing nations lacked mental health policies and legislation. While the authors note that the mere presence of a mental health policy or law does not on its own ensure better health outcomes, having such structures in place is essential to see policy aspirations put into meaningful system-level mental health service provision.

Mental health service provision, particularly in 'low-resource' settings, places such as Samoa and Tonga, continues at a lower level than do other health services (Raviola et al. 2011). The authors point out that only 25% of neuropsychiatric disorders in low-income countries are treated and only 4% of their overall health care budgets is devoted to mental health care –statistics, they argue, that call for a renewed focus on this area. Barriers to successful treatment include 'structural, largely economic and cultural obstacles' as well as 'functional impairment, social stigma, and low health literacy in patients and care givers' (Raviola et al. 2011, p. 1614). They argue, however, that these barriers are surmountable and note other successful interventions, particularly those on HIV/AIDS, as evidence that with the appropriate level of international support and local buy-in, such barriers can be overcome.

Efforts to advance the cause of mental health and wellness on the global policy agenda date at least from the 1990s but have gained momentum in the early 2000s with several high-profile reports and publications in academia and by international institutions. The bulk of this literature is focused on a rights-based and fiscally oriented approach to individuals with mental illness and the burden of mental disease on nation-states. One central theme in these publications involves the mental health consequences of globalisation, both in terms of specific societies bearing the impacts of economic and cultural globalisation as consumers as well as states becoming destinations for migrants and the specific burdens borne by these human participants in global markets.

According to Bhugra and Minas (2007), on average approximately 700 million people cross national boundaries each year, many as migrants, arriving to their destination with their own diverse cultures and languages. These people do not automatically plug into their destination culture and enjoy the economic benefits of their migration. The social costs of such moves can lead to 'increased marginalization, unemployment, erosion of job security, increased poverty, reduced access to health care and education, and reduced social provision' (Bhugra and Minas 2007, p. 1109). These migrations of people often involve individuals from collectivist cultures to individualist ones, such as Australia, New Zealand, North America and Western Europe. At the same time, however, and often overlooked in this literature, the social and economic globalisation factors embodying individualist principles, such as fiscal and corporate policies advanced as part of World Trade Organization (WTO) membership, for instance, send individualist policies to collectivist social contexts. Mental health policies and practices are but one species of this panoply of individualist institutions and structures.

How did mental health become a matter of contemporary international concern? As presented in a 2007 special mental health edition of The Lancet:

> [T]he public health importance of mental disorders, complex links with physical diseases, scarcity of mental health resources, inequity in resource distribution, inefficiency of use, and evidence related to the effectiveness of interventions for the treatment and prevention of mental disorders in low and middle-income countries (LAMICs). Health systems are the core to the delivery of evidence-based mental health care. (Jacob et al. 2007, p. 1061)

Patel et al. (2011) estimate that there currently exists a basic care treatment gap of 90% for individuals with mental disorders or illness in some countries. Critically, they note that this gap is not 'due to insufficient evidence about the effect of mental health problems or their effective treatment but to a range of barriers operating on all levels of health systems, from global policies to local health care provision' (2011, p. 1441). These barriers are apparently attributable to disparities in resources and focus on these problems as relevant policy areas for societal concern. The authors urge greater attention to the specific human rights concerns for individuals suffering from mental illness. They note that the 'even basic entitlements such as freedom and denial of the right to care constitute a global emergency on par with the worst human rights scandal in the history of global health, one which has rightly been called a failure of humanity' (2011, p. 1441).

Patel et al. propose a global treatment approach that would 'discourage' and 'weed out' 'irrational and inappropriate interventions' (2011, p. 1441) to remedy this perceived failure of humanity. Beyond policy and legal language that embodies international human rights norms around the individual and mental health treatments favoured in the community, the focus is now shifting to precise manners of intervention meant to influence medical determinations at the heart of involuntary civil commitments of individuals with mental illness deemed to pose a risk of harm to themselves or others.

Discussions about the nature of mental health, unlike those surrounding communicable disease or finance, tend to directly implicate traditional belief systems. Moreover, many mental illnesses cannot be 'cured' as can most infections. This leads to the conclusion not that Western medicine is flawed, but that the disease, as such, has not been properly identified and is more properly understood through indigenous ways of knowing. In an attempt to inoculate mental health services from these perceived deficiencies, IOs have become increasingly active in mental health policy proliferation over the past 20 years.

This research suggests the nexus of poverty and mental health, as well as untreated mental illness with crippling health system costs. The recognition and publication of these (and other) studies set the stage for international intervention to ensure developing countries would be up to date on contemporary mental health best practices. This was designed to insure against high future health costs that might create extreme fiscal hardships and hence instability in the international system. International, regional and bilateral aid and development organisations, it will be suggested below, served a critical role in confronting this problem by providing technical assistance to many developing countries to bring their domestic institutions and practices in line with international best practices. In order, however, to fully take up what these best practices were and how they were transferred to the developing states of Samoa and Tonga, I first examine how these best practices developed. As will be discussed later in this book, a strand of policy transfer scholarship argues for the elimination of an independent endogenous basis for a policy in order to demonstrate transfer as opposed to convergence or even happenstance.

2.7 Conclusion

This chapter has presented an overview of the historical development and current context of mental health policy in the core regions of North America and Western Europe. This is to provide the necessary policy context for mental health policy's transition from a domestic, state-based policy concern to a global one. Bound up in this discussion has been a consideration of the scholarship on this particular policy area in these countries and the reasons for policy changes over time. Mental health has been seen to be reliant on the social context, with a cultural component the understanding of which is crucial to properly situating it within the constellation of policy problems. Given the underlying ideological assumptions regarding the welfare state and the traditional role of the state in ensuring public safety and providing an environment conducive to maintaining mental health, the state's enduring role in mental health is secure. Mental health is a comprehensive policy area implicating numerous state institutions, from hospitals to prisons and a state's social welfare apparatus. Given this broad-based policy milieu, I propose to use 'mental health policy' as a form of metapolicy framework. This rubric draws together various strands of policy construct (e.g. human rights; state police powers; medical; social welfare; state and private sector care provision) into one mediated construct, which will be packaged and promoted as 'best practice'.

Given these overlapping institutional arrangements, including the affected epistemic and professional networks working within these formal institutions, a consideration of institutional theory was presented with a particular focus on historical institutionalism. Insights from historical institutionalism include the enduring legacies of institutional creation and their stubborn nature even in the face of change. The emergence of the mental hygiene movement – with its underlying ideology of profound belief in state control over the mentally ill – during the early years of the twentieth century would have profound institutional impacts upon recently colonized nations and those reaching independence in the midtwentieth century. Mental health institutions established in these nations would follow a path dependent stagnation for the remaining years of the twentieth century.

In the mental health context, the existence of different policies reflecting different ideological periods has been clearly demonstrated through the moral treatment, mental hygiene and community treatment epochs. Under Hansen and King's (2001) ideational approach, the epochal shifts within the mental health policy core also exhibited the three factors making the ideas to policy transition more likely. Each period was marked by a new ideational structure as to appropriate mental health treatment. The moral treatment, mental hygiene, and community care models were each associated with an accompanying ideological framework concerning best practice. At the same time, each phase was accompanied by a larger fiscal framework that sought to, at one extreme, increase state involvement when state power was at its zenith. As these measures came into question and the costs associated with warehousing increasingly larger proportions of the public in state institutions continued to rise, an antidote emerged in the burgeoning community treatment movement. In other words, the merger of the ideas underlying community treatment also required accompanying fiscal justifications for the shift from facility to community that could be championed by political interests possessing the requisite enthusiasm and institutional position to effectuate change. At the same time, timing is of the essence in placing the proposed policy changes within a preference-reinforcing environment.

Building on the insights offered by historical institutionalism and mental health policy scholarship, I argue that in order to effectively study mental health policies in borrowing or transferor nations, one must examine how policies move from place to place within their specific historical contexts. Institutions established in non-originating cultures as part of decolonisation or other related events must be examined with reference to that context. This merger of ideas, such as those underlying community treatment in mental health, will be justified on one hand by the fiscal concerns facing nation-states in the future. At the same time, the fiscal justification for a policy shift comes to be identified with a moral, human rights, and ultimately cultural notion of appropriate treatment for an individual with a mental disorder. Such transfers of policy easily lend themselves to historical analysis since the existence of the state as well as an implicated policy can be fixed in time. I take up this policy transfer theoretical context and analytical framework in the next chapter, before returning to the mental health policy puzzle in Chap. 4 where I take up the internationalisation of mental health policy.

References

Acharyya, S. (1996). Practicing cultural psychiatry: The Doctor's dilemma. In T. Heller (Ed.), *Mental health matters*. New York: Palgrave Macmillan.

Allen, J., & Laycock, J. (2000). Major mental illness in the Pacific: A review. *Pacific Health Dialogue, 4*, 2.

Barendregt, J. J. (2003). Disability-adjusted Life Years (DALYs) & Disability-adjusted Life Expectancy (DALE). In J. M. Robine et al. (Eds.), *Determining health expectancies*. Chichester: Wiley.

Bass, J., Bolton, P., & Murray, L. (2007). Do not forget culture when studying mental health. *The Lancet, 370*, 918.

Bhugra, D., & Minas, I. (2007). Mental health & global movement of people. *The Lancet, 370*(9593), 1109–1111.

Brown, R., & Connell, J. (2004). The migration of doctors and nurses from South Pacific Island nations. *Social Science & Medicine, 58*(11), 2193–2210.

Busfield, J. (1996). Professionals, the state, and the development of mental health policy. In T. Heller (Ed.), *Mental health matters*. New York: Palgrave Macmillan.

Cortell, A., & Peterson, S. (1999). Altered states: Explaining domestic institutional change. *British Journal of Political Science, 29*(1), 177–203.
Drew, N., Funk, M., Tang, S., Lamichhane, J., Chávez, E., Katontoka, S., Pathare, S., Lewis, O., Gostin, L., & Saraceno, B. (2011). Human rights violations of people with mental & psychosocial disabilities: An unresolved global crisis. *The Lancet, 378*(9803), 1664–1675.
Falleti, T. G. (2010). *Decentralization and subnational politics in Latin America*. Cambridge: Cambridge University Press.
Fennell, P. (1999). The third way in mental health policy: Negative rights, positive rights, & the convention. *Journal of Law & Society, 26*(1), 103–127.
Foucault, M. (1965). *Madness & civilization: A history of insanity in an age of reason*. London: Routledge.
Foucault, M. (1980). *Power/knowledge: Selected interview & other writings 1972–1977*. Brighton: Harvester Press.
Foucault, M. (2006). *History of madness*. London: Routledge.
Foucault, M. (2008). *Psychiatric power: Lectures at the Collège de France* (pp. 1973–1974). New York: Palgrave Macmillan.
Golberstein, E., Eisenberg, D., & Gollust, S. (2008). Perceived stigma & mental health care seeking. *Psychiatric Services, 59*(4), 392–399.
Goodwin, S. (1997). *Comparative mental health policy: Form institutional to community care*. London: Sage.
Grob, G. (2008). Mental health policy in the liberal state: The example of the United States. *International Journal of Law & Psychiatry, 31*, 89–100.
Hall, P., & Taylor, R. (1996). Political science & the three new institutionalisms. *Political Studies, 44*(4), 936–957.
Hansen, R., & King, D. (2001). Eugenic Ideas, Political Interests, & Policy Variance: Immigration & Sterilization Policy in Britain & the U.S. *World Politics, 53*(2), 237–263.
Ikenberry, G. (1988). Conclusion: An institutional approach to American foreign economic policy. *International Organization, 42*(1), 219–243.
Jacob, K., Sharan, P., Mirza, I., Garrido-Cumbrera, M., Seedat, S., Mari, J., Sreenivas, V., & Saxena, S. (2007). Mental health systems in countries: where are we now? *The Lancet, 370*(9592), 1061–1077.
Kagan, R. A. (1991). Adversarial legalism and American government. *Journal of Policy Analysis and Management, 10*(3), 369.
Kendell, E. (1996). The nature of psychiatric disorders. In T. Heller (Ed.), *Mental health matters*. New York: Palgrave McMillian.
Kessler, R., & Usttin, C. T. (2008). *The WHO world mental health surveys: Global perspectives on the epidemiology of mental disorders*. Cambridge: Cambridge University Press.
Kokai, M., Fujiii, S., Shinfuku, N., & Edwards, G. (2004). Natural disaster & mental health in Asia. *Psychiatry & Clinical Neurosciences, 58*(2), 110.
Krasner, S. (1984). Review: Approaches to the state: Alternative conceptions & historical dynamics. *Comparative Politics, 16*(2), 223–246.
Lebra, W. (Ed.). (1976). *Culture-bound syndromes, ethnopsychiatry, & alternate therapies*. Honolulu: University Press of Hawaii.
Lopez, A., Mathers, C., Ezzati, M., Jamison, D., & Murray, C. (Eds.). (2006). *Global burden of disease and risk factors*. New York: Oxford University Press.
Lurie, S. (2005). Comparative mental health policy: Are there lessons to be learned? *International Review of Psychiatry, 17*(2), 97–101.
Mahoney, J., & Thelen, K. e. (2010). *Explaining institutional change: Ambiguity, agency & power*. New York: Cambridge University Press.
Maj, M. (2011). The rights of people with mental disorders: WPA perspective. *The Lancet, 378*(9802), 1534–1535.
March, J., & Olsen, J. (1984). The new institutionalism: Organizational factors in political life. *The American Political Science Review, 78*(3), 734–749.

Marmot, M. (2005). Social determinants of health inequalities. *The Lancet, 365*, 1099–1104.
Marsella, A., & White, G. (Eds.). (1982). *Cultural conceptions of mental health & therapy*. Boston: D, Reidel.
McKenzie, K., et al. (2004). Learning from low income countries: Mental health. *British Medical Journal, 329*(7475).
Mechanic, D. (1969). *Mental health and social policy*. Englewood Cliffs: Prentice-Hall.
Mechanic, D. (1998). Emerging trends in mental health policy and practice. *Health Affairs, 17*(6), 82–98.
Morrissey, J., & Goldman, H. (1984). Cycles of reform in the Care of the Chronically Mentally Ill. *Hospital & Community Psychiatry, 35*(8).
Murray, C., & Lopez, A. (1996). Evidence-based health policy—Lessons from the global burden of disease study. *Science, 274*(5288), 740–743.
Nadesan, M. (2008). *Governmentality, biopower, and everyday life*. New York: Routledge.
Omran, A. (1971). The epidemiologic transition: A theory of the epidemiology of population change. *The Milbank Memorial Fund Quarterly, 49*(4), 509–538.
Patel, V., & Prince, M. (2001). Ageing & mental health in a developing country: Who cares? Qualitative studies from Goa, India. *Psychological Medicine, 31*(01), 29–38.
Patel, V., Boyce, N., Collins, P., Saxena, S., & Horton, R. (2011). A renewed agenda for global mental health. *The Lancet, 378*(9801), 1441–1442.
Peters, B. (2005). *Institutional theory in political science: The 'new institutionalism*. London: Continuum.
Peters, B., & Pierre, J. (1998). Institutions & time: Problems of Conceptualization & Explanation. *Journal of Public Administration Research & Theory: J-PART, 8*(4), 565–583.
Peters, B., Pierre, J., & King, D. (2005). The politics of path dependency: Political conflict in historical institutionalism. *The Journal of Politics, 67*(4), 1275–1300.
Pierson, P. (2000a). Three worlds of welfare state research. *Comparative Political Studies, 33*(6–7), 791–821.
Pierson, P. (2000b). Not just what, but *when:* Timing & sequence in political processes Studies. *American Political Development, 14*, 72.
Raviola, G., Becker, A., & Farmer, P. (2011). A global scope for global health—Including mental health. *The Lancet, 378*(9803), 1613–1615.
Rehm, J., & Shield, K. D. (2019). Global burden of disease and the impact of mental and addictive disorders. *Current Psychiatry Reports, 21*(2), 10.
Rochefort, D. (1988). Policymaking cycles in mental health: Critical examination of a conceptual model. *Journal of Health Politics, Policy & Law, 13*(1), 129–152.
Rochefort, D. (1997). *From poorhouses to homelessness: policy analysis & mental health care*. Westport: Auburn House.
Rogers, A., & Pilgrim, D. (1996). *Mental health policy in Britain: A critical introduction* (p. 1996). Houndmills: Macmillan.
Scheff, T. (1996). Labeling mental illness. In A. Heller (Ed.), *Mental health matters: a reader*. Basingstoke/Houndmills: Macmillan.
Skocpol, T. (1992). *Protecting soldiers & mothers: the political origins of social policy in the United States*. Cambridge: Belknap Press of Harvard University.
Steinglass, P., & Gerrity, E. (2006). Natural disasters & post-traumatic stress disorder short-term versus long-term recovery in two disaster-affected communities. *Journal of Applied Social Psychology, 20*, 21.
Steinmo, S., Thelen, K., & Longsreth, F. (Eds.). (1992). *Structuring politics: Historical institutionalism in comparative analysis*. New York: Cambridge University Press.
Susser, M. (1965). Rationale for the community care of mental disorder. *Medical Care, 3*(1), 52–59.
Thelen, K. (1999). Historical institutionalism in comparative politics. *Annual Review of Political Science, 2*, 369–404.
Tilly, C. (1984). Big structures, large processes, huge comparisons (New York: Russell Sage Foundation) at p. 14.
Tuohy, C. H. (1999). *Accidental logics: The dynamics of change in the health care arena in the United States, Britain, and Canada*. New York: Oxford University Press.

World Health Organization (WHO). (2003). *The ICD Classification of Mental and Behavioral Disorders: Diagnostic Criteria for Research*. Geneva: WHO.

World Health Organization (WHO). (2005). *WHO resource book on mental health, human rights & legislation*. Geneva: WHO.

World Health Organization (WHO). (2007). *Mental health: Strengthening mental health promotion*. Geneva: WHO.

World Health Organization (WHO). (2012). *DALYs/YLDs definition* [online], Available from: http://www,who,int/mental_health/management/depression/daly/en

Chapter 3
Can Policy Transfer Help Us Explain the Global Movement of Mental Health Policies?

This chapter builds on the mental health policy context identified in the policy core countries discussed in Chap. 2. The mental health policy context established above notes a particular rights-based posture for mental health policy in the core regions of North America and Western Europe. This posture is perpetuated through professional training and the community treatment paradigm is considered the best practice model both in terms of professional attitudes to treatment efficacy and from a human rights perspective. This policy consensus will be reflected in the international policy documents to be discussed in Chap. 5, and in the posture of law and policy reforms eventually taken in Samoa and Tonga, is discussed in Chaps. 5, 6 and 7. However, before taking up a substantive review of this process and the resulting policies, a framework for study must first be established. I propose Dolowitz and Marsh's (1996, 2000) policy transfer framework as a means of doing so.

This chapter has two central purposes: firstly, I review the literature on policy transfer, presenting the key topics in the form of various questions designed to focus my discussion on the salient aspects of policy transfer scholarship germane to this book. I begin with an overview of policy transfer and progress by focusing on key variables such as the substance of transfer and identifying relevant actors. Secondly, I adopt Dolowitz and Marsh's policy transfer framework to organise the remaining parts of this book. I consider emerging theoretical and methodological aspects – such as the recent movement towards more constructivist influences within policy transfer scholarship – separately in the following chapter on methodology.

3.1 Explaining Policy Migration: Policy Transfer

In the previous chapter I presented mental health policy in terms of its institutional development in the core regions of Western Europe and North America. That discussion was necessary to properly situate the substantive policy area before considering how mental health policies arose in Samoa and Tonga. The study of how

T. P. Fadgen, *Mental Health Public Policy in Global Context*,
https://doi.org/10.1007/978-981-15-6479-6_3

policies move from one place to another has been the focus of diverse scholarship. Diffusion studies have taken a similar approach and suggested a passivity whereby policies can simply spread throughout the world in the absence of any active search or vetting process, even in the absence of a perceived domestic policy problem (see e.g. Weyland 2007). Others have explained this movement in terms of policy exchange as lesson drawing (see e.g. Rose 1990). Still other researchers have explained this movement in terms of nations converging on a policy solution to a shared area of concern (see e.g. Bennett 1991). These latter approaches proceed from a rationalist perspective and assume policy actors seek out the best possible solution to a locally recognised policy problem.

Diffusion studies tend to focus on the identification of variable patterns such as geographic proximity in relation to policy adoption or resource equivalency between studied cases (Weyland 2007). Previous scholarship, however, has not succeeded in clearly examining the policy transfer as process, instead focusing almost exclusively on policy diffusion between developed countries. While this preoccupation with developed nations has endured, the focus has shifted away from policy diffusion to examining other variables of the transfer dynamic. Moreover, Diane Stone (2012) notes that the diffusion literature's preoccupation with patterns neglects consideration of the alteration of adopted policies. This last point will be seen below to form an important new area of policy transfer research as well.

Richard Rose's (1990) concept of lesson drawing, which also adopts a rationalist approach to policy movement, be-gins with the scanning of programmes in one place and evaluating them for use in the examining country. This rigid emphasis on rationalism leads to what De Jong has described as Rose's 'rejection of the importance of historical, cultural and specific institutional aspects as relevant factors during the transplantation process for fear of culturalism' (2009, p. 145). According to De Jong, Rose argues that 'thick descriptions' of 'individuals, institutional subtleties in the country of origin and historical circumstances leading to the adoption of a policy programme there should be dis-regarded' (2009, p. 147). De Jong (2009) responds that, 'cultural features, also known as "informal institutions", are vital to the way in which new lessons will be embedded into existing regulatory frameworks' (2009, p. 147). Lesson drawing's preoccupation with rational policy search as a prerequisite to demonstrating transfer, together with its rejection of the potential importance of attributes unique to the national context, makes its utility suspicious, particularly in the developing nation context. De Jong's observation suggests that in order to create a comprehensive explanation of the existence of an examined policy within a particular culture, research should consider the 'informal' or cultural context within which those adopted policies emerge. Rose's approach to lesson drawing does not permit such analysis. Similar shortcomings are found in the policy convergence literature.

Colin Bennett's (1991) notion of policy convergence describes a process whereby two or more nations arrive at the same or similar policy selection through one of four processes: emulation, elite networking, harmonisation and penetration. Emulation, like lesson drawing, implies one state looking to another to address an internal problem or concern and drawing lessons from that state's experience.

Convergence and elite networking both involve consensus building by political or policy elites. Bennett argues that harmonisation differs from other processes in that it requires a 'coherent group of transnational actors, a broad consonance of motivation and concern and regular opportunities for interaction; they also require authoritative action by a responsible' international organisation (IO) (1991, p. 225).

These transnational actors, in Bennett's (1991) view, served to shape coordinated responses to shared policy problems 'in order to mitigate the unintended external consequences of domestic policy' (1991, p. 225). Bennett concludes that in order to succeed, emulation and elite networking require information-sharing whilst convergence involves knowledge diffusion concerning policy frames. Harmonisation, in contrast, requires the presence of some international agent, and penetration requires the intervention of an external actor. Ultimately, a researcher must rule out 'domestic factors before concluding that one of the transnational forces must be responsible' (1991, p. 231). Many of these prerequisites to determining whether a foreign policy has been integrated or adopted into a domestic policy structure endure within the policy transfer framework.

Convergence is most likely to occur where countries have common institutional and cultural attributes, amongst other factors (Knill 2005). Similarly, it is thought countries will look to other countries sharing these attributes in deciding on which policies to converge (see e.g. Strang and Meyer 1993). This is especially true for new policy concepts that directly implicate or confront a national culture. Instruments require institutional similarity, meaning those countries with similar governance structures would be expected to 'share preferences' for such institutional change. Like lesson drawing, however, convergence suggests that while nations that share a common cultural heritage might coalesce around a particular policy formulation within a particular area, resulting in a convergence on that particular policy iteration, the process itself still is a rational one, whereby states search for a policy solution and in-stead of a cognitive process of 'learning' there is a search for best-fit that often has a centre of gravity defined by cultural or institutional similarity.

David Dolowitz and David Marsh (1996) originally developed their concept of policy transfer to distinguish their ideas from diffusion, lesson drawing and especially convergence. Their approach would instead focus 'more narrowly upon the transfer of specific policies as a result of strategic decisions taken by actors outside and inside government' (1996, p. 343). Their definition of policy transfer, which has now been widely accepted in the literature, is: "a process in which knowledge about policies, administrative arrangements, institutions in one time and/or place is used in the development of policies, administrative arrangements and institutions in another time and/or place" (1996, p. 344). Mark Evans (2009) adapts this definition and suggests that policy transfer research 'seeks to make sense of the cross-cultural transfer of knowledge about institutions, policies, or delivery systems from one sector or level of governance to another level of governance in a different country' (2009, p. 238). These definitions essentially represent two discrete aspects of a complete policy transfer analysis. Firstly, we must define a 'transfer' by explaining the process of policy movement itself. By identifying a policy as 'transferred' after performing a process tracing analysis to construct the movement of the policy from origin to its point of eventual adoption we can separate the policy under study as an object of transfer rather than the product of some rational, endogenous process. Once this initial step is achieved, Evans's additional interpretive component of policy transfer study can be realised. 'Making sense' of the policies transferred involves not only understanding why they were transferred but also analysing what the imported policy looks like in its new context and, if it has changed, considering how it came to be different.

Spatially, as well as conceptually, policy transfer exists at the 'intersections of society, politics/governance and space' (McCann and Ward 2012, p. 326). These intersections are not merely horizontal in nature. As Betsill and Bulkeley (2004) argue, they can also involve vertical exchanges between various levels of governance, both intra- and inter-state. Additionally, Stone (2012) observes that transfer itself often involves different 'modalities' such as ideals or goals; institutional transfer; regulatory and administrative and judicial tools; transfers involving ideas and ideologies; and personnel transfer (exchange of experts or loaning of policy experts) (2012, pp. 3–4). Policy transfer research often examines, albeit indirectly, the relationship between a nation-state and the international or global society (Gilardi et al 2009). Furthering this observation, Benson and Jordan (2011) argue that the existing policy transfer literature has demonstrated a movement in the 'locus of policy transfer activity' from a primarily government-centred study to a more pluralist perspective, considering many actors and influences (2011, p. 372). This model holds that domestic institutions and structures can gain policy derived from international models through 'global cultural and associational processes' (Benson and Jordan 2011, pp. 144–45).

As these descriptions suggest, policy transfer implicates a foreign policy entering the domestic context. These intersections often implicate cultural variation between transferor and transferee, leading to a rich diversity of policy, reflecting 'diverse histories as well as the institutional and cultural contexts within which [the proffered policies] are undertaken' (Newburn 2010). These transfers are also said to be multi-layered, encompassing various 'policy dimensions' including 'policy sub-elements, such as policy content or policy style' (Heichel et al. 2005). Transfer objects can also be understood as being either 'hard' or 'soft' objects. Hard objects include instruments and institutions, whilst soft transfers might be said to include ideas or ideology. As Stone (2012) has argued, these forms are not necessarily exclusive, and instead coexist within the international policy context (see also Benson and Jordan 2011, p. 370).

Policy transfer scholarship continues to expand to new substantive policy areas as well as geographic regions. Topical diversity has expanded to include such areas as: general institutional transfer (Larmour 2005); health care systems (Leiber et al. 2010); crime policy (Jones and Newburn 2002); transport policy and urban transport policy (Marsden and Stead 2011; Timms 2011); tax blacklisting (Sharman 2010); creative industries policy (Prince 2010) and railway regulation (James and Lodge 2003). Recent expansions in the geographic focus include such diverse studies as public private partnerships in Sri Lanka (Appuhami et al. 2011); restorative and indigenous justice practices in Southern Sudan and East Timor (Banks 2011);

education policy in Armenia (Karakhanyan et al. 2011); and various policies in Melanesian countries (Larmour 2002). Studies have also focused on the movement of policy ideas from a core group of policy leaders to the global level, including microcredit institutionalisation (Aagaard 2011); Organisation for Economic Co-operation and Development (OECD) and bilateral tax treaties (Latulippe 2010); and youth justice regimes (Pakes 2010). These studies adopt various areas of emphasis but typically involve a case study consisting of questions addressing which factors inhibited or contributed to policy transfer. In addition, these studies typically aim to determine when (and if) policy transfer has occurred and what explains successful transfers versus those that failed.

3.1.1 Factors Facilitating or Inhibiting Policy Transfer

Evans (2009) indicates that the existence of certain institutional structures (e.g. IOs, treaties) and ideational structures (such as globalisation; see e.g. Ladi 2005) and the processes that emanate from them are providing the impetus for ever-increasing policy transfer occurrences. These structures are explained through either state-centred or organisational-centred policy transfer perspectives. State-centred perspectives see policy transfer as instrumental in the evolution of the state itself whilst organisational-centred versions tend to focus on rational evaluative frameworks that see dissatisfaction as the main engine behind transfer. Stone contrasts transfer with terms like policy convergence and policy diffusion, suggesting transfer as the result of structural forces. Social or policy learning emphasises cognition and the redefining of interests on the basis of new knowledge, which affects the fundamental belief and ideas behind policy approaches (see e.g. Dolowitz 2018; Hall 1993). Further, Stone notes the danger inherent in causal inter-changeability of lesson drawing and policy transfer – policy transfer is the broader concept encompassing coercion as well as the voluntary activity of lesson drawing.

While these factors have been found to promote effective policy transfer, Rose (1990, 1993) suggests six hypotheses that might constrain policy transfer: (1) programmes with single goals are more transferable than those with multiple goals; (2) the simpler the problem, the more likely transfer will occur; (3) the more direct the relationship between the problem and solution is perceived to be, the more likely it is to be transferred; (4) the fewer perceived side-effects of a policy the greater the possibility of transfer; (5) the more information agents have about how a programme operates in another location the easier it is to transfer; and (6) the more easily outcomes can be predicted the more likely the programme is to be transferred. Further, as Dolowitz and Marsh (1996) note, policy transfer is also dependent upon the 'transferring policy system possessing the political, bureaucratic and economic resources to implement the policy' (1996, p. 354). They suggest that the adopting nation's technical or economic limitations might predict their adoption or refusal to adopt particular policies. A similar inquiry can be made about determining when a policy transfer has occurred and the success or failure of a particular policy transfer.

3.1.2 Determining a Policy Transfer Occurrence and Evaluating Success or Failure

Given this, how might one demonstrate policy transfer and not some mere coincidence of a similar policy emerging as a result of an indigenous political process? Again, Stone (1999, 2000) and Bennett (1991) are instructive. Bennett provides a set of prerequisites for determining whether transfer has occurred, which he developed out of the existing case study literature on policy diffusion and transfer. Accordingly, policy transfer can be substantiated if no 'idiosyncratic domestic factors' are found to account for the policy change, that the changes are not merely due to 'similar modernising forces having the same but separate effects in different states'(Stone 1999, p. 56), where one can demonstrate awareness amongst policymakers in the adopting state of similar changes made elsewhere; or situations where foreign material is relied upon in the domestic policy process. Of course, instances of policy transfer are most obvious where policies, programmes or institutions are copied in toto, but as Stone (1999) argues, while objectives in and of themselves may be transferrable, the form of implementation, the tools and procedures adopted in various locales may result in quite different outcomes. Policy, institutions, and ideas are indigenized. The intensity or degree of transfer needs to be relatively significant to make a valid argument of transfer (1999, p. 56). She concludes that '[t]ransfer is likely to result in implementation problems and failure when a practice or idea cannot be translated into another context' (1999, p. 54). These observations illustrate the importance of context-specific transfer strategies for agents of transfer, an insight to be explored and reinforced in this book.

For most engaged in policy transfer research, the best evidence for transfer is found when a particular policy is actually implemented. However, distinguishing between types of change is necessary when considering a purported area of policy transfer. For instance, Evans (2009) considers 'first order change' as that which affects policy instruments but not the creation of new instruments; 'second order change' involves changes to instruments themselves; and 'third order change' concerns policy objectives broadly (Evans 2009, p. 247). Evans ultimately concludes that the single feature of policy transfer analysis that can distinguish it from other policymaking analytic approaches is its shifting the focus onto 'the remarkable movement of ideas between systems of governance through policy transfer networks and the intermediation of agents of policy transfer' (Evans 2009, p. 263). In other words, a view towards the role of IOs or epistemic communities (see e.g. Haas 1992) in the policy transfer process should be an essential characteristic of policy transfer studies.

Related to identifying when transfer has taken place is addressing whether a policy transfer has been successful or has failed. Policy success is defined as 'the extent to which policy transfer achieves the aims set by government when they engage in transfer, or is perceived as a success by the key actors involved in the policy area'(Dolowitz and Marsh 2000, p. 17). Failure occurs, in Dolowitz and Marsh's view, due to three factors: (1) uninformed transfer (where a transferee adopts a policy on less than perfect understanding of its purpose or necessary contextual or operational prerequisites); (2) incomplete transfer (some, but not all, critical elements of a particular policy are transferred); and (3) inappropriate transfer (incongruity between underlying social and other contexts between transferor and transferee). I argue here that it is only through a historical analysis of a particular policy area that the perspective necessary to determine success or failure is possible.

3.1.3 The Predominant European and North American Policy Transfer Research Focus

As noted above, a further issue with this scholarship has been its European/North American preoccupation to the neglect of the developing world's policy needs or cultural milieu. Marsh and Sharman (2009) argue that the lack of non-European cases is particularly unfortunate since policy transfer studies tend to employ a common case study methodological approach which is particularly apropos in contexts of limited quantitative data (2009, p. 280). In addition, given that many of the identified policy transfer mechanisms (e.g. IO agendas and conditionality), transfer would be expected to be stronger in developing states.

This lack of focus outside of Europe and North America also serves to obscure other areas of potentially important policy transfer research. For instance, Stone (1999) observes the risk involved in Western efforts to market so-called best practices which, even if they are objectively the 'best' manner of achieving the desired outcome, can come to be seen as imperialist or neo-colonialist in nature. These studies implicate the risks of overreliance on transferred policies as well as the issue of finding an appropriate fit. On one side, Evans (2009) notes that 'the con-tent of policy transfers normally reflects areas where indigenous state actors lack expertise. Agents of policy transfer have the capacity to bridge the indigenous knowledge gap can become important players in policy transfer networks' (2009, p. 260). Where indigenous actors lack expertise and foreign expertise is available, then it seems rational and logical for this expertise to be relied upon to solve a particular policy problem.

Huck-Ju Kwon (2009), however, writes of the perils and limitations of overreliance on transferred policy and the effect this has on the domestic policy process. The author looks at the phenomenon in Japan, the republic of Korea, and Taiwan. The focus is on the utility of developmental states adopting Western policy initiatives, but the quick fix available through policy transfers of this nature often comes with the high cost of supplanting the development of domestic policymaking capacity needed to address future unanticipated and unique domestic policy concerns. Kwon argues, however, that health care generally, and as will be demonstrated below in the mental health policy context in particular, is an example of top-down (formal) policy innovation as an 'effort to modernize' and thus shorten the 'development gap' between developing and developed states (Kwon 2009). One arguable consequence of this approach, however, is that the nation adopting the proffered policy does not develop the necessary skills to confront future problems and must continuously rely on such policy imports to address domestic demand.

Similarly, Kerstin Tews (2009) finds concerns in policy transfer involving European Union (EU) expansion. Tews focuses on EU environmental legislation and shows that the process of EU accession raises similar issues. The down-side of policy transfer lies primarily in the reduction in domestic political accountability to respond to emerging policy problems. Tews begins with the premise that the joint notion is that there exists a kind of asymmetrical power relationship between the importer and the exporter of policies—usually resulting in the form that the "weaker" one wishes to gain resources from the "stronger" one, who then conditions access to its resources by making the "weaker" one import its policies (Tews 2009, p. 133).

The problem with such a dynamic lies with the phenomenon that such 'obliged transfers' might well result in imposed lessons without any learning (Stone 2000, p. 8 cited in Tews 2009, p.134). Furthermore, Tews (2009) notes that 'without a domestic approach to prioritizing the development of … legislation … [policy transfer] becomes merely an instrument to prepare for [EU] accession, instead of an instrument to deal with domestic … problems' (Tews 2009, p. 135). There must, in addition to any actual policy transfer, be a transfer of the perception of political need of a transferred policy. Therefore, Tews introduces an additional factor: in addition to ensuring appropriateness of transfer, there must also be some recognition or actual 'learning' amongst policymakers of the importance of the adopted policy in order to set in motion an institution that might respond to future policy needs.

Müller and Slominski (2017) have lamented the dearth of scholarship on how international public policies come to be influenced by domestic politics. They focus on the management scholarship to identify three main ways in which these policy processes exert and experience influence. Lessons from abroad can lend "argumentative power" to pre-existing or even novel domestic policy arguments that favour adoption. These lessons, however, tend to be incomplete and privilege the low-cost/no-cost attributes of policies over those that might be uncomfortable or even painful to adopt. A third way in which this process unfolds is by allowing learning on the policy design to successfully promote a proposed policy for adoption. Lastly, by looking beyond the substance of the policy to more effectively map the process, identify key stakeholders and likely opponents, the messaging around the policy can be refined—another form of political learning. These insights are useful to understand the constructivist turn that policy transfer scholarship has taken in recent years.

These contributions raise important implications for the future directions of policy transfer literature. Implicit in both studies is the importance of domestic policymakers having the institutional ability to respond through innovation to new problems not previously envisioned by other states or whose lessons are not readily available for guidance. On the other hand, these studies also imply that there is often little or even no local consideration of the proffered policies; that the proposals are offered in an in toto form that removes the domestic policymaking capacity in some way. These are all matters worthy of investigation and I next consider several recent studies adopting a critical realist orientation as well as an emerging constructivist turn in policy transfer scholarship that has as its central purpose privileging the role of domestic policy actors in order to better understand the complexities of policy transfers. I discuss the policy transfer framework as developed by Dolowitz and Marsh (1996, 2000) that I use to organise my research. Be-cause of the methodological implications of the discussion on the critical realism and constructivism in recent policy transfer scholarship, I resume the discussion on these topics in the following chapter, where I expand upon the re-search methodology developed for this book.

3.1.4 Other Critiques of Policy Transfer Scholarship

Other critiques of policy transfer scholarship bearing mention here centre around four areas identified by Evans (2009) and an additional element offered by Stone (1999). Firstly, policy transfer analysis cannot be distinguished from normal forms of policymaking in general (Evans and Davies 1999) and rational approaches to policymaking in particular (James and Lodge 2003); secondly, policy transfer analysis fails to advance an explanatory theory of policy development (James and Lodge 2003); thirdly, it fails to provide rigorous tools for evaluating whether transfer has occurred or not (Page 2000); and fourthly, the research isn't relevant to the world of practice (Evans 2006). Stone's (1999) additional criticism of existing literature is that transfer is treated ahistorically. Transfer is presented in the literature as becoming apparent due to globalisation, but, as Stone argues, the occurrence of policy transfer has a much longer history, including imperialistic transfers of legal codes (see e.g. Watson 1993) and systems of government, for example.

Evans and Davies (1999) argue that while policy transfer is not itself an explanatory theory (see also James and Lodge 2003), it is a useful 'analogical model' providing a vehicle for explaining policy change (see e.g. Dolowitz and Marsh 2012). Amongst the criticisms of the existing literature that Evans and Davies note is that the relationship be-tween state structures and agency remains underdeveloped. A notable exception to this is Ian Greener's (2002) analysis of the United Kingdom's National Health Service (UKNHS) reform process. Greener uses policy transfer, social learning and path dependency concepts in an attempt to explain the UKNHS reform process. He uses the under-standing of policy transfer established by Dolowitz and Marsh and defines social learning as a 'process usually involving three central variables: the overarching goals that guide policy, the techniques or policy instruments used to attain these goals; and the settings of these instruments' (Hall 1993 cited in Greener 2002). As Greener points out, social learning and policy transfer scholarship tends to privilege policy change over continuity. Path dependency, in contrast, focuses on what makes certain policies intractable. Greener suggests that the combination of these approaches to the UKNHS reform debate should shed greater light on the policy process.

Greener argues that the policy transfer account suggests the importance of agency in health reform and the danger of an agency-centred relationship, with the incumbent peril of overlooking 'complex power relationships underpinning policy formulation' (2002, p. 177). In sum, he finds that 'lesson-drawing across time and social learning are both central to understanding the health policy process with policymakers learning form their earlier experiences in education reform' (2002, p. 177). Knowing what general conditions are needed to establish a new policy and thus avoid the path dependency trap comes from the policymaker's ability to 'differentiate between those factors that are relatively permanent features of the policy environment' (2002, p. 178). I intend to explore the relationship between state (and international) structures and agency in this book in an attempt to deepen the utility of the policy transfer framework as a tool for analysing policy transfer and for making sense of the form that adopted policies ultimately took in Samoa and Tonga.

Dolowitz and Marsh (2000) also address the general lack of focus in much of the policy transfer literature as to whether policy transfer is used as a dependent variable (asking which factors influenced the transfer process) or an independent one (asking how the policy transfer process impacted the adopted policy). Michael Howlett and Jeremy Rayner (2008) also describe this confusion in dependent/independent variable as confusing the 'what' (object of transfer or diffusion) with the 'how' (process of transfer or diffusion) (2008, p. 386). Dolowitz and Marsh (2000) and Dolowitz (1998), however, maintain that in order to provide a full policy transfer analysis, policy transfer should be examined as both a dependent and independent variable. As Marsh and Sharman (2009) observe, using policy transfer as an independent variable creates a null hypothesis 'that particular national arrangements reflect particular national circumstances, or that even if pronounced similarities can be observed, these are independent reactions to common shocks or trends' (2009, p. 278).

In addition to this focus on the policy as variable, other researchers have argued that policy transfer research should be directed to validating whether transfer has occurred and assessing the extent of transfer (See e.g. Evans and Davies 1999). As introduced above, on the question of isolating a transfer phenomenon from other likely explanations for an apparent transfer, Bennett (1997) develops an account of substantiating transfer by (1) eliminating idiosyncrasies found in domestic factors not independently responsible for policy adoption; (2) ensuring that similar adoption is not the result of cross-national forces with separate effects in different states; (3) demonstrating that policymakers are aware of policies in other areas; and (4) demonstrating that this foreign knowledge is actually used in the host state. I will integrate these insights, notably focusing on critical criteria for ruling out domestic factors for the mental health policy changes adopted in Samoa and Tonga below. The next section outlines the pertinent dimensions of the policy transfer framework to be emphasised in this book.

3.2 The Policy Transfer Framework

Dolowitz and Marsh's central contribution to the study of policy transfer is perhaps in developing a framework for organising policy transfer inquiry. In its initial iteration, Dolowitz and Marsh's (1996) policy transfer framework provided a systematised approach to identifying factors contributing to or inhibiting policy transfer. Their 2000 article added to this framework an evaluative component to assess factors contributing to success or failure (Marsh and Sharman 2009, p. 278). The framework's parsimony is perhaps its greatest attribute. Organising a policy transfer study using the framework approach requires situating the research with reference to several initial determinations the researcher must make. In this section, I set forth the relevant enquiries and discuss several related policy transfer studies employing this approach. I also discuss the determination of pertinent transfer agents (the whoof a policy transfer event which might include policy entrepreneurs, IOs or parliamentarians, to name but a few) as a necessary step in conducting a policy transfer analysis.

Secondly, determining what has been transferred is critical to any policy transfer analysis. A study should focus on a particular object of proposed or completed transfer, whether it is ideological, ideational or a specific pro-gram. I argue that the emphasis must also be on process: How was the proffered policy adopted and how does the adopted version differ from the proposed models and why? The related question as to why this particular policy has been the subject of transfer must also be investigated. With actors and substance identified, a study should endeavour to explain what the motivation of key actors in the process was and whether it impacted the transfer in any significant way.

3.2.1 Determining the Relevant Scope of Transfer Agents: IOs and Individuals

In order to help guide how we make sense of a policy transfer, Dolowitz and Marsh (1996, 2000) begin by posing several questions for organising any research project endeavouring to analyse a suspected instance of policy transfer. Primarily research must identify the universe of relevant policy actors. Dolowitz and Marsh (2000) identify nine actor categories: elected officials, political parties, bureaucrats/civil servants, pressure groups, policy entrepreneurs and experts, transnational corporations, think tanks, supra-national governmental and nongovernmental institutions, and consultants. Not all actors are present in every transfer, so an important first step is to review the transfer artefacts to make an initial determination as to who was involved in the transfer. In this book I focus on government, bureaucratic and non-governmental actors in Samoa and Tonga as well IOs (and their consultants) identified through the relevant literature reviewed in the chapters that follow. In this section I take up two broad categories of possible policy actors: IOs and individuals key policy actors and entrepreneurs.

IOs represented by staff and consultants are often employed to offer expert advice in policy and programme development. In developing countries, the practice of relying extensively upon outside experts and consultants has been long-standing. Countries experiencing colonialism and decolonisation have routinely used outside (mostly bilateral or international agency representatives) sources of best practice in specified policy domains. Dolowitz and Marsh's (2000) observation on this point is that the role of such consultants serves to blur the line between voluntary and coercive transfer (2000, p. 11). Given the long-standing and fundamentally different nature of these relationships in developing nations, the institutional dynamics of such advice-seeking/offering must be viewed as part of both its substantive and temporal context. For instance, in a state with a history of relying on foreign legal advisers to under-take significant changes to that nation's legal structures or institutions, comprehensive research might consider the successive policy transfers as part of a historical process of state-building.

Policy transfer research often examines, albeit indirectly, the relationship between a nation-state and the international or global society (Gilardi et al. 2009). For instance, as Bierstaker (1992) observed, international financial institutions (IFIs), such as the World Bank, often link their financial assistance to a state in exchange for that state's adoption of neoliberal economic reform policy, known as 'conditionality'. It is not however a case of 'weaker' or recipient states universally adopting the prescribed policies. Notably, Weyland's (2007) study of pension reform policy diffusion in Latin America concludes that given the range of variance in Latin American policies, IFI pressure could not adequately account for the reforms (2007, p. 79). This conclusion might, however, be driven by the 'selection effect': IFIs efforts being targeted at 'recalcitrant countries' (Gilardi et al. 2009, p. 14). Other transfer studies in the health care reform context suggest that success, defined as reduced fiscal burden, has led to greater proliferation of reform-inspired policies in the OECD. Dussauge-Laguna (2012) also finds IOs and their role in policy transfer to be well represented in the literature (see e.g. Evans and Davies 1999; Stone 1999, 2004; Walt et al. 2004).

Moreover, Dolowitz and Marsh (2000) make a distinction between individual or private consultants and intergovernmental organisations (IGOs) and non-governmental organisations (NGOs) as transfer agents. The authors note the addition of these actors to the puzzle only serves to complicate transfer study. While it is true that not all consultants represent IGOs or NGOs, such organisations continue to serve an important consultative function in transferee states. A further complicating feature of these actors occurs when they are embedded within indigenous domestic political institutions. Often, expert consultants paid by international and bilateral organisations operate with-in existing indigenous political institutions, for example legal advisers attached to an attorney general's office or Ministry of Finance. Where these arrangements are made the line between organisational and individual consultant contributions to eventual policy adoption becomes even more blurred. In order to explore this relationship, specific consideration of the nature of these relationships within a policy transfer process must be considered.

Walt et al. (2004) combine the policy transfer approach with an analysis of the role of IOs, specifically the WHO and World Bank, in addressing infectious disease policies surrounding tuberculosis (TB) and sexually transmitted infections (STIs). The authors address a theme explored in this book: the formation and promotion of 'best practices'. Their study identifies IOs, their respective staffs, and the epistemic community with which they are affiliated as key actors. Principal organisations in their study and also noted in this book include WHO, World Bank and bilateral donor organisations that, acting in concert with others, make up the relevant policy net-works. Additionally, the authors note the presence of key individuals who move between organisations, strengthening technical links between them and enhancing the sharing of ideas and consensus on new approaches.

Walt et al. (2004) raise important questions about the utility of dropping complexities and more difficult aspects of policies when promoting them as global best practice. Significantly, this practice – identified as the 'point of transfer' when complex policies have been transformed into simple guidelines and are marketed globally as 'best practice' – is the final loop in a long and iterative process. Ultimately, the authors conclude that the process cannot be described as linear, rational, bottom-up or top-down, nor coercive or voluntary, but may display any of these characteristics at different points in the loops. IOs are members of such networks and play different roles at different parts of the looped process. In essence, the structure provided by IOs within which individual actors can collaborate and share best practices was key to understanding policy transfer. Institutions serve important functions both in terms of instigating agenda items and advancing them and in nurturing practice-level collaboration, which is particularly critical in the health services delivery context.

In this IO context, Stone (2012) notes the strong 'normative assumptions' regarding government learning held by IOs. These assumptions can cloud eventual transfer processes through such standardisation approaches. Pol-icy translation offers a more varied tool to ensure policy adaptation in accordance with sustainable objectives. Stone (2012) notes that no matter how authoritative an IO might see itself, in the end it still must have local buy-in to see its preferences implemented (2012, p. 9). Secondly, IGOs provide a forum for such translation processes to unfold. Thirdly, translation also occurs within more 'complex webs' of nation-states, organisations and non-state actors. These international and regional venues provide opportunities for networks to form and for policy information and ideas to be translated within the particular substantive or cultural contexts of the relevant epistemic or 'other' com-munities. This is where what Stone (2012) refers to as 'knowledge' transfer is likely to occur, which is more extensive than policy transfer (2012, p. 495), and is instrumental in creating what Acharya (2004) calls 'interpretative communities' engaged in a 'continuous process of translation and modification' (Freeman 2009 cited in Stone 2012, p. 496). These organisations serve in an institutional role but are nonetheless made up of individual actors, either employees or attached consultants that interact with national counterparts, institutions and individuals in the transferee state. We next turn to a consideration of these individual actors.

In addition to IOs and their agents, indigenous policy actors and entrepreneurs are considered as possible transfer agents in the pages that follow. I will address 'entrepreneurs' first. Kingdon (1995) defines policy entrepreneurs as 'people who are willing to invest their resources in pushing their pet proposals or problems are responsible not only for promoting important people to pay attention, but also for coupling solutions to problems and for coupling both problems and solutions to politics'(1995, p. 20). Further, the existence of either type of problem (perceived or actual) and political 'happenings' open windows of opportunity (critical junctures) for these entrepreneurs to advance their respective issues within the political system. While Kingdon addressed the domestic political agenda, in this book I address both an international agenda setting and a domestic one, on both formal and informal policy levels, with each involving its own set of actors and some crossover between the spheres.

Mintrom and Vergari (1996) observe the importance of policy entrepreneurs as agents of change. They de-fine policy entrepreneurs by what they do and note the commonality with their private sector equivalents as discoverers of 'unfulfilled needs and suggest [ing] innovative means to satisfy them' (1996, p. 420). Importantly, entrepreneurs must bear some risk in pursuing the innovation and serve in a coordinating role between various relevant 'net-works of individuals and organisations' (1996, p. 422). What is meant by 'risk' will necessarily vary by context. For instance, risk of social capital is likely seen as more 'risky' in collectivist societies, for instance, than wagering money (see e.g. Tiessen 1997; Stenholm et al. 2013). Entrepreneurs are also said to possess a defined skill set: knowledge, intellectual ability, knowledge of policymakers, leadership and team-building skills, reputation and contacts, strategic ability and tenacity (1996, p. 424). Success is demonstrated when the entrepreneur both develops a policy innovation and takes action to see the policy change (Mintrom 2000, p. 6).

Policy entrepreneurs are likely to be identified in research in the first instance as key policy actors. When reviewing the information surrounding a particular policy transfer, individuals central to the transfer will likely become apparent (see e.g. Morrison 2012). Their identification, however, as a policy entrepreneur in the sense presented here requires establishing whether or not the key actor meets the criteria established in the literature. As such, this book takes the position that whilst key actors were readily identifiable from the available research, including those revealed in the course of interviews undertaken for this study, refection of their actual role in the policy transfer process must be taken into account in order to determine whether or not they are entrepreneurs in the sense meant here.

Entrepreneurs can be institutional, bureaucratic or independent policy actors. Elizabeth Lightfoot (2002), for instance, examines the internal and external factors leading to the transfer of disability anti-discrimination law and policy be-tween three Western, English-speaking nations in the 1990s, from the United States (Americans with Disabilities Act [ADA]) to the United Kingdom (UK Disability Discrimination Act [UK-DDA]) and Australia (Australia Disability Discrimination Act [Aus-DDA]). Lightfoot adopts the policy transfer frame as a dependent variable used to explain why policy transfer occurs, while identifying constraints on transfer.

She argues that most of the policy learning and transfer literature adopts a rationalist orientation where the adopting nation's actors are 'dissatisfied with the current policies' and overlook 'how institutional and structural variables, such as political or legal structure, can affect policy transfer' (Lightfoot 2002, p. 7).

Lightfoot (2002) first conducts a textual analysis of the respective anti-discrimination laws to support her assertion that transfer had occurred. She notes several similarities between the various laws as evidence that transfer has occurred. In addition, key differences in each context are identified and while offering no clear explanation for these differences per se, the differences are suggested to address the general orientation or predisposition of each adopting nation in terms of receptivity to the rights-based ADA policy. She notes that the United Kingdom lacked critical insider policy entrepreneurs and had an enthusiasm gap amongst key political actors to embrace a rights-based model that contributed to the lateness in policy take-up there. In the United States and Australia, in contrast, policy entrepreneurs at federal level were responsible for adoption of both policies. In Australia, key forerunners were found in several state-level enactments, which had all been enacted in accordance with the United Nations International Year of Disabled Persons in 1981.

In addition, Lightfoot (2002) identifies several important features of policy transfer. Not only was there the presence of a significant, rights-based legislative template in place from which Australia and the United Kingdom could borrow, but she also identifies the importance of having local, enthusiastic individuals vested in the particular policy area available for transfer. These individuals she identified as 'policy entrepreneurs'. Even though all three countries shared a domestic consumer rights advocacy movement, these entrepreneurs, who had passion for the disability rights, were critical in seeing the policy innovations carried forward. Rights-based arguments tend to awaken the moral leanings of policy advocates and the public alike and the ability to frame policies seeking full employment such as disability statutes do make the political selling of the laws much more palatable. This research then draws our attention to another dimension of the framework: determining what has been transferred.

3.2.2 *Determining What Has Been Transferred*

Determining what was transferred is critical for maintaining empirical focus. As introduced above, transfer objects can also be understood as consisting of both 'hard' and 'soft' objects. Hard objects include instruments and institutions, whilst soft transfers might be said to include ideas or ideology. Dolowitz and Marsh (2000) highlight eight categories of policy 'things': goals, content, instruments, programmes (means of adopting policies), institutions, ideologies, ideas and attitudes, and negative lessons. As they argue, it is critical to clearly distinguish between policy and programme in analysing policy transfer content (2000, p. 12). They note policies are best understood as 'broader statements of intention' versus programmes which are 'specific courses of action' meant to effectuate the intentions embodied in policy pronouncements (2000, p. 12). Maintaining this distinction becomes especially important when considering transfers that are comprehensive in nature and contain several substantive transfer categories. As Stone (2010) argues, however, these forms are not necessarily exclusive, and instead coexist within the international policy context (2010, p. 270; see also Benson and Jordan 2011, p. 370).

Transfer of a particular 'policy' most often requires several related levels of policy change to accompany it and bring it into practice, which are sometimes referred to as 'policy dimensions'. For instance, 'health policy' is a generic policy area that contains myriad components such as institutional arrangements, bureaucratic structures, practices in terms of services and administration, and different health subfields requiring all manner of regulatory and legal frameworks to effectively function. In addition, the health sector includes legal frameworks for regulating professional members of the health sector.

There are important cultural changes that often must accompany such changes. For instance, shifting form a free public service to a fee-for-service regime requires changes in organisational, institutional and political cultures as well as many levels of complex policy changes for a successful and comprehensive transfer to take place. As such, the policy transfer framework might include consideration of an area of policy change in both its spatial and temporal context not as an event necessarily fixed in time but as part of a series of transfers affecting the culture, practice, legal and aspirational dimensions of the policy context. This nuance requires consideration of perspectives on policy change from a wider selection of policy actors. These additional perspectives are necessary since many of the actors traditionally engaged in policy formation might not have been instrumental in establishing the normative or localisation components of a successful transfer. Yet the insights offered by these actors are critically important to the study of policy transfer and localisation since the process of rectifying policy attributes in conflict with cultural norms is often the hallmark of successful transfers.

In this book, I am interested in exploring what has been transferred as part of the mental health policy transfers to Samoa and Tonga, which will include consideration of both hard and soft objects. Firstly, through a review of the literature on each transfer, including government publications and official documents, I plan to identify the hard objects such as law, written policies and related institutions. Secondly, I plan to examine whether soft policy has been transferred in either Samoa or Tonga. In addition, I will explore whether ideas about rights or appropriate treatment were transferred along with the policies themselves. These questions suggest another dimension of the transfer framework: determining motivation for transfer.

3.2.3 Transfer Motivations

Once the researcher has identified the substance of the policy transfer and assembled the constellation of key actors the question of motivation for transfer can be addressed. Dolowitz and Marsh (2000) conceive of a continuum to explore the motivation for a particular policy transfer. The continuum ranges from the rational end of the spectrum (les-son drawing), to a middle ground of 'voluntary' transfers that are nonetheless motivated by some perception of need. Coercive or imposed transfer lies on the other end of the spectrum.

As outlined above, this device is framework in nature and many transfers contain both coercive and voluntary attributes. Yet, Dolowitz and Marsh (2000) maintain that understanding policy transfer involves substantive and motivational analysis. Related to gaining this fuller understanding of the transfer process is the aforementioned and related need to identify the key actors since this is the key to uncovering motivations. In addition, the continuum permits deeper analysis that might reveal different actor motivations at different policy levels, giving rise to different policy or programmatic outcomes. As a final point, the authors note that circumstantial context surrounding a particular transfer (e.g. stability vs. crisis) will invariably impact the motivational dimension. They argue change in times of stability will most likely have strong voluntary characteristics whereas transfers as a result of crisis tend to be more coercive. Similarly, a global movement is likely to yield pressure to engage in transfer but not necessarily be coercive in nature (2000, p. 17).

A variation on this framework is offered in Evans (2004, 2009). He notes four types of policy-oriented learning. The first (and rarest) is copying, where a policy is imported and implemented in toto. The second is emulation, where a government accepts a foreign model as best suited to its local problem. Hybridisation is the third (and most typical) type, where a government combines elements of one policy with its own culturally sensitive notions. The fourth is inspiration where an idea inspires fresh thinking and helps facilitate policy change. Evans (2009) notes that there are three distinct categories of transfer processes: voluntary, negotiated and direct coercive transfers. Negotiated transfers are those involving exchange of concessions on domestic policy (brining it in line with some foreign model) for access to structural or other funds. Where a government is 'compelled by another government to introduce constitutional, social and political changes against its will and the will of its people', a coercive transfer has occurred (Evans 2009, p. 245).

Evans and Davies (1999) draw a distinction between the process of voluntary and coercive policy transfer and offer an in-depth explanation of each. The approach they advance is implicitly voluntarist, which they contrast with an involuntary/coercive one without providing similar process-level detail. They note, however, the following elements: regime-pull; regime search; contact agent(s) within epistemic community; emergence of transfer network; process of elite and cognitive mobilisation; contexts of interaction; process of evaluation; decision enters policy cycle; implementation process; and outcome. The distinction between the two approaches is in their origin: internal circumstances typically trigger voluntary responses whereas external factors, which might include IOs seeking non-conforming state compliance with a desired norm or policy objective. IO's often target these nations through regional organisations or other international level venues for demand-creating measures, such as the threats of failure to grant loans for development without adopting neoliberal market reforms.

Evans and Sultan Barkat (2012) argued that successful policy transfer, particularly in fragile, post-war contexts, required two key and perhaps occasionally divergent attributes: the underlying policy content can come from abroad but it must be "culturally assimilated through comprehensive evaluation and piloting, build[ing] on existing organisational strengths and is transferred by high-quality indigenous knowledge elites." (2012, p. 541). This policy "sweet-spot" is, of course, an ideal type but knowing the high probability of unsuccessful or incomplete policy transfers from a policy core to periphery, the key insight here is to perhaps proceed gradually and with all deliberate speed when introducing a new policy in a new context. Sometimes there are indeed no 'second acts' where the policy failures can be tried again. Writing in the context of post-war Afghanistan, Evans and Barkat's conclusions might be tempered by the necessity of adopting policies in such a setting. Governments are quite use to adopting less than optimal policy choices in the so-called fog of war, which, likely extends to the lightening fog of post-war contexts, but what about other contexts where the need is perhaps not so acute? Surely, the same insights as to the centrality of local ownership of both the policy process and substance would apply? Since tit is not difficult to find cases where this imperative is absent, we might conclude that these policy changes are perhaps more important to external actors than to domestic ones. As we explore later in this book, mental health policy and law reform in both Samoa and Tonga, seemed to reflect less the ideal form of Evans and Barakat and more the more pedestrian form of policy reform that occurs in order to modernise a system with which very few citizens are aware or interact. Moreover, a system reform in which there is a strikingly small policy community. And, as we shall see in later chapters, while the transfer of the policy forms, such as a tangible law reform in both countries and a physical policy document being issued in Samoa, the deeper or perhaps more meaningful parts of policy transfer as embodied in implementation, were difficult to identify.

Adrian Bazbauers (2018) addressed the similar question of international organisations and policy transfer from the World Bank. At issue in his study was the very powerful tool of international development assistance funding. The unequal relationship that is reinforced through this mechanism can result in inappropriate policy "fixes" being proposed and advanced resulting in poor fit of solution to problem. Perhaps more profound and often detrimental are the effects this dynamic can have on domestic policy development processes, which become atrophied and responsive only to external pressure and the availability of funds. As we will see later in this book, this is a key attribute of the policy development processes within Samoa and Tonga's mental health sectors. Bazbauers is clearly approaching policy transfer from a constructivist ontology, emphasising the iterative policy development at the heart of the policy mobilities literature and its emphasis on "social interaction, relational dynamics and conflict" between the domestic and international policy domains (2018, p. 37).

Bazbauer promotes an approach similar to that which is at the heart of this book and is discussed at greater length in the chapters that follow. From the policy transfer scholarship, I identify and organise the various components of policy and law transferred over nearly 100 years of policy history in Samoa and Tonga. Organising the various instruments, actors and interests at play at each policy transfer episode allows us to further investigate the complex dynamics of these interactions. The result is a far more systematic presentation of the evolving mental health systems in both countries, over-time, that permits comparison and lesson-drawing to help inform future domestic policymakers and their international champions and supporters about how to approach the next iteration of mental health systems reform. Demands on these systems is likely to increase in the years ahead with the acceleration in the epidemiological transition Samoa and Tonga—and many other emergent middle-income nations—have and will soon endure. Demographic changes are not the only cause for greater demands on national mental health systems. Nation-states will be called upon for ever -greater policy responses to the mental health impacts of lifestyle diseases and disruptions caused to social systems by increasing environmental disasters, including sea-level rise and climate-change driven adverse weather events, greater and more frequent need of state-based responses to buttress languishing community-based mental health response systems.

The extent to which a transfer can be described as truly voluntary or coercive is inherently difficult. Typical examples, such as an organization making a loan contingent on enactment of specific legislative regimes) suggest at least a degree of involuntary behaviour on the part of transferee nation since the proffered policy changes were not done independent of the external inducement. On the other hand, state adoption of a human rights law which might be the result of a rational political process or because it was necessary to adopt such a law to qualify for grant funding or to avoid the international perception as a nation out of step with the mainstream.

3.3 The Constructivist Turn in Policy Transfer Scholarship: Localisation, Translation and Mimesis

As presented in the previous chapter, policy transfer scholarship has not been silent on the need to hybridise policy components, particularly those conflicting with indigenous cultural perspectives. This emphasis on understanding agent-level engagement in and influence on the policy transfer process is at the cutting edge of policy transfer re-search and often constitutes the injection of constructivist tenets into the research approach. Stone argues that constructivist policy transfer analyses emphasise the need for socialisation and development of inter-subjective understandings while translation accounts tend to prefer ethno-graphic studies of policy transfer (Stone 2012).

The consideration of local dimensions to policy transfer, however, is not limited to constructivists. Dolowitz notes the importance of merging indigenous cultural attitudes with legislation proposed for transfer in his seminal work *Learning from America* (1998). His cultural consideration, however, was on the political dimension of selling the discordant values underlying the welfare-to-work legislation to a universal-entitlement culture existing in the United Kingdom until the 1990s

(Dolowitz 1998, p. 86). Amitav Acharya's (2004) contribution on localisation (discussed below) and other related policy transfer literature concerned with the impact of indigenous agents on the policy transfer pro-cess and products offer perhaps a more nuanced consideration of the topic and act effectively as a bridge between globalisation as a process and policy transfer as the study of discrete pieces of a general globalisation process. These approaches allow for (or perhaps demand) greater national and individual agency in the globalisation process. Success in policy transfer often hinges on the capacity of the adopting state to rectify these incongruent aspects of policies proffered for transfer.

David Benson and Andrew Jordan take up an earlier critique of the body of research as being overly positivistic in failing to account for the extent to which 'problems are socially constructed and how this inter-subjectivity might determine where (and what type of) potential solutions are sourced' (Benson and Jordan 2011, p. 374). Benson and Jordan believe this shortcoming endures since only relatively few studies embrace a constructivist approach. However, in reply to Benson and Jordan, Dolowitz and Marsh (2012) engage in an assessment of the state of policy transfer research. Firstly, they reaffirm their intention that policy transfer is intended to be used as a framework and that 'it stands or falls in relation' to the extent that it assists in policy research (2012, p. 339). In addition, they take up the post-positivist dimension of transfer scholarship. As they note, '(a)pproaches to the study of policy transfer … reflect the explicit, or implicit, ontological and epistemological positions [the researcher] adopt[s]' (2012, p. 342), and that employing a constructivist research approach is not necessary to achieve this objective. Marsh, for instance, affirms his critical realist orientation to policy transfer research, which I discuss briefly below. The authors then address the constructivist trends in the literature, engaging Eugene McCann and Kevin Ward's (2012) four critiques of policy transfer literature, of which I address two: agent/agency focus and nation-state preoccupation of existing literature.

Primarily, McCann and Ward (2012) adopt a constructivist critique of the existing literature, maintaining that an agent focus does not amount to an agency focus (2012, p. 343). While not necessarily conceding the point, Dolwoitz and Marsh (2012) again affirm the proper role of the framework: as a means to systematise empirical investigation. Scholars have approached this long-standing debate from several perspectives including: structuralism (maintaining that the structure, not the individual, should be the basis of analysis as agents are merely shaped by structures); intentionalism (arguing that the individual or group is the proper study variable since structure is only the result of intentional behaviour [e.g. rational choice theory]); dialectical approaches (structures and agents are engaged in an iterative process [e.g. structuration theory, morphogenesis]); and postmodernist approaches (arguing essentially that since a discernible 'truth' about the relationship between structure and agency does not exist; the purpose of study is merely to uncover formative discourses).

The dialectical approaches offer the most promise for study when one is interested in examining the complex relationships between structural components and individual behaviour within a discrete policy area. This can be justified simply because it is only the dialectical approach that arrives without preordained assumptions that tend to suggest the outcome. If we accept there are things we can call 'structures' and accept that individuals also act within them, then dialectical approaches offer the most promising opportunity to honestly examine the relationship between them.

McCann and Ward's (2012) second criticism – that the policy transfer literature is too state-focused – is valid but the alternative they propose, that policies emerge from 'unbounded dynamic, relational assemblages' (2012, p. 327) perhaps explains too much. They propose a policy assemblages approach that reflects the fluid nature of the policy process (2012, p. 343). Their proposed methodology is agent-centric and emphasises the 'social construction' of policy meanings (2012, p. 344). Dolowitz and Marsh (2012) maintain that while McCann and Ward's approach is acceptable, it ultimately reflects a 'constructivist/discursive institutionalist position and constructivist ontology', whereby 'institutions, and the policies that they produce, are seen to have no role, independent of the way in which they are narrated or discursively constructed' (2012, p. 344). This perspective is a point of debate and the bulk of transfer scholarship presently adheres to a 'realist ontological and a positivist epistemological position' (Dolowitz and Marsh 2012, p. 344).

This is not the first critique of policy transfer scholarship based on the agent-structure dichotomy. Earlier at-tempts to address this debate include Evans's (2004) use of structuration theory. While the transfer literature tends to privilege the role of agents in transfer, structures of government remain important factors in the process (Evans 2009, p. 274). Marsh and Sharman (2009) argue the fundamental problem with the literature is the 'unsophisticated approach to structure/agency' (2009, p. 275). Critical realist theory has been offered as a sensible compromise to the perceived relativist excesses of the interpretivist tradition and the reductionist tendencies of the positivist perspectives. Instead, Marsh and Sharman argue the path ahead should have research encapsulating the structure/agency relationship as dialectical or 'interactive and iterative' (2009, p. 275). Structures necessarily constrain and enable actor behaviour but actors are able to interpret and possibly change the structures. This discussion raises the possibility, however, that ideas might also serve as factors critical to explaining change within existing institutions or structures and I will first briefly address this issue within the historical institutional scholarship.

The distinction between institutions and the individuals operating within them has taken many forms. The influence of ideas on this relationship has been explored in the historical institutionalism scholarship to explain change. As Blyth (2002, 2004) argues, he and scholars such as Hall (1993) see 'ideas' as analogous to institutions, both existing a priori to individuals. This temporal isolation of these elements permits the study of ideas and institutions with reference to their effect on agent behaviour. Historical Institutionalism's ontology, in this construction, is one in which individuals were the products of institutions, not the producers of them (Blyth 2002 p. 309). Ideas are similar to institutions in that they are not 'reducible to individual preferences but instead determine the content of those preferences' (2002, p. 309).

This dynamic allows for change that is consistent with historical institutionalism's ontology. State institutions provide the context within which individual state policy actors act. Since agents join these already existing institutions, such as the health ministries and IOs at the centre of this book, they necessarily adapt to the respective institutions and can then work to effectuate change. In the study of such dynamics, identification of institutions, relevant influential ideas and key actors or entrepreneurs is key. The historical institutionalist approach, however, as de-scribed by Blyth is not a complete model for analysing complex relationships between existing structures and individual agents. For instance, how can we effectively isolate variables relevant to structure, such as institutions and culture, from the agents themselves? Several scholars have developed different approaches to studying this dynamic process, from varying ontological and epistemological perspectives, including: localisation (Acharya 2004); mimesis (Massey 2009) and translation (Prince 2010; Freeman 2009; Sahlin and Wedlin 2008). I now consider each approach in turn in order to examine the nuance between each approach and determine which approach is best suited to the examination of mental health policy transfer in Samoa and Tonga.

3.3.1 Policy Localisation

Acharya (2004) asks why some transnational ideas and norms find greater acceptance in particular locales than others. In doing so, her focus on agency in norm diffusion emphasises a process she identifies as 'localisation'. Localisation is the 'active construction (through discourse, framing, grafting and cultural selection) of foreign ideas by local ac-tors, which results in the former developing significant congruence with local beliefs and practices' (2004, p. 245). Localisation can also be descriptive of the incorporation of these borrowed ideas within local behaviour. She notes that those ideas that had closer 'fit' to already existing norms or practices stood a better chance of adoption than purely novel ones. Secondly, she identifies an active process in which the indigenous norm-taker aligns indigenous institutions or belief structures with those proposed for transfer, thereby bringing them into line with local practices. This process is particularly likely where the proffered adaptations also serve to enhance an adopting agent's status (2004, p. 245). This process of fitting a foreign norm to the local context is referred to as 'pruning' and is motivated by an interest in strengthening existing institutions, not replacing them. She also notes that cultural predilections, and deeply ingrained beliefs in the importance of existing institutions sanctified by popular beliefs and nurtured through rituals and practices, could not be easily sacrificed without incurring social and political costs.

The localisation process is one of incorporation: transnational norms are brought together with local constructions and practices to form a new hybridised output (Acharya 2004, p. 241). In line with the institutionalist approach discussed earlier, Acharya states that localisation typically begins either with a punctuating event or systemic change (exogenous shock) (2004, p. 247). The most invasive type of change envisioned by this analysis is 'norm displacement' whereby the foreign norm is proposed to supplant a domestic one. She notes that norm displacement fails when challenging a 'strong [indigenous] identity norm' (2004, p. 248). Should the prospective norm-taker, however, determine that their indigenous belief, while perhaps inadequate but not harmful in practice, might be 'broadened and strengthened with the infusion of new ideas', then the probability for successful localisation increases (2004, p. 248). In addition, a key variable in successful localisation is the prestige of the key movers of the prospective norm change within in the adopting culture. The key movers must be of suitable credibility in terms of their insight into 'indigenous cultural traits and traditions and the scope for grafting and pruning presented by foreign norms' (2004, p. 248).

Acharya (2004) distinguishes between tactical adaptation, which might, in some ways, be coercive in nature, and a purely voluntary localisation that yields a more 'enduring' result (2004, p. 251). In contrast to constructivist arguments that local norms are brought into line with international ones, localisation argues 'external ideas are simultaneously adapted to meet local practices' (2004, p. 251). Further, 'localisation is progressive ... reshap(ing) both existing beliefs and practices and foreign ideas in their local context' (2004, p. 252) suggesting a dialectical or iterative process. Local agents promote norm diffusion by 'actively borrowing and modifying transnational norms in accordance with their pre-constructed normative beliefs and practices' (2004, p. 269). Acharya sees the prevailing literature as failing to adequately explain norm diffusion because, unlike her approach, it does not adopt a 'dynamic theory of localisation in which norm takers perform actors of selection, borrowing and modification between that and emerging global norms' (2004, p. 269).

The localisation approach raises several interesting insights and implications for the policy transfer literature. Firstly, when adopting a more inclusive framing of policy as this book does, localisation allows for consideration of normative aspects of policy transfer, such as beliefs and other practices that might pre-date a policy transfer event. Secondly, with its emphasis on a potentially broader class of prospective agents and on their specific role in localising norms and policies vetted in foreign cultural contexts, localisation provides a theoretical link between the Western-centric policy transfer literature and the empirical study of transfer in developing, non-Western nation-states. The re-search questions arising from localisation involve a broad issue of whether localisation can be said to have existed within a particular policy area and whether the localisation element contributed to the transfer itself or the success of the transfer in terms of implementation. In this book, I do not evaluate the efficacy of the implemented mental health policy changes. Instead, I concentrate on the process and actors engaged in the policy transfer process, including the efforts of ensuring sufficient fit between proffered policies and indigenous cultures.

3.3.2 Policy Mimesis

Other research has also sought to address the particular attributes of the transferee's policy process in reconciling potentially conflicting or ill-fitting foreign policies. Massey (2009) presents the concept of 'policy mimesis'. Massey's approach stems from his central contention that policy transfer scholarship privileges the notion of transfer as mere movement of a set policy, essentially in toto, from one context to another. Because of this interpretation, he prefers the term 'mimesis' to policy transfer since mimesis refers to an imitation or reproduction of a policy in a new context (2009, p. 388). Importantly, however, Massey discusses mimesis within the contexts of former colonial countries con-text and argues that the current policy search stems from independence struggles and their associated legacies. He argues, quite rightly in my view, that these transitioning states, particularly those achieving independence through a mediated process, formed various state-run institutions on the understanding that they would be the 'most appropriate mechanism for providing services that were not provided by the private sector' (Massey 2009, p. 388).

This initial institutional decision has long-lasting effects on later policy decisions; most notably the establishment of such entities as state-owned enterprises and state health systems. These decisions were themselves adaptations of the then existing structures, hybrids in many cases of the prevailing notions of the state's role in the economy. Hence, later transfers such as New Public Management and market liberalisation were not straight copies in toto but constituted translations of these foreign models. Successful transfers were successful because they came to integrate the foreign model with 'prevailing social, economic and political institutions, without challenging those institutions' (Massey 2009, p. 389). Massey's is a case study of the privatisation of Kenya Airways and, as he notes, the case suggests the 'role and importance of individuals' as well as cultural context in the mimesis or transfer process (2009, p. 393). Like Acharya (2004), Massey's analysis can be interpreted from an institutional perspective with critical junctures occurring at 'punctuation' points that offer the possibility of change. He argues that the introduction of 'global rules' (punctuation points) enabled local 'constraints' to be overcome. Since there was significant local agency at play, Massey argues this process constitutes mimesis and not straight transfer (2009, p. 393).

3.3.3 Policy Translation

Representing a decidedly more constructivist approach is Freeman (2009), who argues that in policy transfer there is an inevitable process of policy 'translation'. Translation, in the policy transfer context, requires uncovering shared meaning and might be the 'key to policy transfer [success]' (2009, p. 430). Freeman argues that 'local knowledge' necessary for translation practice is defined as 'the very mundane, yet expert under-standing of and practical reasoning about local conditions derived from lived experience' (2009, p. 431). Similarly, Sahlin and Wedlin (2008) also address 'translation' in the policy transfer context. Importantly, they note that in contrast to diffusion's passiveness, imitation is a 'performative' or active process (2008, p. 224). They argue that what is actually being transferred are accounts and materialisations of certain ideas or practices instead of the actual ideas and practices themselves. Such accounts undergo translation as they spread, resulting in local versions of models and ide-as in different local contexts. Related to this point, translation can involve an ideological reframing (Sahlin and Wedlin 2008, p. 227). This distinction is one between 'programmatic or normative' elements and 'technological or operational' ones. Programmatic elements involve 'ideas, aims and objectives' undergirding a policy and technological aspects involve 'concrete tasks or routines' within the proffered policy (2008, p. 227).

Others have examined these policy assemblages in the pacific. Catherine Kingfisher (2018) examined welfare reform in New Zealand and its influence on far-away places such as individual States within the United States. Russell Prince (2010) also looked at transfer in terms of translation of foreign policies into new domestic contexts. He examines the creative industries policy adaptations in New Zealand. In support of his translation model he notes that seldom are transfers in toto adaptations of a foreign model. Instead, local policy actors are actively engaged in a process of tailoring foreign models to local contexts. This tailoring process involves 'essentialising and delocalising policy programmes' (2010, p. 171). Prince (2010) adopts an assemblages perspective similar to that of McCann and Ward (2012). In the policy context, the policy itself is understood as an 'assemblage of texts, actors, agencies, institutions, and networks. They come together at particular policy-making locales that are constituted by a complex of relations, including the increasingly spatially stretched relations constitutive of globalisation' (2010, p. 173). These international and domestic actors engage in a process of translation: "the negotiation of the coexistence of two or more circulating knowledges through the alteration of each to accommodate the existence of others, often resulting in a synthesised form" (2010, p. 173).

Stone (2012) also takes up the related concepts of translation and variation in the policy transfer context. She offers translation as an innovation, advancing policy transfer from the study of the mere movement of policy to the study of nuance in policy interpretation within the new context (2012, p. 5). Translation rejects rationalist preoccupations and instead focuses on context (see e.g. Dwyer and Ellison 2009; Newburn 2010) as well as the need for interpretation or experimentalism (see e.g. Sabel and Zeitlin 2012) in the policy assemblage (see e.g. Prince 2010). Importantly, Stone notes the Public Sector Linkage programme of the Australian Agency for International Development (AusAID) – an important actor in both Samoa's and Tonga's policy transfer contexts, which emphasises 'ownership' and 'local context' as vital to assessing 'lessons learnt' (Stone 2012, p. 6). Stone also observes that 'indigenization' of policy can occur both at policy adoption (transfer) but also occurs over time as policies confront 'endogenous forces' and practices 'mutate' (2012, p. 7).

Common amongst these various approaches is an emphasis on explaining and understanding policy transfer as it unfolds in the adopting country. The research opens new possibilities for investigating former colonies and other developing countries that might have few formal data sources but have rich cultural heritages that are implicated in the importation of government policy. In addition, the focus on the interplay between structures, institutions and individual agents permits the creation of something akin to a 'thick description' of policy contexts and the identification of aspects unique to particular nations and discrete policy areas. Common to all of these approaches is a rejection of any suggestion that policies are commonly adopted *in toto* by a transferee nation. This, however, appears to be a 'straw man' argument as Dolowitz and Marsh (2012) propose, given that most research outside of diffusion studies with large-N design tends to examine case studies and consider individual nation-state variability in adoption.

The contribution, however, of these approaches is to shift the emphasis on comparing proffered and adopted policies as well as the processes through which the proffered policies were adopted (or not adopted). By comparing a policy proposal and the one eventually adopted, in addition to the obvious identification of differences between the two versions, we can also identify actors central to both the construction of the policy proposed for importation as well as that eventually adopted. In addition, these new strands of policy transfer research move the role of individual agents into the centre of the policy transfer nexus. Understanding the attributes and attitudes of these key ac-tors becomes critical to fully explaining policy transfer. In addition, and a matter of particular interest in this book, is the related research question: Do different actors contribute differently depending on the level of policy under study? In other words, do actors engage with structures in the same way across different types of policy transfer or does this experience differ? The purpose of such an analysis might reveal insights for designing similar policy transfer approaches or strategies in future.

3.4 Conclusion

This chapter has set out to accomplish two broad objectives in relation to situating this book within the policy transfer scholarship. Firstly, I reviewed the policy transfer literature with a particular focus on gaps in the current literature, such as its diminishing yet enduring European and North American focus and its emergent application to examine localisation processes in non-Western nation-states. Secondly, I restated the policy transfer framework to be applied in the remaining chapters of this book.

This chapter has laid out how, as Nainggolan (2017) has also emphasised, the catalyst effect of the policy transfer literature on other areas of the policy and comparative politics literatures. As discussed in this chapter, there are many studies in the literature applying the policy transfer model to in-stances of foreign policy adoption or influence. This literature has largely stuck to its Western or Eurocentric roots. Policy transfer studies have examined social rights policy transfer involving national disability policies and its path from an US innovation to adopted policy in both the United Kingdom and Australia has also been reviewed using this research approach (Lightfoot 2002). The unifying theme of these studies is the importance of indigenous cultures and institutions looking to what are perceived to be other, similar exemplars of policy models rather than merely to other developing states more broadly. Similarly, Walt et al. (2004) study the communicable disease prevention policy transfer process from the IO perspective and conclude that whilst IOs provide the critical context, the relationships between various policy actors was critical in the transfer process. Finally, Kwon (2009) and Tews (2009) examine the perils of overreliance on transferred policy. Both argue that overdependence on foreign policy innovation comes at the expense not only of the development of domestic policy solutions to problems, but also of the institutions necessary to confront future domestic policy problems for which a ready-made foreign model might not be found.

In its essence, the utility of the policy transfer framework is its ability to comprehensively account for a number of variables influencing policy transfer analysis in an organised manner. By providing an organised template to guide research on any issue of transplanted public policy it ensures intellectual consistency and rigour across cases. By not being overly descriptive of a wide range of sub-variables it also allows significant flexibility for case-by-case differences that add to the body of knowledge in this growing scholarship.

Given the current posture of the policy transfer literature as presented here, this study has two broad aims: firstly, to ascertain the contours of the mental health policy transfer event as experienced in Samoa and Tonga by fully vetting the relevant actors, their respective roles in the process, and how they affected the respective mental health policy transfers. Secondly, I endeavour to further explore and explain the actual policy transfer processes within the mental health contexts of Samoa and Tonga. From this analysis, I propose to determine whether the existing literature is adequate for fully explaining the policy transfer process or whether further inquiry is required.

As was discussed with reference to the literature on lesson drawing having a preoccupation with single-direction transfer of lessons, the recipient is said to learn from the originator. However, in certain situations and at certain levels of policy, it may be the IOs and consultants in their employ that actually learn. For instance, where a consultant bases his or her recommendations on a policy model to a government based on his or her impressions of the local context, the learning has been done by the consultant, not necessarily by the local policy actors. In other words, I am interested in uncovering how much of the existing law was tailored to fit the local context and by whom. The policy adopters persist in an institutional pattern of deference to the policy expert's judgment. Such a finding would be consistent with both Kwon's and Tews's concerns about unilateral policy transfers.

Consideration of these broad aims reveals several specific questions to be addressed in the pages that follow. These questions are: (1) Did mental health policy transfers to Samoa and Tonga occur? If so, what did the transfers look like and why did they happen when they did? (2) Were different types of actors engaged in different types of policy transfer and how were they involved? (3) Were any of the actors involved in these transfers 'policy entrepreneurs'? Why or why not? (4) Is there any variation in the degree of localisation depending on the policy type and actors involved in transfer? If so, why is there variation? I am primarily interested in identifying the scope for the transfer event or events and asking whether different policy actors become engaged in the transfer process at different points. As such, the next step in analysing the transfer process is to identify the relevant actors and texts forming the international mental health policy context.

Similarly, I am interested in investigating whether these different transfer agents engage in different types of transfer (e.g. statutes, written policies, practices engaged in by policy actors).What do these processes look like and what influences them? In order to examine these overarching research questions, I examine how mental health policy has developed in Samoa and Tonga over time. I also explore whether mental health policy and practice is similar or different in Samoa and Tonga and what might account for the similarities or differences.

References

Aagaard, P. (2011). The global institutionalisation of microcredit. *Regulation & Governance, 5*, 465–479.

Acharya, A. (2004). How ideas spread: Whose norms matter? Norm localization & institutional change in Asian regionalism. *International Organization, 58*(2), 239–275.

Appuhami, R., Perera, S., & Perera, H. (2011). Coercive policy diffusion in a developing country: The case of public-private partnerships in Sri Lanka. *Journal of Contemporary Asia, 41*, 3.

Banks, C. (2011). Protecting the rights of the child: Regulating restorative justice and indigenous practices in Southern Sudan & East Timor. *The International Journal of Children's Rights, 19*, 2.

Bazbauers, A. R. (2018). *The World Bank and transferring development*. Cham: Springer.

Bennett, C. J. (1991). Review article: What is policy convergence and what causes it? *British Journal of Political Science, 21*, 215–233.

Bennett, C. J. (1997). Understanding ripple effects: The cross–national adoption of policy instruments for bureaucratic accountability. *Governance, 10*(3), 213–233.

Benson, D., & Jordan, A. (2011). What have we learned from policy transfer research? Dolowitz & Marsh revisited. *Political Studies, 9*, 366–378.

Betsill, M., & Bulkeley, H. (2004). Transnational networks and global environmental governance: The cities for climate protection program. *International Studies Quarterly, 48*, 471–493.

Bierstaker, T. J. (1992). The 'triumph' of neoclassical economics in the developing world: Policy convergence & bases of governance in the international economic order. In J. Czempiel et al. (Eds.), *Governance without government: Order & change in world politics*. Cambridge: Cambridge University Press.

Blyth, M. (2002). *Great transformations: Economic ideas & institutional change in the twentieth century*. New York: Cambridge University Press.

Blyth, M. (2004). Review: [untitled]. *Perspectives on Politics, 2*(3), 622–623.

De Jong, M. (2009). Rose's'10 steps': Why process messiness, history and culture are not vague and banal. *Policy & Politics, 37*, 1.

Dolowitz, D. (1998). *Learning from America: Policy transfer and the development of the British workfare state*. Brighton: Sussex Academic Press.

Dolowitz, D. P. (2018). Policy learning and diffusion. In *Handbook on policy, process and governing*. Cheltenham: Edward Elgar Publishing.

Dolowitz, D., & Marsh, D. (1996). Who learns what from whom: A review of the policy transfer literature. *Political Studies, XLIV*, 343–357.

Dolowitz, D., & Marsh, D. (2000). Learning from Abroad: The role of policy transfer in contemporary policy-making. *Governance: An International Journal of Policy & Administration, 13*(1), 5–24.

Dolowitz, D., & Marsh, D. (2012). The future of policy transfer research. *Political Studies, 10*, 339–345.

Dussauge-Laguna, M. I. (2012). On the past and future of policy transfer research: Benson and Jordan revisited. *Political studies review, 10*(3), 313–324.

Dwyer, P., & Ellison, N. (2009). We nicked stuff from all over the place': Policy transfer or muddling through? *Policy & Politics, 37*(3), 389–407.

Evans, M. (2004). *Policy transfer in global perspective*. Hants: Ashgate.

Evans, M. (2006). At the interface between theory & practice-policy transfer & lesson drawing. *Public Administration, 84*(2), 479–489.

Evans, M. (2009). Policy transfer in critical perspective. *Policy Studies, 30*(3), 243–268.

Evans, M., & Barakat, S. (2012). Post-war reconstruction, policy transfer and the World Bank: The case of Afghanistan's National Solidarity Programme. *Policy Studies, 33*(6), 541–565.

Evans, M., & Davies, J. (1999). Understanding policy transfer: A multi-level, multi-disciplinary perspective. *Public Administration, 77*(2), 361–385.

Freeman, R. (2009). What is 'translation'? *Evidence & Policy, 5*, 4.

Gilardi, F., Fuglister, K., & Luyet, S. (2009). Learning from others: Diffusion of hospital financing reforms in OECD countries. *Comparative Political Studies, 42*(4), 549–573.

Greener, I. (2002). Understanding NHS reform: The policy-transfer, social learning, & path-dependency perspectives. *Governance: An International Journal of Policy Administration & Institutions, 15*(2).

Haas, P. (1992). Introduction: Epistemic communities and international policy coordination. *International Organization, 46*(1), 1–35.

Hall, P. (1993). Policy paradigms, social learning, & the state: The case of economic policymaking in Britain. *Comparative Politics, 25*(3), 275–296.

Heichel, S., Pape, J., & Sommerer, T. (2005). Is there convergence in convergence research? An overview of empirical studies on policy convergence. *Journal of European Public Policy, 12*(5), 817–840.

Howlett, M., & Rayner, J. (2008). Third generation policy diffusion studies & the analysis of policy mixes: Two steps Forward & one Step Back? *Journal of Comparative Policy Analysis, 10*(4), 385–402.

James, O., & Lodge, M. (2003). The limitations of 'policy transfer' & 'lesson drawing' for public policy research. *Political Studies Review, 2003*(1), 179–193.

Jones, T., & Newburn, T. (2002). The transformation of policing? Understanding current trends in policing systems. *The British Journal of Criminology, 42*(1), 129–146.

Karakhanyan, S., van Veen, K., & Bergen, T. (2011). Educational policy diffusion & transfer: The case of Armenia. *Health Education Policy, 24*, 53–83.

Kingdon, J. (1995). *Agendas, alternatives & public policies*. New York: Longman.

Kingfisher, C. (2018). *A policy travelogue: Tracing welfare reform in Aotearoa/New Zealand and Canada*. Oxford: Berghahn Books.

Knill, C. (2005). Introduction: Cross-national policy convergence: Concepts, approaches & explanatory factors. *Journal of European Public Policy, 12*(5), 764–774.

Kwon, H.-J. (2009). Policy learning & transfer: The experience of the developmental state in East Asia. *Policy & Politics, 37*(3), 409–421.

Ladi, S. (2005). *Globalisation, policy transfer and policy research institutes*. Northampton: E, Elgar.

Larmour, P. (2002). Policy transfer & reversal: Customary land registration from Africa to Melanesia. *Public Administration & Development, 22*, 151–161.

Larmour, P. (2005). *Foreign flowers: Institutional transfer & good governance in the Pacific Islands*. Honolulu: University of Hawai'i Press.
Latulippe, L. (2010). *The influence of ideas on domestic policy choices: The case of bilateral tax treaties*. Doctoral dissertation, PhD Thesis.
Leiber, S., Gress, S., & Manougian, M. (2010). Health care system change & the cross-border transfer of ideas: The influence of the Dutch model on the 2007 German health reform. *Journal of Health Politics, Policy & Law, 35*, 4.
Lightfoot, E. (2002). A comparative study of social policy transfer. *The Social Policy Journal, 1*(4), 5–22.
Marsden, G., & Stead, D. (2011). Policy transfer & learning in the field of transport: A review of concepts and evidence. *Transport Policy, 18*, 492–500.
Marsh, D., & Sharman, J. (2009). Policy diffusion & policy transfer. *Policy Studies, 30*(3), 269–288.
Massey, A. (2009). Policy mimesis in the context of global governance. *Political Studies, 30*, 3.
McCann, E., & Ward, K. (2012). Policy assemblages, mobilities & mutations: Toward a multidisciplinary conversation. *Political Studies, 10*, 325–332.
Mintrom, M. (2000). *Policy entrepreneurs & school choice*. Washington, DC: Georgetown University Press.
Mintrom, M., & Vergari, S. (1996). Advocacy coalitions, policy entrepreneurs, & policy change. *Policy Studies Journal, 24*(3), 420–434.
Morrison, K. (2012). *Penal transformation in post-devolution Scotland: Change and resistance*. PhD Thesis, University of Edinburgh.
Müller, P., & Slominski, P. (2017). The politics of learning: Developing an emissions trading scheme in Australia. *Global Environmental Politics, 17*(3), 51–68.
Nainggolan, A. H. (2017). Key dynamics of internationalization of public policy in the context of policy transfer. *Jurnal Politik, 3*(1), 5–20.
Newburn, T. (2010). Diffusion, differentiation and resistance in comparative penality. *Criminology & Criminal Justice, 10*, 341.
Page, E. (2000). Future governance & the literature on policy transfer & lesson drawing. In *ESRC Future Governance Programme Workshop*.
Pakes, F. (2010). Global forces and local effects in youth justice: The case of Moroccan youngsters in Netherlands. *International Journal of Law, Crime & Justice, 38*.
Prince, R. (2010). Policy transfer as policy assemblage: Making policy for the creative industries in New Zealand. *Environment & Planning A, 42*, 169–186.
Rose, R. (1990). What is lesson-drawing? *Journal of Public Policy, 11*(1), 3–30.
Rose, R. (1993). *Lesson-drawing in public policy: A guide to learning across time & space*. Chatham: Chatham House.
Sabel, C. F., & Zeitlin, J. (2012). Experimentalist governance. *The Oxford Handbook of Governance, 1*, 2–4.
Sahlin, K., & Wedlin, L. (2008). Circulating ideas: Imitation, translation & editing. In R. Greenwood (Ed.), *The Sage handbook of organizational institutionalism*. Thousand Oaks: SAGE.
Sharman, J. C. (2010). Dysfunctional policy transfer in national tax blacklists. *Governance, 23*(4), 623–639.
Stenholm, P., Acs, Z., & Wuebker, R. (2013). Exploring country-level institutional arrangements on the rate and type of entrepreneurial activity. *Journal of Business Venturing, 28*(1), 176–193.
Stone, D. (1999). Learning lessons & transferring policy across time, space & disciplines. *Politics, 19*(1), 51–59.
Stone, D. (2000). Non-governmental policy transfer: The strategies of independent policy institutes. *Governance: An International Journal of Policy & Administration, 13*(1), 45–62.
Stone, D. (2004). Transfer agents & global networks in the 'transnationalization' of policy. *Journal of European Public Policy, 11*(3), 545–566.
Stone, D. (2012). Transfer and translation of policy. *Policy Studies, 33*, 6.
Strang, D., & Meyer, J. (1993). Institutional conditions for diffusion. *Theory & Society, 22*, 487–511.

Tews, K. (2009). From law-making to policy making, The environmental dimension of the EU accession process—Challenges, risks & chances for SEE Countries. *Environmental Policy & Convergence, 19*, 130–139.

Tiessen, J. (1997). Individualism, collectivism, and entrepreneurship: A framework for international comparative research. *Journal of Business Venturing, 12*(5), 367–384.

Timms, P. (2011). Urban transport policy transfer: 'Bottom-up' & 'top-down' perspective. *Transport Policy, 18*, 513–521.

Walt, G., Lush, L., & Ogden, J. (2004). International organizations in transfer of infectious diseases: Iterative loops of adoption, adaptation & marketing. *Governance, 17*(2), 189–210.

Watson, A. (1993). *Legal transplants: An approach to comparative law* (2nd ed.). Athens, Ga: University of Georgia Press.

Weyland, K. (2007). *Bounded rationality and policy diffusion*. Princeton: Princeton University Press.

Chapter 4
What Constitutes the International Mental Health Policy Context?

This chapter builds on our definition and conceptual background of mental health as well as the policy transfer and localisation scholarship discussed in previous chapters. Specifically, I develop here the second stage in the policy transfer process: the internationalisation of both policy problem and solution. This chapter continues the discussion of the substantive mental health policy context as developed in the core regions of Western Europe and North America developed in Chap. 2. The construction of mental health policies, therefore, will bear a particular imprimatur of these core states' policies involving a formalised institutional set of relationships between individual and community as mediated by state institutions – historically the prison and hospital.

In this chapter I identify the key international actors in the advancement of this international mental health policy context. While several organisations were involved in the mental health policy domain, including international banking institutions, regional mental health entities and bilateral development agencies, the WHO was a primary international actor. The policy transfer literature review revealed the critical role such organisations can play in transfers and their presence and influence on mental health policy transfer in Samoa and Tonga must be fully considered. At the same time, other actors must be considered in fully vetting a particular transfer. As highlighted in Chap. 2, the health sector has been identified as a uniquely specialised area of government intervention often requiring (or insisting upon) professional input into both the bureaucratic and service delivery components of reform efforts. This chapter's focus, however, is on the international actors who were active in mental health policy normalisation efforts. Other ac-tors identified in the earlier part of this book will be taken up as their particular roles are explored in the ensuing chapters. I conclude this chapter by summing up the context promoted through economic and fiscal concerns as justification for the subsequent adoption of mental health policy reforms in Samoa and Tonga, which is designed as segue into the empirical case studies and analysis that follow.

T. P. Fadgen, *Mental Health Public Policy in Global Context*,
https://doi.org/10.1007/978-981-15-6479-6_4

4.1 Internationalisation of Mental Health Policy as a Human Rights Problem

IOs can be divided between intergovernmental organisations (IGOs) and non-governmental organisations (NGOs). IOs serve a critical function in a world increasingly defined by the rapid movement of ideas, entertainment and culture from one place to another. Some are regional in focus and work on forging stronger links of cooperation amongst neighbours. This particular variety is present in the Pacific in several fora and plans for expanding these to include such regional entities as a regional human rights tribunal for Asia and the Pacific remain under development (see e.g. United Nations 2007). Other organisations, international in scope, maintain both regional and local presences that are instrumental in policy localisation efforts, particularly the WHO and World Bank efforts to reform health services and to integrate human rights concepts into mental health services and systems.

Michael Barnett and Martha Finnemore (1999) observe that IOs have become central in the construction of international dis-course by providing conceptual consensus around such tasks as 'development', whilst labelling relevant actors in this process (1999, p. 699). They argue there is an intellectual conflict between scholarly perspectives, between constructivists who see IOs as 'promoters of peace, engines of progress and agents for emancipation' even if there is 'nothing about social construction that necessitates "good" outcomes' and neoliberals and realists who posit the cooperative and stabilising roles these groups play (1999, p. 727). Barnett and Finnemore seek the 'theoretical reasons why undesirable behaviour may occur and suggest that normative evaluation of IO behaviour should be an empirical and ethical matter, not an analytic assumption' (1999, p. 727).

The point builds on Finnemore's (1993) work on the United Nations Educational, Scientific and Cultural Organization (UNESCO) and the proliferation of science bureaucracies. In this study she notes that while some of the motivating factors are intrinsic (i.e. demand-driven based on a rational appraisal of interests), this cannot fully ex-plain the spread of such change (1993, p. 565). Instead, she observes that UNESCO adopted a 'teaching mission' in spreading the notion that scientific bureaucracies were both good and desirable, creating an exogenous impetus to adopting such bureaucracies. She concludes that state 'policies and structures' are prone to influence by such 'changing inter-subjective understandings about the appropriate role of the modern state' instigated by an IO acting on the systemic level; hence the IO is a principal actor, not merely an agent of idea proliferation (1993, pp. 593–94).

In a similar vein, Lisa Martin and Beth Simmons (1998) argue for a renewed focus on 'how institutions matter in shaping the behaviour of important actors in the world' (1998, p. 729). They note that at least since the 1950s the 'idea that international institutions can influence state behaviour by acting through domestic political channels' has been widely recognised in scholarship (1998, p. 732). Moreover, they suggest that IOs might serve to substitute some activities previously thought to be within the competency of domestic state government such as agenda-setting and selecting amongst policy options (1998, p. 752). They then consider circumstances under which a national government might 'substitute' the judgments of these external actors for their own. If 'domestic institutions are the source of persistent policy failure [or] prevent the realisation of societal preferences, or if they somehow interfere with the pursuit of mutual benefits with other states', then domestic policy actors might seek to maximise local benefit through essentially 'contracting-out' these governance functions (1998, p. 752).

This theoretical context raises several points for further inquiry. The general role of IOs as actors in policy transfer and the spread of ideas is both substantively diverse and procedurally complex. There are IOs that specialise in certain overlapping policy areas germane to mental health. There are the health-focused specialist institutions, most notably WHO. In addition, where substantive policy areas such as health converge with other areas of institutional competency, for instance bureaucratic reforms associated with neoliberal public sector reform projects, other international entities become active in a particular policy area. Mental health reforms will be seen to fit this pattern of organisational overlap leading to reform. In the next section, I take up the matter of international, bilateral and regional organisations playing a part in mental health policy transfer during the first decade of the twenty-first century.

4.2 IOs Relevant to Mental Health

4.2.1 World Health Organization

WHO is the world's primary international organisation dedicated to health matters generally and mental health in particular. WHO is composed of three main organs, the World Health Assembly (WHA), the Executive Board and the Secretariat. Of these, the WHA, as the representative of member states, meets annually to set policy as well as ad-dress budgetary matters. WHO, however, was conceived to be a remarkably decentralised organisation and acts significantly throughout the world through its six regional offices in Copenhagen, Cairo, Brazzaville, New Delhi, Manila and Washington. The organisation enjoys quasi-legislative power consisting of 'formal recommendations' of the WHA to member governments concerning matters within WHO's jurisdiction. WHO also possesses convention-making authority in the WHA whereby with a two-thirds majority an instrument executed pursuant to 'any matter within WHO jurisdiction' will become 'legally binding'. Amongst other enumerated powers, the WHA has the authority to adopt regulations concerning nomenclatures with respect to disease and standards with respect to diagnostic procedures for international use (WHO 1947).

Since the 1970s WHO's perspective on health has shifted from one based on purely medical approaches to health to one more socially situated and more explicitly developmental in character. Mental health is a relative new-comer to the international health agenda. Mental health became part of the health agenda only after the agenda-setting role of World Bank was well established and the focus on the fiscal burdens of disease, particularly those presented by disability generally, and mental health disability in particular, was clearly identified by World Bank's 1997 Disability Adjusted Life Years (DALYs) innovation discussed in Chap. 2.

Formal agenda-setting at WHO resides in the objectives set forth in its Constitution and through resolutions of the World Health Assembly (WHA) and the Executive Board. WHO relies heavily on the work of expert committees and uses its position as the preeminent international health organisation to bring experts together, form consensus around public health matters, and to pursue a collective agenda around these shared priorities. Beyond the traditional public health concerns of preventing epidemics and chronic illness, WHO has expanded its scope to include mental health. As Shimkin (1946) observed, '[f]or the first time emphasis was laid not upon quarantine and checking epidemics and other defensive measures, but upon positive, aggressive action toward health in its broadest sense' (1946, p. 283). The Preamble of the WHO Constitution declares that 'health is a state of complete physical, mental, and social well-being and not merely the absence of disease or infirmity'. This was understood as one of the fundamental rights of every human being. Further, Article 2(m) states that, as a priority, WHO will 'foster activities in the field of mental health, especially those affecting the harmony of human relations'(WHO 1946, p. 1). In later years, when combined with the principles set forth in the Universal Declaration of Human Rights (1948), be seen as providing the foundation of mental health treatment existing within a context respectful of individual human dignity.

In particular, the dual objectives of establishing 'international nomenclatures' and 'standardising diagnostic procedures' stand out as particularly germane to the mental health discussion. Mental health diagnosis is often an imperfect endeavour relying almost entirely on subjective impressions, self-reports and similar information in reaching an appropriate diagnostic label for an individual. Although one might argue that standard categories of mental illness might exist that are capable of inter-cultural categorisation, the same is difficult to argue for homogenising diagnostic criteria. These matters are better left to the debates amongst medical and psychological professionals. WHO's broad mandate to 'foster activities' related to mental health gives it moral footing to adopt and then advocate for a particular set of protocols surrounding mental health and illness.

These centrally coordinated activities are then filtered throughout a global organisation by way of regional offices. The Western Pacific Regional Office based in Manila, Philippines, serves as the WHO regional headquarters. Policy and programmatic pursuits that are initiated in Geneva move through information systems through the regional offices and then to individual country missions. By way of internal list-serves, separated by WHO's various health focal areas, priorities and other information is shared throughout the organisation. WHO maintains small country offices in both Samoa and Tonga. Illustrative of the situation in both Samoa and Tonga, a WHO country representative commented.

> I am the only international staff here, I have general staff supporting me, they do not have professional activities, the way things, the way we operate here, in country offices we work closely in collaboration with the Ministry of Health in support of their priorities and their priorities focus basically on non-communicable disease, life-style diseases which are very pressing issues.

Whilst the purpose of the in-country mission is to work closely with the respective Ministry of Health, the assistance is primarily focused on the implicated international health agenda items. Mental disorders are not a common feature of this collaboration. Yet, as will be seen below, WHO has been heavily involved in the production of mental health texts meant to assist regional offices and member states in developing strategies, policies and programmes based on global best practices.

WHO's work is on-going and remains a concern of member nations as represented in the WHA. As recently as May 2012, the 65th WHA issued a pronouncement on the global burden of mental disorders. This latest pronouncement once again linked mental health to the broader non-communicable disease (NCD) context, emphasising the tremendous fiscal and social burdens it poses for nation-states. The WHA reiterated the need for nation-states to adopt appropriate policies and practices in regard to mental health as well as to do more to provide proper surveillance of mental health within their respective states. Moreover, the continuing role of WHO in coordinating efforts at the global level was affirmed.

4.2.2 The World Bank

Christopher Murray and Alan Lopez (1996) note the collaboration between WHO and World Bank on matters germane to the health sector. Since at least 1990 World Bank had been concerned with international development matters and poverty's relationship to escalating health costs. This interest increased in particular regard to mental health matters when neuro-psychiatric disorders, which were first thought of as 'heavily underestimated' at 6.8% of total DALYs lost in the 1990s, were discovered to constitute an estimated 13% by 2003 (Thomas 2004). World Bank itself notes its engagement in mental health and development since 1999 (Thomas 2004). With its longstanding commitment to poverty reduction and the emerging data connecting mental ill health with poverty, World Bank maintains that poverty reduction efforts must incorporate consideration of the mental health dimension.

World Bank is technically a group of five organisations with slightly differing functions. These organisations are technically owned by World Bank's 188 member nations, including Samoa and Tonga, which have the ultimate decision-making power within the organisations on all matters, including policy, financial or membership issues. The daily operations of World Bank, however, are controlled by the Boards of Governors and Boards of Executive Directors. Member states participate in agenda-setting through a weighted-voting system. Based on the member's economy size and resulting contribution paid for membership, the member is assigned a voting quota, with the largest most prosperous countries having a weightier vote in agenda direction.

World Bank's involvement in health care matters is a continuation of Organisation for Economic Co-operation and Development (OECD) interest in the health sector reforms undertaken by many OECD nations in the 1990s (see e.g. Tuohy 1999). The efforts of World Bank specifically sought to globalise what had been a concern amongst the most economically advanced nations. These efforts, advanced through World Bank's World Development Reports, notably beginning in 1993, reflected the neoliberal and new public management principles then prevailing in the public realm. Mental health became an important aspect of the World Bank's economic assessments as reflected in the DALYs measure noted above.

World Bank first officially became involved in mental health matters in 1994 when the mental health dimension was first specifically addressed in several World Bank programmes, notably the health sector reform efforts of the time. The Global Burden of Disease Study (GBD) (Lopez et al. 2006) and the World Development Report (1993) both emphasised disease burden in terms of national costs associated with all manner of disease revealed the tremendous cost (and social) burden of mental disorders, including accounting for four of the top ten causes of global disability (Thomas 2004, p. 5). The attention these reports drew to this burden effectively pulled the World Bank into the universe of needing to address mental health concerns head on. Within 2 years of the GBD's release, World Bank created a 'Mental Health Specialist' position to organise and disseminate knowledge in the area of mental health to World Bank members as well as to provide technical support to its projects and to develop institutional relationships with WHO and other international entities (Thomas 2004, p. 5).

Since 1994 and World Bank's first foray into mental health matters with its Early Child Development Project in Argentina, World Bank efforts have tended to have operational, analytic and knowledge-management orientations. Law reform efforts were undertaken containing a mental health component in Sierra Leone and health sector re-form initiatives containing a mental health component were advanced in Albania, Lithuania, Romania, Zambia, Trinidad, Tobago, Thailand, Afghanistan and Lesotho (Thomas 2004, p. 33). In offering its own assessment of its work, however, World Bank admits its results have been mixed. For instance, HIV/AIDS interventions have long been an important aspect of World Bank's work in Africa and other regions where it has been involved in 'advocacy, analysis and lending' but this 'broad array of . . . initiatives [has] fail[ed] to address mental health' (Thomas 2004, p. 63). In other World Bank projects, the mental health dimension is often a relatively insignificant component. However, the importance of mental health to some vocal members of the international community, including World Bank bureaucrats championing the fiscal and social costs associated with mental disorders, has effectively placed it on the organisational agenda albeit in a relatively subdued position. The importance of mental health in World Bank's agenda is tied to its poverty reduction nexus. As the evidence base of the association of the two grows along with the evidence of successful policy interventions, World Bank may yet take a larger role in mental health policy and best practices proliferation. From this global IO level, I turn to the role played by regional organisations in the Pacific in mental health policy transfers to Samoa and Tonga.

4.3 Regional Organisational Emphasis: The Pacific

Stewart Firth's (2006) edited collection of essays on globalisation in the Pacific Islands gives a good overview of some of the international institutionalist literature and provides a necessary link to the Pacific regional context as setting for the present study. Claire Slatter's contribution to this edition focuses on the ideas undergirding neoliberalism, specifically the 'belief in individualism, free enterprise, lowered taxes, deregulated economies and labour markets, and small government … [that privileges the] private sector at the expense of public interests and welfare' (2006, p. 24). For Slatter, 'neo-liberal discourses on "growth", "efficiency", "reform", and "governance" emerging from World Development Reports have come to dominate development thinking' (2006, pp. 24–25). This conceptual shift accompanied an increasing emphasis on the active participation of NGOs that began in the 1990s and led to the 'emergence of new frameworks for global policy-making (particularly the rights-based approach) as a result of understanding and agreements achieved through negotiations that took place within them' (2006, p. 25). These changes were only possible, however, with the rise of the nation-state in the Pacific.

Peter Larmour (1992) observes that the state as both a legal entity and abstract notion is a relatively recent invention in the Pacific. He notes that 'proto-states' have evolved in the Pacific since about the time of European contact in the eighteenth and nineteenth centuries, marked by increasing stratification in several polities, including in Tonga. Be-ginning in the late nineteenth century, European missionaries arrived on the scene, impacting the indigenous political consolidation processes. Related to this, Larmour argues, is the construction (and division) of traditional ethnic groups into states during the colonial period. New states, such as Samoa, emerged from these colonial states over the course of the twentieth century. At the same time, Jacqueline Braveboy-Wagner (2009) notes that upon independence, 'the nations of the global south inherited patterns of economic, political and cultural dependence arising from colonialism, and postcolonial strategies of counter-dependence or counter-hegemony have been adopted to try to bring about change' (2009, p. 212). Consequentially, the political and economic dominance exerted by the traditional 'Western' powers served to constrain 'the sphere of action' in these Pacific Island states (2009, p. 214). These are precisely the institutional at-tributes examined in this book in the context of mental health systems.

Slatter has also suggested a practical 'consensus among multilateral and bilateral aid donors in the [Pacific] region' (2006, p. 25) when it came to economic reforms in individual states beginning in the mid-1990s. In her research, this consensus was forged around several factors. Firstly, two influential World Bank reports on economies in the region (published in 1991, 1993) contextualised the regional development discourses as part of the emerging neoliberal economic world order. Secondly, were the 'urgings of neo-liberal policy advocates in Australian and New Zealand academia'; finally, 'the [public sector] restructuring experience of New Zealand' (2006, p. 26). These soft factors combined with the slightly more suggestive elements of specific lending programmes initiated by the Asian Development Bank (ADB) through a lending programme that has regrettably saddled many Pacific Island states with significant and previously non-existent debts (2006, p. 27).

In addition, the Pacific Island Forum (PIF) was instrumental in bringing about these reforms. PIF 'function[ed] as a channel for the diffusion of neo-liberal economic ideas and thinking among Pacific Island leaders and as the principal implementing agency in the externally driven program of reforms' (Slatter 2006, p. 27). Beginning in 1999, shortly before Tonga undertook wide-ranging health sector (and other) reforms and also pre-dating the later Samoa reforms, the work of the PIF Secretariat focused on 'trade liberalisation and compliance with WTO principles and trade rules' (2006, p. 27). These efforts coincided with an increased focus on forging an independent 'Pacific' regional identity continues, at least at the institutional level. Elise Huffer (2006) argues for forging a common Pacific identity based on a common core of regional values revolving around 'concepts of solidarity and reciprocity; the fostering and maintenance of kinship net-works and relationships; attachment to land and sea; respect and care for others; the upholding of human dignity; and consultation and shared leadership' (2006, p. 50). As might seem implicit from the statement or summary of com-mon regional values, and more apropos to the topic of governance, Huffer notes the centrality of the local community as opposed to the central government providing much of the 'regulatory agen[cy]'.This was due to the fact that traditional governance institutions were spared destruction during the colonial and decolonisation projects. Linking these often-disparate governance levels has found its most recent iteration within regional organisations driven by a more bottom-up approach, as evidenced by the design of the Pacific Islands Mental Health Network (PIMHnet).

4.3.1 Pacific Islands Mental Health Network

In 2005 the PIMHnet, a joint initiative of the WHO Regional Office for the Western Pacific and WHO Headquarters in Geneva, was established as a regional intergovernmental organisation focused on mental health policy planning and promotion to enhance capacity within the region. The Pacific need for such a network is focused on the perceived increase in drug and alcohol abuse in the region and the association of such abuse with mental ill-health (Hughes 2009, p. 177). Amongst its other areas of emphasis are policy, legislation and planning, as well as efforts to develop the research capacity of mental health units throughout the region. The organisation's official launch was in 2007 and includes 18 member nations in the region, including Australia, New Zealand, Samoa and Tonga. Each member state designates a national focal representative who is supported by an in-country team. The network functions through information-sharing between member states effectuated by the facilitator. As information becomes avail-able throughout the network and from the founding entities in Geneva and Manila, it is filtered through the network of national focal points and through their respective mental health action teams.

PIMHnet's role is to raise mental health as an issue for public concern in Pacific governments and populations. As one senior official commented, initially, PIMHnet primarily focused on 'support[ing] member countries to develop ability to be responsive to mental health primarily focusing on mental health policy then on legislation'. The organisation, funded in large part by the New Zealand Aid Programme (NZAID) and based in Wellington, New Zealand, collaborated with NGOs such as World Organization of Family Doctors, the colleges of psychiatry in Britain and Australasia, as well as formed several other alliances. These networks, in turn, collaborate with in-country NGOs as well as national governments. Typically, NGO partners would include groups often competing against one another for limited international funding and donor money, such as women's groups, domestic violence organisations, addiction groups and self-advocacy organisations.

When the organisation formed in 2005, none of the original 12 member states had a policy and 80% of the region had either an antiquated law that did not encompass contemporary human rights protections or no mental health legislation at all. In 2012, after only 6 years in operation, 15 of 16 current members would have a policy (Tonga as the sole outlier). The central theme of this organisation is the human rights aspect of mental health and this has been the general thrust of statutory and policy interventions in the region. One PIMHnet official opined that these governments have 'little interest in mental health or the mentally ill, so there's no budgets, the countries themselves don't give any money to this area of health, they just think if it needs to be done they'll just go to a donor or nothing needed to be done.'

The organisation completed situational analyses of each nation's mental health policy. Once these parameters were known, the organisation, acting only on a commitment from the interested government to reform their mental health policy, set out to, as a PIMHnet official observed:

> work with the national focal contact, because that is their policy, not our policy, we would give them the technical support. We got all the countries together and had a 3 day workshop in Samoa and we talked about the, about what mental health policy was, through the guidance packages from WHO, and we talked to them about the process, what content they put in there was basically up to them but they needed to have some clear guidance of content that needed to be there, so things that would protect people's human rights, things that moved to support community care and not institutions, things that allowed access for people to psychotropic drugs, things that created education for communities, things, basic things would expect to see in a mental health policy, processes that they needed to run, that they would lead but we would support them on, so you couldn't do this in your office in your department of health, you needed to have a meeting with your stakeholders, so they needed to identify the stakeholders, and talk to NGOs, to people with mental illness and their families, with police and corrections, as they are the organisations by default that dealt with mental health.

The organisation uses much of its resources to produce materials for the member states, including 'informed consent packages' and makes the bulk of material available electronically, sharing the templates on policy, legislation and clinical guidance and information brochures on USB sticks to key contacts in the member states. In addition, a central database is maintained of each member state's developments for sharing with other members and the organisation does not copyright its forms or other publications, allowing for ease of access and reproduction.

PIMHnet recognised the benefits of its association with the prestige of WHO and its physical presence in New Zealand with its perception as both a 'neutral' in the region and a major donor as critical to achieving its tasks. The perception that these entities were acting in concert was seen as crucial to the organisation's mission to ensure local development and ownership of devised mental health policies. As a representative reported:

> Everything is about creating ownership and supporting them to understand more about mental health and its role in their countries success[...] Giving them time, not putting lots of pressure on them, listening to them very clearly about the kinds of things that they need and hat one model will not fit all. Yes, there are key ingredients of policy that need to be in there but how they get there may be quite different.

PIMHnet's continuing role as a known regional entity dedicated to mental health policies framed around a particular human rights construction of the state's role in mental health service provision has been critical in the regionalisation of these mental health policies and norms. This organisation and its impact on the mental health policy developments in Samoa and Tonga will be taken up later in the book.

4.4 Bilateral Aid and Development Agencies: Australian Agency for International Development (AusAID) and New Zealand Aid Programme (NZAID)

Australia and New Zealand are both active in the development context within the Pacific region. Aid and development initiatives originating in these countries are administered throughout the Pacific by their national aid and development agencies, AusAID and NZAID. AusAID, an executive agency under the Ministry of Foreign Affairs and Trade, began in 1974. Its stated aims are simply to combat poverty in the Asia-Pacific region. This broad approach has led to a plethora of development and aid projects undertaken in the Pacific region over the past several decades. Health sector reforms were a large undertaking and began in the late 1990s with a particular Pacific regional emphasis. The process of aid tends to involve a formal request made by a regional government. In response to a specific aid re-quest, say in the health sector, AusAID dispatches a consultant project identification team. This team analyses the situation within the health sector and makes recommendations jointly to AusAID and the requesting government about the aims of any intervention. In addition, AusAID has recently added a 'lessons learnt' debriefing element to all aid programmes. The idea behind this measure is to ensure institutional intelligence is perpetuated from project to project. This same general approach was adhered to in both Samoa and Tonga. On the basis of the project team's visits, projects were developed aimed at improving the planning, management and resource capacity of each respective Ministry of Health. The extent of each development agency's involvement in Samoa and Tonga will be discussed further below. The general role of aid and development agencies, particularly those with long-standing relationships with affected governments, requires further investigation to understand the nature of their role in the policy transfer and localisation processes in Samoa and Tonga.

Wyber, Wilson and Baker (2009) undertook a comprehensive review of the literature on NZAID's role in Pacific development with a particular focus on health initiatives. NZAID, as presently constituted, was established in 2002 as a semi-autonomous agency within New Zealand's Ministry of Foreign Affairs and Trade. New Zealand's official development assistance (ODA) programme has long had a Pacific regional focus. A significant proportion of Pacific ODA funds are distributed by way of bilateral agreements. Wyber et al. note that health sector investment within bilateral Pacific arrangements has been relatively small and has been primarily targeted on non-communicable diseases, communicable diseases, and human sector human resource development.

AusAID's contribution to both Samoa and Tonga's current mental health policy context has been critical. It was widely recognised by respondents involved in this project that both Samoa and Tonga's laws were based on Australian state laws from South Australia and Victoria. Tonga's international consultant was funded by WHO but was an Australian lawyer who relied upon state laws to form the basis of her proposals. Samoa's consultant, as dis-cussed further in Chap. 6, was provided by AusAID and was also an Australian lawyer and former judge with a significant background in mental health law.

In sum, the universe of organisations actively engaged in mental health policy transfer in Samoa and Tonga is relatively small. This review has identified the relevant global institutional actors, primarily WHO and to a lesser extent World Bank. Together, these actors have been engaged in health care reforms for many decades. World Bank has primarily promoted overall health sector reforms whereas WHO has sought to normalise training and nomenclatures. WHO has been particularly invested in regional action and policy promotion. WHO regional activities are coordinated out of the Western Pacific Regional Office in Manila. These global IOs have been augmented in the mental health policy transfer process by regional and bilateral aid entities. Notably, PIMHnet's work and the continued engagement of bilateral development agencies from Australia and New Zealand were observed in both Samoa and Tonga. These entities not only issue grants and other funding streams to nations in support of policy reforms, they are also actively engaged in creating and advancing texts in discrete policy areas. I next consider the global policy textual context with emphasis on the particular framing of mental health as a human rights cause.

4.5 Constructing the Global Mental Health Context: Relevant Policy Texts

In this section I review the global mental health policy context through the second of the two central aspects of the international system: textual artefacts. The mental health policy textual context is rooted in the UN-initiated human rights instruments and pronouncements of the mid-twentieth century. These important documents formed the foundation upon which later rights-based arguments in support of discrete subclasses of individuals would be erected. One such subclass includes those with disabilities. The category 'disability' includes a wide range of physical, cognitive and mental health conditions and was first held together under this one rubric. These documents, however, serve an important link between generic human rights as inalienable rights of the individual and special rights owed to a particular group based on particular attributes of the affected class. As the general disability construct yielded nuances in disabilities and there was a recognition that not one label could envision the particular obstacles confronted by all individuals and their respective disabilities, further subgroups began to emerge. One such subgroup included individuals with mental disorders. This chapter proceeds by outlining the key instruments established along the way to the contemporary global mental health context to provide a sufficiently detailed textual context to fully consider the subsequent policy transfer and localisation efforts in Samoa and Tonga.

WHO's current focus in the area of mental health involves the concept of mental health promotion (WHO 2004b). WHO finds common ground between the traditions of public health promotion and the new endeavour of mental health promotion. To this end, it advances a definition of mental health as being 'a state of well-being in which the individual realises his or her own abilities, can cope with the normal stresses of life, can work productively and fruitfully, and is able to make a contribution to his or her community' (WHO 2004a, p. 16).This same policy document finds that mental health disorders are the result of 'multiple and interacting social, psychological and biological factors' and that the social factors include poverty, low levels of education, poor housing and income. Factors such as rapid social change and physical ill-health can exacerbate mental disorders and the best way to support mental health is to form a society that 'respects and protects basic civil, political and socio-economic and cultural rights' (2004a, p. 12).

Moreover, WHO prescribes mainstreaming mental health promotion into policies and programmes in 'government and business sectors including education, labour, justice, transport, environment, housing and welfare, as well as the health sector' (WHO 2004a, p. 12). WHO's role will be to 'support governments by providing technical material and advice to implement policies, plans and programmes aimed at promoting mental health' (2004a, p. 12).How these prescriptions are entirely consistent with more detailed technical information that is disclaimed as not providing recommended policies or statutory language is considered below. Firstly, however, I consider the broader rights-based context for mental health policy.

4.5.1 Constructing the International Rights-Based Mental Health Context: Generic Human Rights Instruments

Development of a rights-based mental health context occurred rapidly over the latter third of the twentieth century. While inspired, in part, from consumer/patients' rights movements in the core regions as delineated in Chap. 2, and often effectuated through court action and framed in constitutional, substantive fundamental rights language, universal human rights have now found their way into international norms and various formal written instruments. Numerous international instruments concerning human rights, health and mental health provide the framework within which IOs and their voluminous policy documents operate. Key rights and principles include the right to equality and non-discrimination; to privacy and individual autonomy; and to freedom from inhuman and degrading treatment, as well as the principle of least restrictive environment and the rights of information and participation (see e.g. Burns 2009; Saraceno et al. 2007; Dawson 2006; Keilitz and Roesch 1992; Pacific Island Secretariat 2004).

There are two broad categories for international human rights documents: first, those that are legally binding to those who have ratified them (e.g. the 1966 International Covenant on Civil and Political Rights [ICCPR] and the 1966 International Covenant on Economic Social and Cultural Rights [ICESCR]) and second, international hu-man rights 'standards' which are considered guidelines enshrined in international declarations, resolutions or recommendations issued by international bodies (e.g. Mental Illness Principles 1991). In addition, treaty bodies, such as those established by the European and Inter-American human rights systems, have mechanisms for considering individual complaints. Moreover, individual Pacific Island Countries (PICs) participate in select international human rights regimes and instruments. On 25 September 1992 Samoa became the first regional state to ratify the UN Convention on the Elimination and Discrimination against Women (CEDAW), and, on 15 February 2008, acceded to the International Covenant on Civil and Political Rights (ICCPR). Finally, in November 2007 Samoa acceded to the Rome Statute of the International Criminal Court. Meanwhile, on 23 September 2007 neighbouring Tonga signed on to the Convention on the Rights of Persons with Disabilities (for a full discussion of these events, see Jalal 2009).

The category of legally binding provisions contains a trio of international human rights documents referred to collectively as the International Bill of Rights (IBR). The IBR consisted of the Universal Declaration of Human Rights 1948; the ICCPR; and the ICESCR. From here, international bodies entrusted to review and interpret these documents from time to time issued what are known as general comments on the interpretation of a particular provision contained within an underlying treaty, declaration or recommendation. In 1996, for instance, the International Committee on Economic Social and Cultural Rights adopted General Comment 5 detailing the applicability of the ICESCR to people with mental and physical disabilities. This manner of interpretive decree is non-binding but reflect-ed the 'official view' as to proper interpretation of the Convention. The UN Human Rights Commission (UNHRC), first established in 1946, was charged with monitoring the ICCPR, which, while it has not issued a specific comment on mental disorders, has issued a general disability comment (Comment 18) under Article 26.

However, application of general principles to specific situations leaves room for disagreement as to the particular application of a right to a particular context. As illustrated by these examples of attempted application of generic human rights to the particular context of disability context, individuals with disabilities often have much more specific needs than do members of the community as a whole. Individuals with disabilities often suffer social isolation due to social stigma as well as institutional barriers. As such, general rights to dignity or liberty require specific elaboration if they are to have particular meaning to this population. Hence, human rights discourses took a 'disability turn' during the 1970s and this is discussed in the next section.

4.5.2 *The Disability Thematic Shift in Key International Human Rights Texts*

International policy surrounding persons with disabilities, specifically those pertaining to the rights of these persons, had historically been driven by the UN along with other IOs. The turning point in this evolution of attitudes occurred in the late 1960s with a new concept of disability emerging out of the disability community discourses that focused on the connection between social context and attitudes and the prejudicial experiences of individuals with dis-abilities. This now long line of policy statements began with the 1975 Declaration on the Rights of Disabled Persons (discussed below), and the resulting International Year of Disabled Persons in 1981. From the latter developed the World Programme of Action concerning Disabled Persons, which was adopted by the UN General Assembly in 1982. The UN Decade of Disabled Persons (1983–1992), which yielded an expert-vetted World Programme of Action concerning Disabled Persons at the Mid-Point of the United Nations Decade of Disabled Persons in 1987, followed these earlier international initiatives. The outcome of this expert meeting was the unifying orientation of subsequent disability policy to recognise of the rights of persons with disabilities. In 1993 the Standard Rules on the Equalisation of Opportunities for Persons with Disabilities were developed. These were founded upon the principles embodied in the International Declaration of Human Rights (1948).

The 1975 Declaration on the Rights of Disabled Persons, defines a 'disabled person' in reference to the individual's ability to secure the requirements of both individual and social life which could be due to either a physical or mental incapacity. This Declaration further established the right for persons with disabilities to have access to legal assistance where required, including that court procedures should take into account an individual's disability and accommodate him or her accordingly. Further, the Declaration is one of the first internationally recognised embodiments of the inclusion not only of individuals with disabilities but also of organisations of disabled persons into the policy-making process.

In 1993, the UN General Assembly adopted the Standard Rules on the Equalisation of Opportunities for Persons with Disabilities (SREOPD). Amongst its findings, the SREOPD noted that persons with disabilities endured '[i]gnorance, neglect, superstition and fear' that have 'isolated persons with disabilities and delayed their development' and that the SREOPD resulted from intellectual and policy developments surrounding disability occurring over the past 200 years (UN 1993).States were encouraged to advance positive portrayals of individuals with disabilities in mass media campaigns and produce inclusive policy regimes. This measure consists of a total of 22 Rules plus a monitoring mechanism to check on compliance established to affirm the ability of individuals with disabilities to participate in their respective societies, including fully exercising their rights on an equal basis. Together, these Rules symbolise an emerging international consensus of proper and just treatment of individuals with disabilities, including mental illness.

Building upon these general human rights principles, member states negotiated the 2008 Convention on the Rights of Persons with Disabilities & Optional Protocol (CRPD-OP) to deal directly with the disability and mental health context. This Convention recognised the continuing need for persons with disabilities to be guaranteed their full enjoyment without discrimination, in particular the acute needs of women and girls, children, those in poverty, minority populations or religions. In order to secure non-discrimination of those with disabilities, states signing on to this Convention are expected, amongst other responsibilities, to "adopt all appropriate legislative, administrative and other measures for the implementation of… rights… [and] to take all appropriate measures, including legislation, to modify or abolish existing laws, regulations, customs and practices that constitute discrimination against persons with disabilities …" (UN 2006).

Further, community inclusion is a central right of the broad-based disability rights movement and this Convention demands states implement laws and policies and engender practices designed to achieve fuller participation in the civic and work environments in each nation by offering support services to individuals requiring them. The Convention, again following the precedent established in WHO's regional structure, sets forth the principle of a 'Regional integration organisation' which is 'an organisation constituted by sovereign States of a given region, to which its member States have transferred competence in respect of matters governed by this Convention' (UN 2006). Tonga is one of the 144 treaty signatories while Samoa has not signed. These conventions and other official documents of the international community have created the institutional structure within which IOs operate and serve as the path-ways along which these actors seek to transfer the norms, policies and laws from the global to local levels.

As mentioned, until 1991, disability initiatives generally dealt with physical, intellectual and mental disability under the generic 'disability' label. Even a cursory review of the initiatives leading up to the landmark Principles for the Protection of Persons with Mental Illness and Improvement of Mental Health Care (MI Principles) in 1991, demonstrates the overall thrust of these measures was dealing with physical disabilities and removing barriers to full inclusion within the community. But with the adoption of the MI Principles, the separate category of disability related to mental illness was set forth on its own independent path of recognition, which was followed by specific endeavours by WHO in 2001. These included making mental health the subject of that year's World Health Report and culminated in the 2008 CRPD-OP, to be discussed below.

4.5.3 *Establishing Mental Health as Human Right: The International Context*

4.5.3.1 United Nations Principles for the Protection of Persons with Mental Illness and for the Improvement for Mental Health Care (MI Principles) (1991)

The MI Principles represent the first unified effort in the specifically mental health disability context. While not actually defining mental illness, they define 'mental health care' to include 'analysis and diagnosis of a person's mental condition, and treatment, care and rehabilitation for a mental illness or suspected mental illness' (UN 1991, p. 1). Principle 1 states that all persons have the right to 'the best available mental health care, which shall be part of the health and social care system' (UN 1991, p. 2). And as in other provisions addressing disability generally, the MI Principles carve out an exception for those measures aimed at securing the advancement of persons with mental ill-ness by defining them as non-discriminatory. Also, as in the general disability measures, the MI Principles reinforce the due process of law protections for persons with mental illness in cases where there is an allegation of loss of legal capacity, including involuntary hospital admission. In such cases, the individual shall be entitled to free legal representation. In the case of an involuntary hospitalisation, the law must reflect that the individual is subject to the hospitalisation because of a mental illness that results in serious likelihood of immediate or imminent harm to any person or be-cause the person's judgment is limited by the mental illness to the point that the failure to retain the individual would 'likely to lead to a serious deterioration in his or her condition or will prevent the giving of appropriate treatment' (Principle 16).

MI Principles begins with the premise that where the state confronts a person with mental illness and wishes to detain the individual, the person is protected by human rights protections that require adherence to natural jus-tice principles. These principles are balanced against the state power to protect the individual from him or herself as well as to protect the public at large. If the person at the centre of such a process does not (or is unable to) give consent to treatment, then he or she has right to counsel, that informed consent to treatment must be sought in the first instance, the person is entitled to an independent review of the merits of the case and any determination to detain the individual is subject to judicial review. Ultimately, involuntary admission to hospital is warranted only if necessary to prevent harm and to care and treat the individual in question.

Identifying and treating an individual's mental illness is to be done with a careful focus on maintaining his or her personal autonomy. Any determination that a person has a mental illness must be reached consistently with inter-nationally accepted medical standards. Any subsequent treatment must be suited to the 'patient's' cultural back-ground in the least restrictive environment and with the least restrictive means necessary for both the patient and for the protection of the community. Prescribed treatment must be discussed and embody an individual plan and be subject to revision. To that end, the focus should be on voluntary treatment; involuntary treatment should only be undertaken with due process of law. The MI Principles discourage the use of restraint or involuntary seclusion except where it is done to prevent immediate or imminent harm. Psychosurgery is never to be carried out in the absence of the patient's informed consent and sterilisation is never to be performed.

As Sylvia Bell and Warren Brookbanks (2005) argue, however, the notion of normalising domestic mental health law around the *MI Principles* can be problematic: any definition in a health context that refers to individuals as 'patients' as the *MI Principles* does, is suspect. The human rights perspective advances a construction of the individual which privileges the person him or herself over the person's medical diagnostic status. Related to this, the *MI Principles* did not offer a definition of either mental illness or mental disorder. The guidelines require that no determination of mental illness be made on the basis of political, economic, or social status or membership of a cultural, racial, or religious group; or from any family or professional conflict or non-conformity with moral, social, cultural, or political values or religious beliefs prevailing in a person's community. A diagnosis shall also not be made on the grounds of past treatment or hospitalisation; nor shall any person or authority classify a person as having a mental illness except for persons directly related to such diagnoses. Even then, this shall not happen unless the determination is consistent with internationally accepted medical standards (Bell & Brookbanks 2005). The suggestion left by these limitations is that notwithstanding those behaviours that the community finds deviant or bizarre, the individual must manifest a mental illness as the primary basis for any proposed confinement and must additionally pose either a risk of harm to him or herself or others. The next international document dedicated to mental health as a particular policy concern was WHO's 2003 *Mental Health Context.*

4.5.3.2 The Mental Health Context (2003)

In 2003, WHO published The Mental Health Context. The publication emerged at the behest of the 55thWHA held in 2002 that called on member states to commit to improving the mental health of their respective populations and to engender greater cooperation on an international level in pursuit of better mental health outcomes.

Further-more, the WHA sought support for WHO's Mental Health Global Action Project in 'providing a clear and coherent strategy for closing the gap between what is urgently needed and what is currently available to reduce the burden of mental disorders' (WHO 2003, p. 11). The Mental Health Context is in fact part of a larger guidance package de-signed to speak to a multiplicity of policy and service components with particular attention to the developing nation context. The package is comprehensive in scope in that it addresses developing a policy, developing a mental health plan, developing a mental health programme, and implementation issues for policy, plans and programmes.

That report identified its contributors as experts: policymakers, service providers as well as civil society organisations representing the range of consumers, their family members, medical professionals, and local ministries of health. The overall objective was to raise the profile of mental health on the domestic agendas of less developed country (LDC) policymakers. Here, despite disclaimers that the package is mere guidance and not specific statutory language to be adopted, the module on mental health legislation and human rights 'set[s] out the activities that are required before legislation is formulated' (WHO 2003, p. 7). In addition, the preferred content of model legislation is provided, including language for ancillary policy areas such as drugs policy. Moreover, proposed processes for up-dating a nation's mental health law are prescribed from drafting procedures to implementation.

The tenor of these pronouncements presented two central factors for a nation-state's consideration of direct and indirect economic costs of mental disorders. Because mental disorders often have prolonged and repeated therapies there is an on-going cost associated with treatment over the course of an individual's lifetime. Direct costs are costs directly associated with treating the individual's condition whilst indirect costs, which are estimated to be far higher, stem from lost employment and decreased productivity. For illustrative purposes, the report cited US$148 billion as the estimated annual US direct cost associated expense in 1990 (WHO 2003). Direct expenses will be predictably lower in developing countries simply because there are fewer opportunities for treatment. Consequently, indirect treatment costs are projected to increase in large part due to the on-going and untreated nature of these disorders. Moreover, indirect costs outweigh direct costs in developed countries by two to six times and are likely to be even higher than this in LDCs (WHO 2003). The findings painted a concerning picture for the mental well-being of the future world. Mental disorders were presented as accounting for nearly 12% of the GBD, a percentage expected to jump to 15% by 2020 (WHO 2003). The downside of public health's success in managing, and often eradicating, many communicable diseases and infant health issues is that developing countries are 'likely to see disproportionately large increase in the burden attributable to mental disorders in the coming decades' (WHO 2003).

There are perhaps many reasons for this anticipated rising burden in developing countries. Firstly, longer lives enjoyed by many in the developing world are expected to bring about many of the mental disorders found in ageing populations such as depression and dementia. In addition, demographic and social factors ranging from 'rapid urbanisation, conflicts, disasters, and macroeconomic changes' (WHO 2003,

p. 12) must also be considered. The process of urbanisation is typically accompanied by 'increased homelessness, poverty, overcrowding, higher levels of pollution, disruption in family structures and loss of social support,' (WHO 2003b, p. 12) all of which are risk factors for mental disorders. Finally, according to 2000 estimates, mental and neurological disorders accounted for 6 of the 20 leading causes of disability worldwide (WHO 2001). Depression is expected to become the second most important cause of disability in the world (see e.g. Murray and Lopez 1997). As mentioned above, developing countries with poorly developed mental health care systems are likely to see the most substantial increases in the burden attributable to mental disorders.

4.5.3.3 Resource Book on Mental Health, Human Rights, and Legislation (2005)

Shortly after the Mental Health Context is published, WHO issued its Resource Book on Mental Health Human Rights and Legislation (Freeman and Pathare 2005) to assist policymakers in drafting conforming legislative frameworks. The publication was careful not to argue that the recommendations were sacrosanct but rather were meant merely to draw policymakers' attention to widely accepted international standards and practices in the area of mental health law. To that end, the resource book stated that 'good legislation' was central to improving the lives of those with mental disorders. 'Good legislation' was defined as those laws within the 'context of internationally accepted human rights standards and good practices' (Freeman and Pathare 2005, p. xv).The fundamental aim of good mental health legislation is therefore to 'protect, promote and improve citizens' lives and mental well-being. A mental health law will be deemed 'well-conceived' if it addresses the following six points: (1) it establishes high quality mental health facilities and services; (2) provides access to quality mental health care; (3) protects the human rights of consumers; (4) develops robust procedural protections; (5) integrates those receiving treatment into the community; and (6) promotes mental health throughout the society.

The international instruments recognise the need for these principles to become enshrined in domestic law. To that end, these domestic laws should.

> empower people with mental disabilities to make choices about their lives, give legal protections relating to the establishment of and access to quality mental health facilities, as well as care and support services, established for procedural mechanisms for protection of those with mental disabilities, ensure the integration of persons with mental disabilities into the community, and promote mental health throughout society. (Freeman and Pathare 2005, p. 220).

The Resource Book builds on the MI Principles and other core human rights instruments such as the Standard Rules for the Equalisation of Opportunities for Persons with Disabilities. Good legislation is viewed as the catalyst of human rights in the given community by providing the positive justification for further policy development around the core concepts of human rights and anti-discriminatory principles protecting those suffering from mental disorders. The existence of poorly worded legislation, on the other hand, can have the opposite effect: laws not expressly providing for community treatment will often tie the hands of progressive elements within ministries of health because there is no statutory guidance or precedent for state-sponsorship of such programmes. The Resource Book provided an anatomy of a quality mental health law, which should include a preamble, objectives or purpose statement for the law, and a definitions section to set forth clear and hopefully unambiguous functional definitions of all important or operative terms.

Chief amongst these difficult yet necessary terms requiring definition is 'mental disorder'. As the Resource Book authors state,'[d]efining mental disorder is difficult because it is not a unitary condition but a group of disorders with some commonalities' (Freeman and Pathare 2005, p. 20). This raises a fundamental question for the drafter of any such law: Should the law take a negative approach to definition and purpose? For example, are we assuming a broad amount of civil liberty which we are seeking to narrow in only a certain set of circumstances and contingent upon certain conditions precedent? Or are we to take a positive approach? For example, a rights-based purpose that guarantees rights in addition to a general category of rights available to all citizens?

In either form, there are several major obstacles facing an LDC looking to craft a progressive (by Western standards) statutory scheme dealing with mental disorder. The first is the almost complete absence of reliable data or other information about mental disorder prevalence within a particular LDC, as well as very little information on variance within individual LDCs. The Resource Book authors cite the existence of this data as a vital first step to crafting a meaningful law. A second key obstacle is the absence of one of the primary engines for this type of reform: a mental health professional community. In many countries the driving force behind legislative reform in the area of mental health comes out of a concerned professional association trained in the field of mental health and familiar with both current domestic practices and what are deemed best practices on the international level as a basis for that local structural reform.

The Resource Book offers a litany of mental health care shortcomings that may exist in countries and which can be overcome by the crafting of a revised mental health legal framework in line with its recommendations. These shortcomings centre on central themes of inadequate or unattainable mental health care and services, lack of judicial process for involuntary admissions and the securing of individual rights in such areas as housing and education, and the existence of stigma and other society-based discrimination. The presumed hope is that the process of law creation, through a public debate and education component, will yield a shift in attitudes that will be reinforced through punitive measures designed to ensure the law's recognised rights. Only a more careful analysis of the policymaking process in several LDCs will reveal if these barriers, which undoubtedly exist in all LDCs to a certain extent, can be overcome or reduced as a result of the policymaking process and subsequent policy that comes out of it. The top horizontal boxes are my identified themes. Under each of these themes are the key words together with weighted percentages for each term.

In the Pacific context, the WHO Western Pacific Region oversaw the production and publication in 2002 of its Regional Strategy for Mental Health (WHO Western Pacific Region [WHO-WPR] 2002).This report adopts an inter-sectoral approach to mental health promotion as well as the prevention and treatment of illness. Additionally, it calls for the integration of mental disorder treatment into the general health services. A related objective is to achieve a more informed understanding of mental health throughout the broader Western Pacific community. The central call to action here arose out of what the Regional Strategy authors identified as negative social conditions linked to mental disorders, the high economic cost associated with mental illness, and the high rates of suicide throughout the region. There are several factors that affect mental health including poverty, minority status, uncontrolled urbanisation, disasters, armed conflict, refugees and displaced persons and the weakening of the family structure. These factors, which exacerbate mental illness, result in enormous economic cost to the nation and pose extreme challenges to the health, social services and criminal justice systems throughout the region.

The Regional Strategy identifies three basic goals: (1) to reduce human social and economic burdens; (2) to promote mental health; and (3) to give appropriate attention to psychosocial aspects of health care. These goals are pursued through six approaches, outlined in the body of the study: advocacy, service provision, mental health pro-motion, policy and legislation, encouraging research, and suicide prevention. Advocacy should be used to increase awareness of decision-makers and the general public of both the importance of mental health and stigma associated with being labelled with a disorder. Mental health service delivery is to be streamlined throughout the region by prioritising the integration of mental health with primary care. Moreover, the Regional Strategy adopts the de-institutionalisation model because 'asylums cannot provide modern services close to where people live, and in the least restrictive environment possible' (WHO-WPR 2002, p. 16). Instead, the Regional Strategy embraces the com-munity-based treatment model of care and advances this approach as the preference for member nations.

To this end, the Regional Strategy also identifies the gap between the public and non-governmental sectors in many countries in the region as an area for improvement if this objective is to be realised. There was also a need to accept that people in the region with mental illness and their families often consulted traditional healers and leaders and, as such, this area of service provision needs to be better understood and incorporated into the governmental plan. The lack of health workforce experience and training in many of the countries is also mentioned as an area of particular need. Finally, governments need to promote and develop both family and consumer self-help and advocacy associations in order to assist with the goal of improving service delivery and reducing stigma and discrimination. Mental health promotion should seek to enhance the view of mental health in the community in order to improve out-comes on the policy end of the process.

The policy and legislation focus sought to achieve congruence between domestic law and current international best practices (WHO-WPR 2002).The Regional Strategy addresses inadequacies and omissions in regard to treatment of people with mental disorders. In particular, the focus is on ensuring normalisation of the ethos of law: respect for the rights of individuals with mental disorders to receive only dignified and effective care with a preference of voluntariness. The focus of new policy initiatives in this area should be integrating mental health and general health services.

Again, both cost-effectiveness and human rights narratives are evident in the call for consumer-stigma reduction and in the recognition of the potentially symbiotic relationship of traditional healers, community leaders and the health system. Because improvement in mental health care often depended on first understanding the scale and scope of the particular issues within a particular nation, WHO is encouraging the development of a research culture and capacity. Currently, statistics are not readily available throughout the region, making agenda-setting and fundraising particularly problematic for these nations. Finally, similar to the more general objectives of the research culture objective, suicide prevention will require careful analysis of individual national data in order to understand and address the problem. This deficit in information and the apparently pervasive and grim nature of suicide throughout the region warranted it having its own separate billing as an objective.

4.5.3.4 Situational Analysis of Mental Health Needs and Resources in Pacific Island Countries (2005)

In 2005, WHO commissioned a further regional mental health study entitled Situational Analysis of Mental Health Needs and Resources in Pacific Island Countries. The report was drafted for the WHO Regional Office and meant to 'enhance the ability of countries in the Western Pacific region to undertake mental health reform and planning by providing key people in those countries with training and support around mental health service organisation and de-livery' (WHO-WPR 2005) by developing a pilot project for implementation of both a mental health policy and mental health plan in a subset of nations of the larger 19-nation region. The smaller pilot sample includes Cook Islands, Fiji, Samoa, Tonga, Papua New Guinea, Vanuatu and the Solomon Islands. A 'mental health policy' is defined in the re-port as a broad-based vision that sets forth a vision, values, principles and objectives as well as determining areas for action and the primary roles and responsibilities of responsible parties. The process also involves data collection and organisation as well as evidence-based strategy. The 'plan' is more specific in terms of strategy development and set-ting timeframes to be adhered to; this stage includes costs and specific programmes and activities, as well as budgetary considerations.

The Situational Analysis proposed culturally appropriate technical support in partnership with countries to achieve objectives in a culturally appropriate manner. The support should follow WHO implementation protocols and is likely to take two forms: direct, in-country support by consultants with relevant expertise and experience, and on-going distance support. In addition, a common thread for each pilot would be legislative and legal reviews at the national level that reflect 'the unique circumstances and culture of each country, are comprehensive, contemporary in nature and mindful of international obligations' (WHO-WPR 2005, p. 4). The pilot project sought to address the identified major needs of developing a specialised mental health and general health workforce whilst increasing both understanding and awareness of mental health matters amongst indigenous populations. On the systemic level, emphasis is placed upon the mental health service delivery system, including community care programmes, and there is renewed emphasis on management and development of relevant law and policy frameworks.

The report includes the South Pacific Nursing Forum's observations on regional mental health priorities. This feedback revealed a series of common problems, including inadequate training of doctors and nurses; unavailability of psychologists for in-patient and community services; growing suicide rates, growing alcohol and other drugs problems, especially for students/youth; lack of legislation and policy; lack of medications and services; budgetary restrictions/constraints; and an overall lack of political will. In addition, Pacific health systems tend to be heavily reliant on families and communities, making the stigma and neglect associated with mental disorders more debilitating and making it harder for individuals to get adequate and timely treatment. Mental health is not high on the health politics agenda, given other more important needs, and health professionals are generally untrained in the field and uninterested in it.

The Situational Analysis notes, however, that most Pacific countries are well positioned – due to the lack in most instances of highly entrenched, centralised medical structures – to develop their primary health care systems. Thus, the systemic structure appears to be in place and can be preserved, largely intact, as mental health systems are created or migrate from segregation to a central aspect of the primary health care system. Successful mental health service initiatives often depend on the presence of a comprehensive legislative and policy framework addressing such logistical matters as planning, funding, organisation, and delivery of services. Common obstacles in each country are the reality that mental health is often not perceived as a major health priority by many countries as they address more pressing (and tangible) health needs. Note a marked difference in the emphasis on education, information and research capacity in these regional documents from the international documents summarised above.

4.6 Conclusion

The mental health policy context is broader than the traditional health sector. Government policies concerning poverty, urbanisation, unemployment, education and criminal justice all influence mental health and need to take into ac-count mental illness in their particular missions for society. Poverty is one of the strongest factors affecting mental health because poor people suffer environmental and psychological adversity that increases vulnerability to mental disorders (Patel et al. 2011). Urbanisation leads to increased risk of mental disorders because of its disruption of family life, reduction in family supports, and increases the risks of homelessness (another risk factor), poverty and expo-sure to psychological distress (WHO 2003). Public education that permits early detection of mental disorders can be one of the most useful means of preventing the long-term debilitating effects of disorders. Finally, the criminal justice system and people with mental disorders often come into contact with one another; those in prison are more likely than the general population to suffer from a mental disorder. As such, treatment and care in prison is commonly understood as a state policy concern.

The international context of globalisation and internationalisation involves numerous potential actors implicated in the proliferation of mental health ideas and norms beyond national borders, including ideas on the proper state role in population mental health. These actors include the state and intra-state actors as well as IOs and other international actors, including national aid and development agencies that operate ostensibly as extensions of a particular nation's foreign policy apparatus yet at the same time operate in a substantially similar manner as IOs in an aid recipient state and many other entities. I briefly discussed the IO literature before turning to the substantive international texts and agents engaged in international mental health systems proliferation. Specifically, I identified the key international documents relevant to mental health as an area of international concern and addressed the question of how IOs have predominantly been involved in the Pacific region. Finally, I took up the issue of institutional legacies of colonial and postcolonial institutions in the Pacific.

The elevation of mental health to the international health agenda may have been brought about by the fiscal policy emphasis of the neoliberal discourse concerning health policy and planning advanced by the World Bank, but once established this discourse found a ready partner in the form of the human rights discourse concerning the men-tally ill, which was well established by that point in time (see e.g. World Bank 1993). The convergence of these two discourses advanced the mental health agenda where the human rights discourses alone had failed to effectively influence policy and law prior to the neoliberal health system reform being firmly entrenched on the international policy agenda. The following chapters examine whether Samoa and Tonga have recognised the human rights implications of the treatment of the mentally ill and whether those attitudes have materialised into either policy or law innovations in each nation.

As noted, WHO was the primary actor and worked in informal collaboration with World Bank and other organisations in terms of organisational involvement in global-level mental health policy transfer. As discussed, World Bank was critical in injecting the OECD focus on health sector reform amongst the policy core countries into the development policy context. Over the course of the 1990s and early 2000s World Bank was actively engaged in producing reports and promoting programmes designed to facilitate health sector reform in the developing state. WHO was observed to have long been engaged in global health matters and to that end has been involved in mental health policy and service best practice proliferation for many decades. There has been a convergence of these two groups, with World Bank's emphasis on economic and fiscal matters related to controlling health costs and encouraging government efficiency and WHO's focus on mental health, particularly adopting the increasingly human rights-oriented mental health framework steadily developed in international instruments since the 1970s.

The activities of these two large IOs provided the impetus for regional efforts in the Pacific to reform health care and, by implication, reform mental health systems through policy innovation. In order to achieve these goals, regional development partners were enlisted in the efforts. AusAID and NZAID have long had a presence in PICs, maintain diplomatic missions in these countries, and have historically had large populations of Samoans and Tongans residing within their respective nation-states. As will be seen, AusAID's involvement in mental health reforms in both Samoa and Tonga has been clearly more significant than formal involvement by any of the other international actors. Still, IOs sought to promote mental health through policy-sharing and best practices promotion by creating an institution, PIMHnet, and through the development of two large-scale regional analyses on mental health needs in the region, the Pacific Regional Strategy for Mental Health and the Situational Analysis of Mental Health Needs and Resources in Pacific Island Countries. These two reports clearly establish the need for updated policies by noting that most regional states either lacked a policy or law altogether or had antiquated laws and policies. The recognition of a looming global mental health crisis and its particulars in the Pacific region, together with the identification of the seriously deficient legal and policy structures necessary to effectively equip the state to manage the crisis when it arrives, helped stir government leaders into action. Amongst the nations selected to pilot a mental health policy and plan were Samoa and Tonga. I examine the results of the piloting in the chapters that follow.

Besides this enquiry, however, the existence of numerous international instruments and other documents meant to underline the importance of mental health as a policy issue and to advance the particular framing of state responsibilities regarding mental health in human rights terms raises the inevitable question of how much these documents took into account the indigenous policymaking process. Did policymakers and other stakeholders refer to or rely upon these documents in making policy decisions? Again, did policy actors primarily raise cost justifications for developing a mental health policy or law or did they frame policy decisions in terms human rights? Or were policy decisions thought of in terms of their 'fit' or appropriateness in the local context? These are all questions to be taken up in the remaining chapters of this book.

Despite WHO's 2001 World Health Report prioritising such areas as community care, treatment in primary care settings, the making available of psychotropic drugs, and the establishing of national policies programmes and legislation, many of these areas have remained underserved. Saraceno et al. (2007) conducted a survey of international mental health stakeholders to identify barriers to mental health service development, noting such institutional barriers as the prevailing public health priority agenda and its effect on funding, a situation continuing the trends noted in this chapter from the perspective of IO agendas. The strongly centralised component of such policy coordination efforts overlooks the human rights values inherent in the new approach to mental health such as those efforts to include individuals with mental disorders, their family members and interested community members without formal professional training, in both service provision and advocacy activities.

The concepts bound up with the 'mental health system' are embedded within a complex set of medico-legal relationships existing under the guise of state responsibility. This system emerged from a particular construction of mental health and illness and state responses to manage the social phenomenon of it. As will be discussed, from the domestic level of construction, such policies were advanced throughout the colonial era and decolonisation projects of the mid-twentieth century. Over the course of the twentieth century, the role of mental health norm advancers increasingly fell to IOs in various capacities and, in practice, these forged an international mental health policy context around acceptable and best practices. This global context was advocated by diverse civil society groups to IOs, such as WHO and World Bank. As national aid and development agencies increasingly became involved in neoliberal economic re-forms to various state sectors, these discourses were advanced by national aid and development projects in various developing nations, particularly AusAID and NZAID in Samoa and Tonga. Traditional formal institutions, such as the presence of a Western-style health system, and mental health system in particular, together with formal institutions (e.g. hospital and prisons) embedded in legal frameworks (e.g. mental health laws), staffed by medical and legal professions with their respective knowledge structures (e.g. doctors, nurses, lawyers and judges and their influence over legislative and regulatory frameworks as well as professional practices), served as the institutional pathway to ensure continuity and had the potential to enable policy change. This potential, as we shall see, required the forerunner of significant policy shift in Western nations to influence this eventual international contextual shift.

References

Barnett, M., & Finnemore, M. (1999). The politics, power, & pathologies of international organizations. *International Organization, 53*(04), 699–732.

Bell, S., & Brookbanks, W. (2005). *Mental health law in New Zealand.* Wellington: Brookers.

Braveboy-Wagner, J. (2009). *Institutions of the global south.* New York: Routledge.

Burns, J. (2009). Mental health and inequity: A human rights approach to inequality, discrimination, and mental disability. *Health & Human Rights, 11*(2), 19–31.

Dawson, J. (2006). Fault-lines in community treatment order legislation. *International Journal of Law & Psychiatry, 29*(6), 482–494.

Finnemore, M. (1993). International organizations as teachers of norms: The United Nations educational, scientific and cultural organization and science policy. *International Organization, 47*(4), 565–597.

Firth, S. (Ed.). (2006). *Globalisation & governance in the Pacific Islands.* Canberra: ANU E Press.

Freeman, M., & Pathare, S. (2005). *WHO resource book on mental health, human rights and legislation.* World Health Organization.

Huffer, E. (2006). Regionalism & cultural identity: Putting the Pacific back into the plan. In S. Firth (Ed.), *Globalisation & Governance in the Pacific Islands.* Canberra: ANU E Press.

Hughes, F. (2009). Mental health in the Pacific: The role of the Pacific Island mental health network. *Pacific Health Dialog, 15*, 1.

International Covenant on Civil and Political Rights [ICCPR]. (1966).

International Covenant on Economic Social and Cultural Rights [ICESCR]. (1966).

Jalal, I. (2009). Why do we need a Pacific regional human rights commission. *Victoria University of Wellington Law Review, 40*(177), 177–195.

Keilitz, I., & Roesch, R. (1992). Improving justice and mental health systems interactions: In search of a new paradigm. *Law & Human Behavior, 16*(1), 5–26.

Larmour, P. (1992). States & societies in the Pacific Islands. *Pacific Studies, 15*(1), 99–121.

Lopez, A., Mathers, C., Ezzati, M., Jamison, D., & Murray, C. (Eds.). (2006). *Global burden of disease and risk factors.* New York: Oxford University Press.

Martin, L., & Simmons, B. (1998). Theories & empirical studies of international institutions. *International Organization, 52*(4), 729–757.
Murray, C., & Lopez, A. (1996). Evidence-based health policy—lessons from the global burden of disease study. *Science, 274*(5288), 740–743.
Murray, C., & Lopez, A. (1997). Mortality by cause for eight regions of the world: Global burden of disease study. *The Lancet, 349*(9061), 1269–1276.
Pacific Island Secretariat. (2004). *Review of policy & legislation on disability in Pacific Island countries.*
Patel, V., Boyce, N., Collins, P., Saxena, S., & Horton, R. (2011). A renewed agenda for global mental health. *The Lancet, 378*(9801), 1441–1442.
Saraceno, B., van Ommeren, M., Batniji, R., Cohen, A., Gureje, O., Mahoney, J., Sridhar, D., & Underhill, C. (2007). Barriers to improvement of mental health services in low-income & middle-income countries. *The Lancet, 370*(9593), 1164–1174.
Shimkin, M. (1946). The World Health Organization. *Science, 104*(2700).
Slatter, C. (2006). Treading water in rapids? Nongovernmental organisations & resistance to neo-liberalism in the Pacific Islands. In S. Firth (Ed.), *Globalisation & governance in the Pacific Islands*. Canberra: ANU E Press.
Thomas, R. (2004). Mental health and the global development agenda: What role for the world Bank? In *Proceedings of a November 2003 seminar: An overview of World Bank*. Washington, DC: Interventions in Mental Health, World Bank.
Tuohy, C. H. (1999). *Accidental logics: The dynamics of change in the health care system in the United States, Britain, and Canada*. New York: Oxford University Press.
United Nations. (1948). Universal Declaration of Human Rights. (December 10, 1948).
United Nations. (1991). *United Nations principles for the protection of persons with mental illness & improvement of mental health care (the MI principles)*. New York.
United Nations. (1993) *Standard rules on the equalisation of opportunities for persons with disabilities.*
United Nations. (2006). Convention on the rights of persons with disabilities (CRPD). *May, 3*, 2008.
United Nations. (2007). *Advancing the implementation of human rights in the Pacific: Compilation of recommendations of the UN human rights treaty bodies to the countries of the Pacific.* Suva: Self.
World Bank. (1993). *World development report, 1993: Investing in health.* Washington, DC: Oxford University Press.
World Health Organization (WHO). (1946). *Constitution of the World Health Organization.* New York.
World Health Organization (WHO). (1947). *Chronicle of the World Health Organization.*
World Health Organization (WHO). (2001). *World health report*. Geneva: WHO.
World Health Organization (WHO). (2003). *The mental health context*. Geneva: WHO.
World Health Organization (WHO) 2004a, Promoting mental health: Concepts, emerging evidence, practice. In *Summary report/a report from the World Health Organization, Department of Mental Health & Substance Abuse in collaboration with the Victorian Health Promotion Foundation (VicHealth) & the University of Melbourne*. WHO: Geneva.
World Health Organization (WHO). (2004b). Prevention of mental disorders: Effective interventions & policy option. In *Summary report/a report of the World Health Organization Department of Mental Health & Substance Abuse; in collaboration with the Prevention Research Centre of the Universities of Nijmegen & Maastricht*. WHO: Geneva.
World Health Organization-Western Pacific Region. (2002). *Regional strategy for mental health, Manila.*
World Health Organization-Western Pacific Regional Office. (2005). *Situational analysis of mental health needs & resources in Pacific Island countries*. Auckland: University of Auckland.
Wyber, R., Wilson, N., & Baker, M. (2009). New Zealand's impact on health in the South Pacific: Scope for improvement? *Journal of the New Zealand Medical Association, 122*, 1291.

Chapter 5
How Has Samoa's Mental Health System Developed Over Time?

This chapter explores the establishment of Samoa's mental health system. Firstly, I outline Samoa's key governmental and health system institutions and provide a historical overview to the mental health policy setting. This section includes consideration of Samoa's indigenous governance institutions and the period of German colonialism with its introduction of state structures, law and regulation. These have both contributed significantly to the contemporary mental health policy context by introducing official attitudes and indigenous constructions of mental health and German colonial introduction of the hospital, prison and public health ordinances, including the government's right to confine individuals under the guise of quarantine regulations. New Zealand's administration of Samoa is also considered.

With these institutional aspects of Samoa's development over the early twentieth century in place, I proceed to consider of the specific mental health policy context. Mental health policy transfer in its earliest forms in Samoa will be seen to involve essentially 'hard' policy in the form of direct foreign law applied in Samoa (from New Zealand) followed by an early ordinance passed in 1961 with the leadup to Samoa's independence in 1962. These laws will be seen to continue an ethos empowering the state to confine individuals but with little consideration of individual rights or natural justice. From 1962 until 2005 the domestic mental health context remained essentially silent in terms of hard policy change.

Beginning in 2005, however, the policy changes were rapid and significant. During that short span of time, Samoa developed, vetted and implemented a mental health policy and passed a new Mental Health Act. I explore these policy artefacts, the supporting material, and the perspectives of key policy actors engaged in the policy development process, including local and foreign policy actors. The emphasis on hard policy transfer, however, belies the other half of the mental health policy transfer experience in Samoa. The decades between the Mental Health Ordinance (1961) and Mental Health Act (2007a, b) witnessed significant 'soft' policy changes that are not reflected in any formal government policy yet instituted many of the community care principles outlined earlier in this book. These changes will be seen to occur on the practice level and involve an individual actor engaged in mental

T. P. Fadgen, *Mental Health Public Policy in Global Context*,
https://doi.org/10.1007/978-981-15-6479-6_5

health service delivery. In this context I also draw attention to the importance of professional networks in proliferating best practices on this informal policy level and for providing a possible forum for policies and practice to be repatriated, albeit with the latest iterations bearing the imprimatur of the transferee nations as well as those of the country of inception.

5.1 Samoa: An Institutional Overview

Beginning in the 1830s, the Samoan islands were 'opened' to Europeans by whalers and missionaries. Samoa's geographically lies on a direct route between San Francisco and Australia and New Zealand, a location vital along the trade route. Used by ships as a coaling depot, it became a coveted strategic possession. The Berlin Treaty of 1889 was the international legal document that formally set the now two Samoas on different paths. It divided up Samoa with America granted Tutuila and other islands east of longitude 171 W of Greenwich and Germany those islands west of longitude 171 W.

Increased trade and national agendas in Europe brought increasing encounters and the arrival of many semi-permanent adventurers, entrepreneurs and other drifters. The European notions of land ownership for economic purposes were put into practice and a virtual land rush, together with misunderstandings and perceptions of the deals being struck over rights to such land, ensued. European powers attempted to assert some semblance of control and authority in Samoa, as elsewhere. In Samoa, however, fundamental misunderstandings of the culture and efforts to intervene and establish a monarchy led to many years of violence and turmoil. Two formal attempts were made to subdue the political violence in Samoa. The first, finalised by 14 June 1889, was the Final Act of the Berlin Samoa Conference, which created a power-sharing arrangement between the tripartite powers of Great Britain, Germany and the United States from 1889–1899. Due to its inherently diffuse structure, the Final Act failed and was ultimately replaced with an arrangement whereby Germany was awarded sovereignty over Samoa, the United States retained its interests in Tutuila and Manua, and Great Britain retained its interests in Tonga.

The European arrivals throughout the nineteenth century coincided with the expanding reach amongst other indigenous regional leaders to establish control over neighbouring island groups. In an effort to solidify indigenous and by extension European government control over the territory, European advisers recommended the adoption of written constitutions and legal codes for regulating the far-flung populations (Corrin and Paterson 2011; Hills 1993). In the 1880s, Malietoa of Samoa made a claim to be King of Samoa, a claim recognised by the tripartite powers engaged in European realpolitik in the region: Germany, Britain and the United States. This recognition was followed by the promulgation of written laws for Samoa in 1880, the earliest such codification.

Often regarded as an area of social control, Christianity is central to the Samoan identity post-European contact. Its integration into the local culture has been much studied and is instructive as an example of early cultural transfer and localisation.

Thomas Bargatzky observed that the Samoan conversion to Christianity was 'rather smooth[...] and incredibly speedy', formally beginning in the 1830s (1997, p. 83). The transformation was so successful, in fact, that in 1861 London Missionary Society missionary George Turner offered that 'in a remarkably short time, under God's blessing, hardly a vestige of the entire [heathen] system was to be seen' (1997, p. 84). The reality, however, and a common lament of the missionaries and later anthropologists, was that the indigenous institutions had merely co-opted Christianity, rather than the religion displacing the institutions. Bargatzky argues this occurred because the traditional religious practices were 'constitutive for the organisation of the body politics, the polis (*nu'u*)', as reflected in the traditional Kava Ceremony, an event similar in both form and substance to the Christian Mass (1997, p. 89). Perhaps more important for subsequent governance in Samoa, is Steinmetz's (2007) observation that the missionaries took a different approach to Samoan traditional governance structures than did the colonial powers. This might be simply the result of practical, yet shrewd, political judgments insofar as missionaries needed to work within traditional governance institutions in order to be effective, a lesson learnt well in other Pacific Island contexts. The layering of Christianity on top of the indigenous religious traditions in Samoa offers a parallel to the creation of national governmental structures on top of Samoa's traditional governance institutions.

5.1.1 Traditional Governance Structures: Fa'aSamoa

The central component of traditional Samoan governance, the *fa'aSamoa*, which serves 'social, economic and political functions' in Samoa (Iati 2000, p. 71; Meleisea 1987). The *fa'aSamoa* system is based in the Samoan village (*nu'u*) and has, at its functional heart, the *fono a le nu'u* or village council providing local governance. Samoan traditional governance is formed around the complementary institution of *fa'amatai*, or the traditional leadership structure. Furthermore, as a factor in providing economic governance, the *fa'amatai* encourages community-oriented economic action, with the 'profits' predominantly consumed within and by the community itself (2000, p. 73).

As Iati (2000) has elsewhere argued, *fa'aSamoa* has a particular focus on the provision of welfare. This factor alone places Samoa in a category separate from most of its policy and law-exporting partners in the West since these are predominantly modern welfare states where the central government has the lead role in welfare distribution. Related to this is the issue of remittances (Fitzgerald and Howard 1990, p. 43) and their profound importance in the Samoan governance structure and economy. This issue of remittances will be discussed further below.

As Meleisea (1987) and later Iati (2000) explain, governance in Samoa centres today around four types of service (*tautua*): to one's family, village, church, and national government. The family in Samoa is a broader concept than the Western one, including parents, children, biological and adoptees, descendants and extended kin. The family is headed by a *matai* (titled person) elected by the family for a term of life, unless, for very select reasons, the family should decide otherwise. The matai's responsibilities include representing the family in the *fono* (village council of matai), settling family disputes, protecting family interests (such as lands and titles), upholding and advancing family prestige and honour, and providing leadership in the family. From here, the village consists of many families, each with a matai, who then meet in the *fono*. The *fono* decides all matters related to the village and performs the traditional law-making, executor and judicial functions of a municipality in doing so. In addition, the village is a partner in executing central government programmes. The church persists as a centre of Samoan cultural life, occupying much of the village's attention and identity. The state has an all-encompassing influence over each of the other levels of governance.

Another critical component of effective governance in Samoa hinges on the place of women in the territory. The traditional women's role in village governance was intrinsically linked to her husband's titular position within the village (Fairbairn-Dunlop 2000, p. 226). Village groups of women, known as women's committees, initially developed around sharing the knowledge of *i'etoga* or fine-mat weaving. The modern women's committees (Komiti Tumama or health committees), at least those since the 1920s, were comprised of all village women, were initially formed to 'improve maternal and child health care and village hygiene' (2000, p. 225; see also Scholeffel 1977, p. 15). These groups served as a critical link with central government, though they traditionally worked through such village institutions as the *matai*, *fono* and *pulenu'u*, and have been central to Samoa's governance and development regimes since at least the 1930s. While Samoan villages continue to operate as semiautonomous polities under the leadership of the village *fono* and the *Komiti Tumama*, recent health sector restructuring has 'contributed to a fragmentation of the NGO community, including marginalizing traditional women's NGOs' (Fairbairn-Dunlop 2000, p. 98).

Beginning in the 1930s, New Zealand administrators co-opted the *Komiti Tumama* into its 'national system of shared responsibility for village development' (Fairbairn-Dunlop 2000, p. 99). Building on the historical presence of the women's meeting groups, the 'women's health committee' was introduced in every village with the aim of ensuring that families, even in the most isolated rural areas, had access to essential public health services and information. These efforts were so successful that New Zealand's Director of Health described the health partnership as 'the most brilliant illustration of the possibilities of preventative medicine' (Lambert 1928, as cited in Fairbairn-Dunlop 2000, p. 100). The structure of this 'partnership' was simple: Samoa's Department of Health (DoH) held the national policy vision whilst *Komiti Tumama* focused on village-level service and information delivery (Fairbairn-Dunlop 2000, p. 99). This was a trailblazing model that serves as the template for most modern public health intervention strategies in the developing context. In an interesting parallel to this book, the frontier between traditional and state governance structures was initially navigated by a 'very remarkable pioneer group of district nurses' (2000, p. 101) – a group later to become the

Samoa Nurses Association, members of which would be, as discussed later in this chapter, pivotal in the development of Samoa's mental health system. Yet, these indigenous governance systems have continued to evolve in relation to introduced government institutions and systems a topic to which we now turn.

5.1.2 German Colonial Policies in Samoa

Samoa has often been seen as a laboratory for all manner of research, social and natural (Hempenstall 1997, p. 66). Samoa served in a similar capacity for the construction of colonial policy and, by extension, I argue here, for development policy in our time. Samoa was to become the centre of the German colonial enterprise in the Pacific and has been described as a 'living ethnographic museum' (Hiery and MacKenzie 1997) whilst under German occupation, where 'the colonizers protected traditional culture from the depredations of capitalist modernity' (1997, p. 15). As Hiery also observes, however, the Germans attacked 'any aspect of Samoan culture that threatened [their] authority' (1997, p. 15). The colonial government's stated aim was to 'stabilize Samoan custom rather than simply allow it to exist and evolve undisturbed.' (1995, p. 17) They did this through a process of translating and codifying Samoan customary law.

As illustrative of this contradictory position, Wihelm Solf, Samoa's most significant German colonial administrator, opined that Samoan's 'don't think like us, [they] have different emotions, and therefore have to be handled differently'. He argued that 'each individual colony ha[d] to develop on its own with no analogy to the other protectorates and should be given specific laws corresponding to its conditions' (Steinmetz 2007, p. 346). Solf sought to maintain the system of titles and matai; the use of forms such as *ifoga*, *malaga*, *mavaega*, *avaga*, *fono*, *kava* drinking, the distribution of fine mats, support for traditional building materials, Samoan land ownership and communal rather than individual forms of labour, amongst others (2007, p. 346). This colonial policy has been described as 'regulated tradition'. Solf offered this explanation for his approach:

> I have often told natives that the German government wishes them to be ruled, not according to the white mans [sic] ideas, but according to the Faa Samoa…for this reason I do not wish to interfere in your Samoan titles and such things. (as quoted in Steinmentz 2007, p. 319)

As set forth above, however, the Germans had, in fact, since the very beginning of their occupation, done quite the opposite through the establishment of courts as well as the Land and Titles Commission, which was established solely to address questions of Samoan matai titles and land disputes (Steinmetz 2007, p. 321). This was again, however, borne of a realisation that most of the civil strife in Samoa occurring over the period of time beginning with European contact was motivated by seemingly intractable disputes to titles and associated land claims.

Europeans had tried and failed for decades to form a single central authority similar to Tonga's monarchy. The Germans now took the opposite tack: eliminate any trace of centralisation. Solf argued that colonial governance was 'missionary work, in the broadest sense of cultural education' (Steinmetz 2007, p. 334). He argued not for assimilation, but for the Samoans to emulate to the extent that 'their mental and spiritual character' would allow (2007, p. 334). Internal Samoan legal affairs were handled according to Samoan custom by the *fa'amasino*, *pulenu'u* and the Land and Titles Court. There was very limited access to justice against Europeans and virtually none against the colonial government itself. Furthermore, Stenmetz notes an enduring division between those privileging the colonisers' treatment of specific indigenous practices and those emphasising the structural components of law and governance (see also Hiery and MacKenzie 1997). German officials sought to leave the imprint of Imperial Germany on the Samoan culture not through overreach, but through regulation (Steinmetz 2007, p. 331). The colonial state, as was observed by the final German executive in Samoa, was trying to preserve the Samoans' social structure while destroying their political system (2007, p. 332). It does not appear that Germany succeeded on either count. While they were attempting to do so, circumstances surrounding the outbreak of World War I would shift the trajectory of European affairs in the world and Samoa's place in it.

5.1.3 New Zealand's Mandate, Law and Constitution Making, and an Independent Samoa

The New Zealand journalist Michael Field, writing on Samoa's independence movement, the Mau, begins his book on the subject by explaining an important milestone in Samoa's colonial history: its transition in 1914 from being a German colony to that of New Zealand, acting at the direction of Great Britain. Field outlines how the island group was seized by the New Zealand squadron, which consisted of 3 P-class British cruisers, all ageing but still formidable Naval vessels, each boasting eight 10 centimetre guns and capable of reaching speeds of 20 knots (1984, p. 10). Perhaps auspiciously for this focus of this book, the squadron was led by the *HMS Psyche* demanding unconditional surrender. The German 'yoke', such as it was, was cast aside in August of 1914 and in its place, New Zealand took steps to deepen European influence over the functions of the State. In the years between the cessation of German rule and independence in 1962, the first iterations of state categorisation and control over mental illness would emerge and take root. The arrival of *HMS Psyche* thus set Samoa's institutional views of the individual psyche on a new course.

New Zealand established its military occupation of Samoa on 29 August 1914 and maintained military control until 1920. The Treaty of Versailles granted Great Britain dominion over Samoa as a Class C Mandate. New Zealand assumed administrative responsibilities and ruled via a legislative council under the mandate until

1946, when the UN trusteeship process succeeded. The legislative council was composed mostly of Europeans, civil servants and residents of Samoa and served at the pleasure of the Governor-General of New Zealand (Meti 2002). It was a body ostensibly empowered for law-making for Samoa on a wide range of matters but whose power was, in actuality, severely restricted by its mandate; it required assent from Wellington on any significant matter of policy. As Samoa headed towards independence under the UN-inspired process, Lieutenant-Colonel F.W. Voelcker, the newly minted Administrator of Samoa, echoed Solf's earlier pronouncements on European policy intentions in Samoa: "It is in no way my desire nor that of the New Zealand Government or the trusteeship Council to give you a paplangi plan to govern your country. This is your country and you should make the plan. When you have produced this plan it is for us as good friends to discuss it and to see any weaknesses that may make trouble in the future." (Verbatim record of the Fono of Faipule as referenced in Meti 2002, p. 26). New Zealand had essentially been on this track and had virtually recognised village autonomy since 1929 after its forces killed seven Mau political protesters and leaders, including Tupua Tamsese Lealofi, one of the paramount titleholders. This event became known as 'Black Saturday' and led to immediate changes in approach to Samoan affairs, including this withdrawal from the day-to-day Samoan affairs of the village (Meleisea 1987, 1992).

The historian A.H. McDonald (1949), writing on the trusteeship arrangements in the Pacific, emphasised that Samoa's case as a trust territory sets it apart from other such territories in that within a month of its accession to trusteeship status on 13 December 1946, the Secretary-General of the UN received a petition requesting self-government, not only for what was geographically and politically Western Samoa, but for all of Samoa and the American possessions. This request included provision that New Zealand maintained the role of 'protector and adviser' similar to that of Great Britain with neighbouring Tonga (McDonald 1949, p. 47). Article 5 of the Trusteeship Agreement called for the establishment of 'free political institutions suited to Western Samoa … as may be appropriate to the particular circumstances of the Territory and of the peoples …' (1949, p. 47). In response to this request, the Trusteeship Council resolved to send a 'mission of experts, men with practical experience of colonial administration' (1949, p. 49). After spending 2 months in the territory, the mission reported that Samoa should become self-governing, while acknowledging several shortcomings in the population including 'the absence of national unity and discipline, inadequate education and lack of political experience and organisation' (1949, p. 51). They argued, in essence, that risks would be necessary in order to educate the population on self-government because what was needed was 'actual experience' in governing (1949, p. 52). This report coincided with several recommendations being simultaneously considered in Wellington, resulting in the Samoa Amendment Act, 1947. Samoa's struggle for independence carried forward by the Mau and advanced with deliberate speed by the international community would still take many years to achieve. Finally, in 1962, the independent nation of Western Samoa emerged. A discussion of how these events set the stage for Samoa's first mental health law, the Mental Health Ordinance 1961 – the mental health law that would prevail in Samoa for decades to come – is discussed in the following sections.

5.2 Mental Health in Samoa

This section builds on the historical insights provided in the previous section by applying the broad precolonial, colonial and postcolonial institutions of the 'Samoan context' and the development agenda into the particularly culturally bound context of mental health law and policy. While Samoan traditional beliefs about mental health and contemporary attitudes towards mental health treatment are interesting topics and have been addressed elsewhere (see e.g. Tamasese et al. 2005; Schuster 2001; Macpherson and Macpherson 1990; Mageo 1998), the emphasis here is on the institutional policy context for Samoa's formal mental health system. I discuss contemporary Samoa's institutional context using relevant illustrative data juxtaposed with interview responses from policy process participants charged with forging a mental health system for Samoa couched in competing cultural values such as the centrality of the family in the mental health context. The construction of the 'Samoan context' will be argued to constitute a filter through which successive foreign policy actors have prepared policy and law for Samoa. First, the international policy context around health systems and the related mental health system reforms in Samoa is considered, as well as the rapid process from issue identification on the Samoan policy agenda to its adoption.

5.2.1 *Samoa's Mental Health System: Context Provided by Historical Legacies*

Before turning to the 2006 policy and 2007 Act, it is important to provide the necessary historical context for these reforms. First, as discussed in the previous section, German institutions were established for the primary benefit of the colonial project in the region but they also laid the institutional framework with which the current health sector, and its mental health sector would later operate. This was a primary, coercive policy transfer experiment that brought not only physical structures (e.g. prisons and hospitals) but also discursive institutions such as medicine and law and set dual categories of European and Samoan (and in the case of the hospital, a third Chinese category). This period marked the transition from disorder and civil war in Samoa. New Zealand's Samoa Act 1921 is a second brand of direct coercive policy transfer marked by direct legislation for Samoa, though the period between 1921 and 1961 saw a gradual devolution of political responsibility to local institutions. Hence, the official health sector has its roots in the German institutions and the New Zealand regulatory framework provided by the Samoa Act 1921, policies largely turned over to Samoa at the leadup to independence through numerous ordinances. In particular was the Mental Health Ordinance was transferred in 1961 along with several other health-related Bills, a practice to be repeated in 2006 and 2007.

In the mid-1990s individuals with mental illness prone to violence continued to be housed at the Tafaigata prison since the hospital was ill-equipped to hold them and no other treatment regimes were then available. Further, the medical superintendent at that time, Dr. Frank Smith, noted the rise of the homeless population with mental illness after Samoa began to follow New Zealand's homebased treatment model without 'adequate government support for families newly entrusted with the care of serious cases' (as quoted by Peteru 1996). In other words, the community model was being implemented on a practice level of service delivery but the official government position and practice had not caught up with it, leaving the efforts hamstrung. This issue will be explored further later in the book.

Samoa's health sector reforms, which the Government of Samoa had prioritised by since at least 1990, coincided with the broader turn towards market liberalisation and universal suffrage. World Bank credits these reforms with 'macroeconomic stabilization and comprehensive structural reforms, which contributed to rapid real economic growth of 4 percent per annum' between 1993–2006 (World Bank 2008, p. 1). The political decision to focus on this sector, coupled with the availability of structural funding from international sources to support health sector development, helped to see gains in indicators such as life expectancy; maternal, infant and child mortality rates; reductions in infectious diseases; and the achievement of high immunisation coverage. Success in regard to these concerns, however, has given rise to new health concerns due to the epidemiologic transition. These include the constant increase in urban population resulting in substandard living conditions and limited access to health services, the rise in NCDs, poor nutrition, the persistence of communicable diseases, and the increasing costs to government of maintaining secondary and tertiary health care brought about by changing disease patterns and demographic profiles.

During these years, mental health services were offered through the Mental Health Unit at Motootua and include clinical services at the neighbouring Tupua Tamasese Meaole Hospital (TTMH) on Upolu. The clinical unit contained a four-bed ward for inpatient treatment of people with mental disorders. According to the Government of Samoa, these beds have never been used and instead serve as day-care facilities as well as offices for the unit. Moreover, there are no dedicated beds in the hospital for people with mental disorders and hospital admission is possible only where the individual is deemed not to pose a 'significant risk'. While the majority of admissions to the Mental Health Unit are by way of family referral, the policy describes the admission process for 'violent patients':

> People with a mental disorder who are at risk to others are detained by the police and taken to the police cells until psychiatric care is arranged. Where possible, the person receives treatment as a day patient from the mental health unit and is returned home to their families with community support or, if their behaviour is very disturbed, they may remain in custody until their symptoms stabilize and the risk of harm to themselves or others is reduced. (GoS 2006, p. 6)

This is the typical mental health admission process for Samoa's residents.

Samoa's health system has long had links to the relevant international and regional policy actors. The Australian Agency for International Development (AusAID) funded the Samoa Health Project (SHP) to enhance the overall health sector. The New Zealand Aid Programme (NZAID) supported primary health care (with the Child Health Project) and human resource development through various staff exchange schemes. Both aid agencies contribute to regional programmes delivered through multilateral and regional agencies focusing on public health priorities. WHO provided technical assistance in many areas; the UN Population Fund (UNFPA) supported adolescents, reproductive and sexual health, and family planning; the UN International Children's Fund (UNICEF) has provided support to strengthen the immunisation program; the Japan International Cooperation Agency (JICA) supported infrastructure and provided technical assistance; whilst World Bank funded the Health Sector Management Project from 2000–2006 to develop financing and health infrastructure needs (World Bank 2008).

These international actors continue to be involved with projects in Samoa's health sector as a continuation of these major initiatives. World Bank itself argues that it 'has built a record of development experience' in Samoa. In support of this claim, World Bank points out that since Samoa's membership in June 1974, 15 IDA credits totalling US$87.8 million have been made to support agriculture; telecommunications and power; finance; transportation; and health sectors (the first health sector being the 20,002,006 round). In fact, World Bank cited 'lessons learnt' from the Health Sector Management Project and the AusAID/NZAID financed Samoa Health Project were used in developing subsequent projects pursued in 2008 (World Bank 2008). World Bank's effectiveness is brought about through its relations with AusAID and NZAID and their collective efforts were instrumental in seeing the various aspects of health system reforms of the early 2000s come to fruition.

5.2.2 *The International Policy Context of Samoa's Mental Health Policy Reforms*

In early 2002, ostensibly at the request of the Government of Samoa, WHO sent a short-term consultant to Samoa to gather information on the nation's mental health system with an aim to develop a collaborative approach to establishing a suitable mental health programme in Samoa. The consultant was specifically charged with analysing 'the situation with Government and other local people and recommend the means of achieving and supporting the required change, e.g. advocacy, policy, legislation, programme introduction and evaluation' (WHO 2002, p. 2). The consultant's report made several recommendations for Samoa including to develop a national mental health programme (since there was none) and to 'carry out legislative and regulatory reform and enforcement in the areas of alcohol and consumption, antidiscrimination legislation, and mental health legislation' (2002, p. 3). The report referenced the move to community-based mental health services that occurred in the 1980s and 1990s but raised the persistence of several problems including the lack of a psychiatrist (a situation, which, at least for the time being, has been addressed); limited medication availability; limited nexus with alcohol and drug abuse or dependency matters; and rural transport complexities.

The consultant introduced mental health promotion as a conceptual framework with several key individuals. This framework was adapted from Australia's Victorian Health Promotion Foundation's Mental Health Promotion Plan, 1999–2002 (Victorian Health Promotion Foundation [VHPF] 1999) and included 'interventions' (policy development, legislative reform, research, monitoring and evaluation, communication and advocacy, project development and funding). The goal of this framework was to reduce the overall stress, anxiety, and depression levels in the population through these interventions, which would thereby reduce the overall occurrence of certain mental illness, including depression and anxiety. In addition, these reductions, and others, would result in decreased risk behaviours associated with drug abuse and crime, amongst other factors.

Further recommendations included the formation of a 'multisectoral, multidisciplinary committee' charged with review of the existing mental health services, which was not 'part of the terms of reference'; that Samoa establish some capacity for basic research and surveillance of mental illness including drug and alcohol abuse; that Samoa engage in project development on such topics as mental health counselling and mental health promotion, support for children with special needs attending schools, and mental health care givers (WHO 2002, p. 10). In addition, the Government of Samoa should raise the public understanding of the link between suicide and mental ill health and 'explore further assistance [with mental health initiatives including] facilitating support from potential international donor agencies' (WHO 2002, p. 10–11).

Following this report, in February 2003 the WHO issued a Country Cooperation Strategy for Samoa. This made note of Samoa's epidemiological transition and the accompanying rise in NCDs. In addition to identifying these diseases and others conditions, the Country Cooperation Strategy for Samoa notes that

> Insufficient understanding of mental health disorders within the community can cause difficulties for the families burdened with the daily care of the patient. Although community based mental health nursing services are being delivered the services and guidance of a psychiatrist and psychologist are not available. Additionally, a review of the mental health legislation and the development of a comprehensive strategy, policy and mental health promotion framework could be beneficial in dealing with the problem effectively. (WHO-WPR 2003, p. 6).

The report notes that since 1983 Primary Health Care, Health Promotion and the Healthy Island Principles (all WHO inspired initiatives) have been behind health sector development (WHO-WPR 2003, p. 7). Building on these, Samoa's economic and public sector reforms since 1996 are cited as central to Ministry of Health planning. In particular, the Health Sector Strategic Plan 1998–2003 (GoS 1999) is referenced for its aims at strengthening health institutions, primary health care and health promotion on NCDs and women and children's health, as well as quality improvement through infrastructure and facilities development. Identified needs include specialist medical care (which would include psychological and psychiatric professionals) and the accompanying drain on the economy since high fees are paid to treat individuals overseas, as well as the professional drain where locally trained professional staff move overseas in search of higher remuneration.

In the Country Cooperation Strategy for Samoa WHO identifies its key areas of work in Samoa as 'human resource development' accounting for 49.1% of its allocated budget, with a further nearly 26% dedicated to 'health sector reform' (WHO-WPR 2003, p. 17). Human resources development includes sending individuals on fellowships or trainings off-island. These accounted for nearly 70% of the programme component in Samoa in 2002–2003 (2003, p. 17). Upon deeper inspection, the fellowships included funding for 'clinical attachments for nurses in mental health in Australia' and 'mental health ... workshops for nurses [and] postgrad training for nurses in mental health' (2003, p. 18). These fall under the guise of the 'Noncommunicable Disease programme' and are designed to 'see the improvement of mental...health through technical support and the provision of teaching aids and books' (2003, p. 19). These efforts were well received in that the policy development team and those with whom I spoke discussed the availability of numerous resource texts on policy development in the SNHS library.

WHO's structure is an important consideration in examining local buy-in for these endeavours. Headquartered in Geneva, WHO relies heavily on its regional and intercountry teams for policy and programme implementation. While there seems to be little question that the overall direction and agenda of WHO is set in Geneva, there is considerable discretion in the regions in arranging the implementation priorities based on local demands, interests and concerns. These tiers

> provide participants from Samoa with regular opportunities to participate in international regional and sub-regional meetings, workshops and trainings thereby enabling the sharing of information and experiences, updating skills and knowledge, and establishing consensus to WHO technical strategies, plans of action and joint action (emphasis added). (WHO-WPR 2003, p. 20)

The World Health Assembly reaffirmed the 'Health for All' policy in 1998 with an added emphasis on 'humanitarian action and human rights' (WHO-WPR 2003, p. 20).WHO, in pursuing the overall policy, dedicated itself to a number of goals, amongst which is to 'develop[] an enabling policy and institutional environment in the health sector'. It has identified 'limited specific priorities' which are based on the 'potential for a significant reduction in the burden of diseases using existing cost-effective technologies' and include mental health along with several others (2003, p. 21).

Applying this broad context to Samoa, from 2003–2007 WHO pursued a policy of supporting government work on healthy communities and populations; health sector development; and continuing focus on combating communicable disease (WHO-WPR 2003, p. 22). It engaged in a 'significant shift in roles, functions and modalities of support' to legislative and policy technical advice provision as well as broadening its training support for health workers and nurturing 'multisectoral collaboration and partnerships' and 'play[ing] an increased role in coordination of donor assistance' and resource mobilisation (2003, p. 23). Under the 'building healthy communities and populations' rubric, NCDs are specifically said to include mental health and WHO will assist 'in the (re) drafting and reviewing of existing legislation, policies and strategies to be more in line with present practices in the field of NCDs in general and mental health… in particular' (2003, p. 23). Furthermore, the effort will extend to developing 'technical guidelines to address risk factors and to ensure the delivery of quality community-based services for … mental disorders' and a mental health promotion framework (2003, p. 23). Within 3 months of the issuance of this report, a mental health symposium was held in Apia (discussed in below) gathering together key actors in Samoa for establishing broad directions and needs in mental health.

This section has presented an overview of Samoa's governmental and traditional governance institutional contexts. In addition, the framing attributes of the international milieu have been presented as forming an overarching structure within which Samoan governance takes place. Samoan policymakers have confronted these institutions and their agents since contact with Europeans. A recurring theme of these encounters beginning at least with German colonial attitudes and perpetuated by the New Zealand administration of Samoa was stated to permit Samoan self-governance to flourish so long as it was consistent with the foreigners political and policy objectives. As we next turn to an examination of the particular mental health policy transfer, we will observe a continuation of this general institutional framing of Samoan policymaking scope as part of a localisation process. This process is intended to reconcile indigenous perspectives with international policy objectives. I will address how this process unfolded in the mental health policy context.

5.3 Samoa's Mental Health Law Development: An Institutional History

In this sect. I will first consider formal policy transfer in Samoa of mental health laws beginning with origins in German colonial administration and New Zealand's UN Mandate for Samoa. In addition, Samoan independence is considered and the development of mental health law to its most recent changes in 2007. As part of the overall Samoan health institutional context, mental health policy will be seen over time to require macrolevel moments of opportunity in order to change. I will next address Samoa's adoption of a written mental health policy. The mental health policy was developed contemporaneously with the Mental Health Act 2007 yet will be seen to demonstrate greater participatory attributes than the process surrounding the adoption of the Mental Health Act. The process leading to the policy's eventual adoption and the policy itself are considered below. Finally, this chapter addresses mental health policy change which predated these formal and quasi-formal changes at the practice-level. Key policy actors are considered within the Samoan context and their individual contributions to the implementation of a community care regime prior to these more formalised policy changes is discussed.

Specifically, I consider below several law changes and the Western influence over Samoan mental health matters since the Samoa Act 1921 (NZ) through to the Mental Health Act 2007 (Samoa) and how the policy language used in Samoa, at least in the area of mental health, was very strongly influenced by Western institutions, beginning via direct legislation and evolving to the more subtle form of influence of IOs (Fadgen 2019). This section examines the case of Samoa's Mental Health Ordinance 1961 and its successor the Mental Health Act 2007 and compares the Ordinance with the Mental Health Amendment Act 1961 (NZ) and the Mental Health Act 2007 with the MI Principles (UN 1991).

5.3.1 German Colonial Ordinances, Mental Defectives Act (NZ) 1911 and the Samoa Act (NZ) 1920: Colonialism, Mandate and Mental Health

The Mental Defectives Act 1911 (NZ) served as the basis for Samoa's Mental Health Ordinance 1961. The 1911 Act had itself, however, was the object of a policy transfer from the United Kingdom and previous New Zealand mental health law was rooted in a transplant from Australia. The provisions of the Mental Defectives Act were first applied to Samoa under the Samoa Act 1921 (NZ). A 'mentally defective person' was first defined in the 1911 Act as 'a person who, owing to his mental condition, requires oversight, care, or control for his own good or in the public interest'. The law first found its applicability to Samoa under Part XII of the Samoa Act 1921, dealing with 'Persons of Unsound Mind' and a separate section for those deemed 'Criminal Lunatics'. 'Persons of Unsound Mind' could be arrested and sent to hospital or 'other places' in Samoa (as well as, under certain circumstances transported to New Zealand), which invariably meant the Upolu prison, where they would be housed alongside 'criminal lunatics'.

Following the Mental Defective Amendment Act 1921 (NZ) and the Samoa Act of the same year, the New Zealand portion of mental health law changed radically over the years between 1921 and 1961. These changes included at least 11 subsequent Amendment Acts, including the significant 1954 amendments, which changed the more offensive title from 'Mental Defectives Act' to 'Mental Health Act' the title used in all subsequent amendments and new legislation. The law itself, despite the many amendments, did not undergo a significant redraft until 1969. Prior to this major overhaul, however, Samoa became an independent country and the Samoa Act 1921, as amended, ceased to apply in Samoa. For reasons lost in the intervening decades, the 1961 Ordinance used the older 1911 definition and terminology over the more recent 1954 updates. The statute adopted the definition of 'mentally defective person' as found in the 1911 definition, only without the subclasses of individual found in the initial Act. Significantly, while the overhauled New Zealand Mental Health Act would go on to be significantly amended, nearly 14 times through 2007, the Samoa Mental Health Ordinance was not amended until it was repealed and replaced in its entirety by the Samoa Mental Health Act in 2007.

While no definitive record apparently exists of any explicit mental health regulations for the German colony of Samoa, we do know that German occupation provided the foundation for several institutions integral to the modern mental health system, such as police, prisons and hospitals, as well as ordinances providing for detention due to health status (quarantine) (Archives of German Samoa [AGS] 2011). The law and other institutions imported with the German colonial administration sought to enshrine order through certain liberal economic principles whilst assigning traditional Samoan affairs such as lands and titles to specialised judicial institutions. Amongst these economic developments adopted between 1 March 1900 and 15 August 1914 were public order provisions (liquor and opium regulations, theft, police, prison and press regulations, roads); laws on various aspects of agriculture and animal maintenance (plants, poultry, and pig enclosures); public health laws (quarantine, plague, and rats); commercial laws (Samoa Trading Company, Seaman's Coastal Ordinance, tariffs, transport, weights and measures); and a category of 'Samoan Laws' which presumably contained rules designed ostensibly for the protections for Samoan culture (AGS 2011). When New Zealand took possession of Samoa during the World War I and later under a UN mandate, it continued the economic development practices begun under the German administration.

Between 1920–1962 New Zealand employed various policies to further promote Western-style government and institutions in Samoa. One element to this policy and law foundation was the inclusion of Part XII of the Samoa Act 1921 providing orders of medical custody for persons of unsound mind. Similar to the Mental Health Ordinance 1961, Part XII empowers a 'chief medical officer' with making applications to the court for civil commitment. The part requires a medical examination and the production of a certificate to the court that the individual is in fact of 'unsound mind' and such custody is necessary 'in his own interests or the safety of other persons'. The court must find both elements to issue an order of medical custody for a period not to exceed, in the first instance, 6 months, with possibility of six-month renewals. Additional provisions in Part XII permit the removal of an individual (presumably a European) who is under an order of medical custody to New Zealand. Arrest without warrant was authorised so long as the individual was brought without delay before a 'Judge or Commissioner of the High Court'. Most striking is the provision labelled 'Criminal Lunatics' dealing with individuals accused of crimes who are thought to have acted as a result of their mental illness. These sections are, with only minor revision, the exact language adopted in the Mental Health Ordinance 1961.

5.3.2 Samoa's Mental Health Ordinance 1961

In the leadup to independence, the transitional government enacted a host of laws, known then as 'ordinances' since they were pursued under authority of the Samoa Acts (as amended). The Honourable Tufuga Fatu introduced the Mental Health Ordinance 1961, which had its first and second reading and committal all on the 14 December 1961 (Samoa Legislative Assembly Record of Debate on Mental Health

Bill (Government of Samoa 1961b, pp. 118–24)). The Bill had its third reading on 19 December 1961 and received assent on 29 December 1961, only 3 days prior to independence.

During the process there was an interesting and lively committee debate over a provision that made it a crime to have sexual intercourse with a 'mentally defective female', first in the form of a hypothetical using one of the delegate's wives as the unfortunate specimen to have 'contacted insanity' and left her husband without recourse to this marital right (Government of Samoa 1961b, pp. 118–24). The comment led to a perceptive comment that the provision itself was terribly 'one-sided' in that it proposed to protect a woman but not a man and that might not the provision read better as 'mentally defective person'? At the time, however, one would not engage in 'sexual intercourse' with a man and a woman was incapable of performing sexual intercourse on someone so the language meant exactly what it purported to say and was left alone. At one point in the debate there must have been the perception that the topic of sexual intercourse had become a bit of a joke: the Speaker admonished the assembled men of title to remember to 'speak with respect on this matter as it deals with sick people, the mentally defective person' (1961, p. 120).

Further, as support for leaving the language as it appeared, Fatu offered the following: 'I wish to say that this new Bill was passed on the actual wording of the Samoa Act 1921, Article 127' (Government of Samoa 1961b, pp. 118–24). Notwithstanding the desire for consistency between the New Zealand law and the proposed ordinance, further arguments on behalf of the 'future generations' of unborn children that the wording be changed form 'female' to 'person' throughout the Bill ensued. Here again, the argument met with resistance because it is not possible to have 'sexual intercourse with a person' only for a male to have it with a female, therefore the language should stay as it is. It was at this juncture however that another representative referred to a 'Mental Health Explanatory Note' that apparently accompanied the proposed legislation provided by its drafters to explain the purpose of each clause of the proposal and how it related to provisions of the Samoa Act 1921. The proposed change from female to person was defeated by only 15 votes (there were 13 in favour and 28 opposed to the proposal). There was no other debate on the Bill and it was passed on 15 December 1961, a little over 2 weeks prior to independence.

The 1961 law did not reflect the best practices on mental health of the time. In effect, the law created the legal mechanism for detention, or 'control and treatment' as the ordinance referred to it, of those with mental illness. The ordinance had the early reflection of the need to secure rights by establishing a visiting board entrusted with supervising the personal welfare of individuals kept in medical custody. The ordinance emphasised the primacy of the 'medical practitioner' as a qualified medical and a 'mentally defective person' as 'a person who owing to his mental condition, requires oversight, care, control of himself or his property for his own good or in the public interest'. If a medical practitioner feels an individual is a 'mentally defective person' then he can either conduct or cause the individual to be transported to the capital for evaluation. If the person is uncooperative and seemingly dangerous then a constable is required, to transport the individual to Apia, acting on a warrant issued by the medical practitioner. There, two medical practitioners must examine the individual and then issue reports to the Director-General of Health. Based on the findings, the Director-General then either discharges the individual or applies to the Supreme Court for an order of medical custody.

The court would determine whether the individual is 'mentally defective and [whether] his detention in medical custody is necessary for his own interests or for the safety of other persons'. If it found that individual was, the court ordered the person to be held for up to 6 months with the possibility of renewal for 6 months (but could remain in custody indefinitely with six-month reviews). Further, the ordinance provides that 'any person believed on reasonable grounds to be of unsound mind and to be dangerous to himself or others may be arrested without warrant by a constable or any other person' provided the individual was brought 'forthwith' before a judge or magistrate who could order the individual held pending an application for medical custody and the process outlined above. The ordinance also contained, unlike its 2007 successor, provisions for determining criminal culpability (which was restated in the criminal law and which are also currently under consideration by Samoa's Law Reform Commission). In fact, sections 11–15 of the Ordinance deal with this concern. In essence, these provisions create a rebuttal presumption of 'sanity' that can be overcome by evidence establishing that the individual is a 'natural imbecile[]' or 'of similar condition rendering him or her 'incapable of understanding the nature or quality of the act' or 'knowing that [it] was wrong'.

5.3.3 *Mental Health Act 2007: An International Legacy*

The need for updating the existing law was well recognised by the respondents in this study. As one former government official framed the problem,

> we inherited a piece of New Zealand legislation that was already 50 years old, so it never in my view, it never was effective or implemented and part of that is because we never had, before the 90s, we never had mental health professionals that could be or could undertake the sort of requirements and the responsibilities under the old act, we still don't. But, what's changed is that the new Act is intended to update the options in terms of mental health and the community, the inpatient or the community treatment order, is an attempt to ensure that recognizing the role of the community and mental health issues is formalize in some ways what is happening now and I think is an intent to bring it into the mainstream health system.

Recognising the need to reform, however, did not result in legislation. The health sector reforms, as mentioned above, presented the opportunity for a foreign consultant with extensive expertise in mental health to be embedded in the Samoa Attorney General's office. This key actor was an Australian attorney and former judge with extensive disability law experience who served as Parliamentary Counsel from 2000 to 2005 and as a legislative drafting consultant from 2006 to 2007. During this latter attachment the consultant was tasked specifically with the drafting of health legislation, including the Mental Health Act. AusAID funded both of the consultant's placements, who noted that:

> [t]he genesis of the Samoa Mental Health Act and policy behind it came from my time as Parliamentary Counsel in Samoa. I identified the need to update the legislation with a new Act and obtained the approval of the Attorney General and CEO of the Ministry of Health … Together with [the nation's lone psychiatrist] we worked to develop the Mental Health Act using our Australian experience and contacts in Samoa. I used the Victorian and South Australian Mental Health Acts as the models for the Samoa Act and adapted the legislation to address the Samoan [context] … a draft …was sent out for discussion and consultation with interested persons and organisations … Following the consultations I amended the draft Act and submitted it to the CEO Health, Attorney General, Minister of Health for their consideration and approval. Following further input from [the psychiatrist] and the Samoan health professionals, the draft Act was finalised and submitted to the Minister of Health, CEO Health and the Attorney General for their final approval [obtained].

The consultant cited several 'cultural and other factors' constituting the 'Samoan context' that influenced his approach to the reform: a general reluctance in Samoa (as elsewhere) to openly deal with mental health; a distrust of health care and hospitals; limited resources; the need to empower nondoctor health carers and family; the need to avoid a court-based system due to lack of resources and reluctance to use courts; the small geographic area and population facilitating the ability of individuals to see nondoctors in the first instance; and the need to keep the system as uncomplicated as possible due to very limited resources.

Many of these cultural factors cited above by WHO and AusAID consultants are reflected in the current Act. For instance, with the limited stock of psychiatrists and psychologists, a 'health care professional' refers not only to a medical practitioner but also to nurses, psychologists and social workers. The Act maintains a medical definition for 'mental disorder' which 'includes a mental illness and means a medical condition that is characterised by a significant disturbance of thought, mood, perception or memory'. Voluntary care is a stated preference for mental health treatment as is meant to occur in the family. If this cannot be achieved, due to particular risk to the family or community, then the person with mental disorder may be treated on an involuntary basis.

Where an individual is proposed for involuntary treatment, an initial assessment is performed by a 'health care professional' on the recommendation of a 'concerned person' to determine whether the person under observation appears to have a mental disorder. Involuntary treatment results when the person appears unwilling or unable to be assessed on a voluntary basis; appears to require care, support, treatment or protection; and it is in the interests of the person or others who might be at risk. If the person cannot or will not be assessed voluntarily, the police or health care professional is empowered to 'apprehend and transport' the person for purposes of evaluation. If the individual is determined to meet the criteria set forth above, then a detention may occur for a period of up to 72 h and during that time if the person does not meet the criteria, they are to be released; if the person does meet the criteria they are placed under a 'Community Treatment Order' or an 'Inpatient Treatment Order'. If they do not meet the criteria for compulsory care, the health care professional can, of course, still provide voluntary treatment.

The relevant sections setting forth the Community Treatment Order (introduced in concept in Chap. 2) and Inpatient Treatment Order operate similarly to those sections of law in many other Western jurisdictions: utilising a least restrictive means test. This means that the treatment must be in the least restrictive manner available for the person's particular needs (e.g. in the individual's home). The criteria for being subject to the Act's jurisdiction is constant: mental disorder when coupled with an unwillingness or inability to receive care voluntarily results in the individual requiring care, support, treatment or protection for his or another's' benefit or safety.

A Community Treatment Order, which provides for compulsory care in the community (the family home, typically), can last for 12 months and may, after further evaluation, be renewed for a further 12 months. The order may be revoked at any time by any 'duly directed mental health care professional' if, in his or her opinion, the individual no longer meets the criteria. The Inpatient Treatment Order is the most restrictive tool available. The same general test as the Community Treatment Order is applied but here it is assumed that the individual cannot be safely and effectively treated in the community, hence no less restrictive manner of custody and care is possible. These orders are effective for 6 weeks at a time.

Part 6 of the 2007 Act defines the person's rights as well as the availability of review of adverse orders. The person subject to the Act is to be given a copy of the order; a written statement of the person's rights in Samoan and English (as set forth in regulations); and a copy of the relevant application for review. Individuals subject to a Community Treatment Order may seek judicial review by making an application that is processed by a health care professional or mental health care professional and filed with the Registrar.

Review of an Inpatient Treatment Order may be made by the individual or a person of interest and must then conform to the same procedural rigours as the Community Treatment Order. Finally, similar to predecessor legislation, the Act also contains provisions for the administration of property for individuals with a mental disorder or mental incapacity who are unable to make 'reasonable judgments' and who, as such, are in need of an administrator. The new Act, as mentioned above, does not contain the criminal law elements.

5.3.4 Bringing the Bill Forward: Parliament and the Mental Health Act 2007

On the morning of 31 January 2006 a press release from the Prime Minister's office announced the Cabinet approval of what was then called the Mental Health Bill 2005, which would provide for

> the care, support, treatment and protection of persons with mental disorder and for related purposes…to minimize the restrictions upon the liberty of persons with a mental disorder and interference in their rights, dignity and self-respect…(and) works towards eliminating discrimination against, and abuse, mistreatment and neglect of persons with a mental disorder. (Samoa Government Press Secretariat 2006)

It would, however, take a further 10 months for the Bill to achieve its first parliamentary reading. On 16 November 2006, the Prime Minister rose to move for a second reading of the Mental Health Bill 2006, a Bill of '39 clauses' and not 'much volume' (Samoa Parliamentary Debate Records [SPDR] 2006, p. 867). The need for an update was apparent since as the Prime Minister observed in the proceedings that the original law, the Mental Health Ordinance, had not been amended since its implementation in 1961. He suggested that 'up to this hour, it seems that there have not been any specific conditions for the care of these people and now the Government has prioritised it' (SPDR 2006, p. 867). The Prime Minister goes on to note a personal anecdote as evidence of the need for the Bill. He tells of a trip where he was rushing along the airport road when

> I passed a vehicle coming into town. The driver of the vehicle however had called out an obscene language to a man who was walking along the side of the road. This man in return picked up a rock and threw it straight at the vehicle. The problem was, his rock did not hit that vehicle but broke the windshield of my car…I asked him, 'Why are you like that?' The man who seemed to have been 39 years old at the time replied, 'I was angry at the car that went past'. When I looked at his face, I saw that he seemed to be a mentally ill person. We do not have many people suffering from mental illness. Some people are well known by our locals as mentally ill people, but he could be the only person unaware of his own condition. People tend to look down on these people in society, but we have come to the time when we must specify laws and guidelines so that people suffering from mental illness can also be treated. Mr Speaker that is the main objective of this Bill. (2006a, 869)

The motion was then approved and referred to the Health and Social Services, Internal Affairs, Community and Social Development Committee (Samoa Parliamentary Committee on Health and Social Services, Community and Social Development 2006). The Bill joined several others related to the health system in Samoa, including the Pharmacy Bill; Healthcare Professions Registration and Standards Bill 2006; and Nursing and Midwifery Bill, which would, upon adoption, constitute a wholesale rewrite of the Samoan health legislation framework.

This Committee is charged with 'consider(ing) any bill… to examine the policy, administration and expenditure of the ministers and associated government organisations related to matters in Health and Social Services, Internal Affairs, Community and Social Development' (Standing Orders of the Parliament of Samoa, No. 174). They invited public submissions and while there is no record of these proceedings, those who were disclosed as offering testimony include four senior Ministry of Health officials including the Chief Executive Officer; the Assistant Chief Executive Officer for Strategic Planning and Development; the Assistant Chief Executive Officer for Nursing and Midwifery Services; and the Assistant Chief Executive Officer for Health Promotion and Preventive Services. Despite the efforts undertaken in the policy process to include various policy stakeholders, the legislative process received input only from bureaucrats after the initial vetting process.

The Committee spent '[five] sitting days in considering the Bill' and 'noted that [it] provides for care, support, treatment and protection of persons with mental disorders… [T]he main objective [is to] help encourage non health care professional [sic] to be responsible in offering care and support to persons with mental disorders' (SPDR 2006c). Besides clerical adjustments to the Bill, no changes were submitted.

The Bill's committee report occurred on 19 December 2006 and was adopted without amendment; this was followed by a third reading on 16 January 2007 at which time it passed the Legislative Assembly (SPDR 2007, p. 1010). Occurring contemporaneously with the official law vetting process was the development of Samoa's written governmental mental health policy. The process of developing this policy will be found to be more participatory in nature as set forth below.

5.4 Samoa's Mental Health Policy

'Localisation' and 'translation', as set out earlier in this book, refer to the practice of taking the international and making it local. In the mental health context, this involves taking international best practice on mental health policy, including scientific bases for mental health diagnoses and human rights claims for the appropriate treatment of individuals suffering from mental illness, and interpreting these central policy components in the indigenous context. The policy transfer process necessitates the involvement of domestic actors engaged in mental health broadly. Respondents indicated the central role the international context played in the localisation of mental health in Samoa. As one respondent suggested, the idea for the formation of an initial policy group of key stakeholders emerged from the influence of international relationships between IOs and the Government of Samoa. The attention to mental health occurred because

> [d]uring the reforms, mental health was an issue, because at the time it was much highlighted at WHO Assemblies, governments were attending and then consultations by the WHO, it's very well known, but when it comes to implementation, it's not, I think we are caught in having very limited budgets at the same time, I think it all comes down to the people who are driving the service.
>
> […]
>
> This policy development process took place just when I joined them and so it was part of the reforms, and so I think the government and Department of Health were looking at using WHO guides to look at types of acts and laws that could be considered priorities for countries. And mental health was a dominant theme of WHO Assemblies since 2001, you know like the 'New Hope', the name of that WHO Report in 2001, and another Report in 2006 or 2005, you can easily download them from WHO and they highlight a lot on the needs of mental health people. They were talking about DALYs and that kind of thing.

This context provided the basis for the policy development process. As an initial step, a Mental Health Symposium was organised to bring together key stakeholders for input on forming a mental health policy in Samoa.

5.4.1 Samoa's Mental Health Symposium

Many respondents in the current study cited the 'National Symposium on Mental Health Issues in Samoa' held in April 2003 in Apia as one of the originating forums in the process of mental health policy development (Petaia 2003). The conference that brought together many key actors from government and civil society for a focused discussion on various aspects of the nation's mental health situation, context and needs. Leaders from churches, villages, courts, and international funders participated. Amongst other things, the symposium was designed to attend to Samoa's mental health services by identifying needs and problems and proposing a course of action to address them.

The symposium considered six key dimensions including advocacy; service provision, mental health promotion; policy and legislation; research; and suicide prevention. The policy and legislation prong saw recommendations to prioritise policy and law development. Indeed, many participants recommended the development of a policy as instrumental. The local newspaper, the Samoa Observer, covered these proceedings and reported under the headline 'Moves to improve mental health care' that the symposium, which was sponsored by the WHO and spearheaded by the Mental Health Unit and the Planning and Policy Division of the Ministry of Health (under local leadership in collaboration with AusAID), identified that the WHO definition of health as 'a state of physical, mental and social wellbeing' was complemented in the Samoan context by including the spiritual dimension (Samoa Observer 2005). Due in part to the assistance of a WHO consultant, a medical doctor well-travelled in mental health policy development, the symposium produced recommendations that would serve as the basis for the mental health policy. The following principles were also established: mental wellbeing is grounded in the *aiga* (family) and *nu'u* (community); respect for individual rights; appropriate care without discrimination; the 'recognition that mental, physical, social and spiritual health are indivisible'. The overall goal was to develop quality mental health services in Samoa. Again, it is significant that this symposium closely followed the issuance of the WHO Country Cooperation Strategy for Samoa in February 2003. The combination of these two well-publicised events firmly placed mental health on the collaborative agenda.

5.4.2 Policy Development

The policy development process proceeded with deliberate speed. From its inception with the symposium, the next stage was to form a Mental Health Policy Working Committee, a local stakeholder group who started work in March 2005 and produced a first draft of the policy in December of that year (SMoH 2006 p. 3). This draft, crafted in collaboration with the WHO, adopted a typical policy document structure and adopted two definitions of 'mental health' – both from international sources. The first is provided by the WHO and states that mental health is a 'state of wellbeing in which the individual realizes his or her own abilities, can cope with the normal stresses of life, can work productively and fruitfully, and is able to make a contribution to his or her community' (WHO 2001); a definition offered repeatedly by book participants. The third paragraph of the draft begins with the notion that '[m]ental health as a concept needs to be considered within the context of the Samoan culture' and affirms the association of 'mental disorders'[a term undefined] with physical illness, suicide and social ills such as 'violence, criminality, addictions, homelessness and poverty' (SMoH 2006, p. 3).

The draft policy sets forth a vision that 'all people in Samoa enjoy mental wellbeing that is grounded in the aiga and nurtured through a multi sectoral approach …' (SMoH 2006, p. 3), which precedes the 'values and principles' portion of the document. These 'values and principles' include that 'mental wellbeing is grounded in the aiga and the community'; and that the 'Samoan understanding of dignity and self-esteem is collective and relational in nature' (2006, p. 3). Further, that

> [w]hat is achieved or lost by the individual, is felt by the Aiga. In this context, the aiga is natural and appropriate health care setting for the promotion of mental health and the management of mental disorders, with the exception of some severe disorders requiring hospitalization or seclusion. (2006, pp. 34)

The document identifies, amongst other areas, the need for the development of institutional structures for the continued necessary diligence in this policy area and proposes a mental health board to organise indigenous actors into an institutional arrangement to ensure continued attention to this policy area. In addition, the need for legislation and human rights and focal areas including suicide prevention; drug and alcohol abuse; sexual abuse/child and adolescent abuse; domestic violence; and dignity of the family are all formally recognised as key areas for action (SMoH 2006, p. 4).

The policy also reasserts the 'Samoan context' from a policy perspective under the heading 'Mental Health Services in Primary Care' as

> based on the aiga and this should be the focus of mental health assessment and management. Thus the preference should be for treatment in the community rather than in hospital or health centres. (SMoH 2006, p. 6)

This is a powerful statement in that the basis for community care is not based on an international best practice (though this is also the international model at the moment) but on a key strength of the Samoan culture. This tracks closely with Enoka's (2000) introduced informal practices as embodied in SMoH service models beginning in the mid 1980s to be discussed below. Furthermore, this theme has been continued in recent responses to the 2009 tsunami (Radio New Zealand International 2012) and on developing mental health services in Samoa generally (Enoka et al. 2012).

The informal mental health sector in Samoa is said to consist of a 'wide range…of services…including NGO's, religious organisations and traditional healers' (SMoH 2006, p. 7). These groups address issues ranging from suicide awareness and abuse victim and alcohol abuse services. These services are described as a vital gap-filler between specialist and primary services. Yet, these informal services are not linked to the formal health structure as reflected in no identifiable referrals coming from the informal sector. In addition, as one observer mentioned, in Samoa there were no 'self-help groups for the mentally ill or their families' and people are left to 'wander aimlessly in town and public places'. This last observation is one that came up time and again in the interviews conducted in the research for this book. As one respondent observed,

> We saw a lot of mental people walking the streets and we were concerned. I said, 'it's good we are working on your policy now, because I noticed a lot of women, which is our concern'.
>
> INTERVIEWER: Have you noticed an increase?
>
> Yes, about 2 years ago, when the policy was coming in, so I spoke to [the psychiatrist] and I was concerned. He said many of them were because they are on the marijuana and all that. This is our concern because when they come in to see us, we take them up to [the psychiatrist].

Related to this in the draft policy is a separate subsection dedicated to 'private services' of which there are few in Samoa; counselling services to women were one type available at the time of this research. This section contains, however, the most comprehensive discussion of suicide in the document. It is pointed out that there is no 'suicide prevention strategy or program' and this section contains other areas of association with other social ills including the relationship between mental disorder and substance abuse; domestic violence being associated with 'stress related disorders'; and sexual and physical abuse being correlated to mental disorders in victims in their teenage and adult years (SMoH 2006). These items read more as fact-statements that would seem to suggest a call to arms, though this is not made explicit. Instead, the section shifted into the matter of stigma and discrimination in the community, noting that

> [c]urrent cultural beliefs present a stigmatized view of mental health disorders [that] compromise[] the dignity of families involved and the individual with a mental health disorder [which in turn] acts as in impediment to treatment as well as producing its own stresses. (SMoH 2006, p. 8)

In justifying a mental health policy, the draft policy borrows from many themes advanced in the international literature as influencing the prevalence of mental disorder: urbanisation; economic disadvantage; substance abuse and migration – all of which have been outlined in earlier chapters and all of which are related to the Samoan context as factors influencing mental health and wellness there.

This discussion culminates in the draft policy in the identification of mental health system areas of need. Besides the ever-present need for greater financial resources, legislation tops the list of needs, followed by leadership, and expanding specialist services, including the need for 'acute psychiatric beds'. There is, as mentioned earlier, the need for substance abuse treatment and for the promotion of mental wellbeing and for the prevention of the incidence of mental illness. It is in this portion of the draft policy that a second attempt to define mental health is found. The draft notes that

> every person at some point will experience some form of mental unwellness[reflecting] the notion that mental health exists on a continuum where good mental health is located on one end, and mental illness on the other [where] most people fluctuate. (SMoH 2006, p. 15)

It further opined that

> Mental health should be explained in terms that are acceptable to all communities. Religious, traditional, and western scientific/medical perspectives should all be recognized as having a role in healing people who are mentally unwell or ill. One discipline should not be prioritised over the other. Instead the National Health Sector should develop a collaborative strategy. (2006, p. 15)

In addition, the document suggests that 'research' should be carried out as well as 'education and awareness programmes' in the community, including schools, workplaces, health workers and Parliament, which shall 'give equal emphasis to the traditional, religious and western scientific/clinical perspectives' (SMoH 2006, p.15).

Under the heading of 'Advocacy', the importance of individuals with mental illness participating in policy and law-making processes is affirmed. Antidiscrimination and stigma policies should be adopted throughout government and individuals with mental illness should be 'consulted on all drugs brought into the country to treat them' and be supported 'within a medium that they feel most comfortable' to ensure that their voice is heard. In addition, these people should receive the 'best care and treatment in any facility' and they should not be 'penalized as criminals nor should they be incarcerated within the local prisons' (SMoH 2006, p. 16).

The draft policy recognised that

> [t]here is a strong political and organisational commitment in Samoa to develop a mental health policy. A mental health policy needs to be informed by broader policy frameworks and be consistent with the objectives of the Ministry of Health. Changes in the social and economic structures within Samoa appear to contribute to an increased prevalence of mental disorders. Mental health policy should be formulated aiming at reducing the burden of mental disorders in the aiga and the community. (SMoH 2006, p. 17)

The section titled 'Constraints' formally recognises the dearth of data on mental health in Samoa and that the application of the 'abundance' of overseas data to the Samoan situation is either 'uncertain or unknown' (2006, p. 20). It is at this point that a further definition of mental health is offered. This definition is taken from the Pacific Regional Strategy for Mental Health document on mental health and is presented in the draft as the

> [f]oundation for the wellbeing and effective functioning of individuals. Mental health is the ability to think and learn and the ability to understand and live with one's emotions and the reactions of others. It is a state of balance within a person and between a person and the environment. This balance is a product of a number of interrelated factors, including physical, psychological, social, cultural and spiritual. (2006, p. 20)

The report noted that 'mental illness' refers collectively to all mental disorders. It is the second leading cause of disability and 'premature mortality' (SMoH 2006, p. 20 (See also, So'o 2006)). Mental disorders are, in turn, defined as 'health conditions that are characterized by alterations in thinking, mood, behaviour or some combination thereof associated with distress and/or impaired functioning' (2006, p. 21).

5.4.3 Community Consultation of Policy

This final version of the policy went out for community consultation in February 2006, a process that included the 'Samoa Community, government ministries, non-governmental organisations as well as the Ministry of Health staff' (SMHPT 2006, p. 3). Four consultations were held, two on the main island of Upolu and two on neighbouring Savai'i. Two of these were public and two were open only to SMoH staff. In the latter presentations were made and small group sessions held to address a set of questions including the policy's relevance to Samoa and any omissions or other thoughts on effective implementation and monitoring (SMHPT 2006, p. 3).

The key findings of this consultation process included public support for a mental health policy in order to 'encourage the Samoan people to support and respect the rights of those with mental disorders' (SMHPT 2006, p. 4). Further, central issues raised by participants related to staff training, making available adequate resources for care, and expanding specialist care (2006, p. 4). Amongst the issues missing, participants indicated a need to 'improve … communication and [that] there should be an independent board for Mental Health' (2006, p. 6) and increased public awareness through trainings for the community and through media campaigns to promote individual rights (2006, pp. 56).

Additionally, several groups commented that Ward 9 (the old mental health unit) should be reactivated and that there should be a 'special ward for mental disorders'. In addition, it was felt that the existing Mental Health Unit should be relocated away from the hospital. Participants also encouraged the establishment of a 'mental health council' to support the policy and the creation of 'a support group for mental health patients and their families. The participation of other ministries and NGOs to support mental health should also be encouraged (SMHPT 2006, pp. 78). From here, the Mental Health Policy Working Committee referred to the consultation outcomes and finalised the draft mental health policy before submitting it to the Cabinet Development Committee, where it was finally adopted in August 2006.There appear to be only minor changes to the draft policy and the final version as most of the public comments did not appear to any significant degree to form the final product. The policy is only part of the mental health system story; the Mental Health Act 2007 completes the recent mental health policy transformation in Samoa.

5.5 Practice-Level Change: The Indigenous Professional as Agent of Informal Transfer

The years between 1962 and 2007 were not without significant changes to Samoa's mental health service delivery model. This research uncovered significant contributions to the community treatment model promotion in Samoa, particularly since the late 1980s with the return to Samoa of a New Zealand-trained, Samoan psychiatric nurse. In fact, any account of mental health policy in Samoa without due consideration of the contributions of this key actor, Matamua Iokapeta Sina Enoka (Enoka) would be incomplete. Moreover, here counting of her work in the creation of a 'culturally appropriate mental health care service in Samoa' that was published in a report of the 'Measina A Samoa 2000' conference is a key milestone along the path to the creation of the Samoa's current mental health system.

Enoka was commonly mentioned as one of the main driving forces behind Samoa's current mental health system and its community-based treatment focus. She reported that her profession

> is nursing, as a nurse trained in New Zealand. I came [back] to Samoa in 1984 and I worked in the mental health area from 1984 to about 1990. Currently, I am now a lecturer in the Faculty of Nursing and Science teaching mostly psychology, mental health and research…as a matter of fact I am the only psychiatric trained nurse in the country.

She remembered that she became interested in mental health because it was.

> …just my interest growing up really. My background, my father was a Minister in the church but my father was more an inspiration to myself that he would always talk of how people should settle their own grievances and how people should look at themselves and heal themselves rather than just leaving it to the open and having strange people to come in and talk about their own problems, I think that through that are and my education I was more interested in the mind rather than the body that really sort of drove me to think that I could be that person to help in this area.
>
> […]
>
> My interest is in mental health, everything to do with mental health is my interest, even the development of the community mental health service and looking at standards of nursing and how to deliver the services, it drives my interest to write things about policy, at that particular time, we were the only people who were interested in psychosocial areas.

When, in 1984, she returned to Samoa as a trained registered psychiatric nurse from New Zealand, she found an antiquated colonial holdover system based on custodial and institutionalised care (Enoka 2000, p. 25). The image of the individual separated from his or her family and community resonated with her. A very deep stigma existed not only amongst the community but caregivers as well.

As introduced above, central to the Samoan sense of self is the *aiga* (extended family), which is a broad concept that extends both backwards and forwards in time. It encompasses customs, traditions, the land of origin, and eventual burial (Enoka 2000, p. 26). Enoka advances a construction of Samoan philosophy which holds than an individual has three parts: *mauli* (part of the subconscious active when dreaming); *aitu* (creative inner self also understood since contact as 'ghost', see also Aiono 2003); and *olla* (the physical body). An imbalance in any of the three results in *tagata vale* (disorder) (see generally Aiono 2003). Health is understood as *soifua maloloina* (optimum wellness in life) (Enoka 2000, p. 26). Spirit possession (*fasia*) is understood as occurring where an *aitu* takes possession of one's body and causes disruption to the individual's thinking. Enoka argues that mental illness is culturally defined, and as such, '[k]nowledge of the beliefs, customs and how to use these as effective tools for implementation of health care is transferable to other cultures' leading her to the conclusion that, given the social context in Samoa, 'the approach to care in the Samoa society is not the use of institutionalisation or removal from society but the use of society family and the strength of Samoan culture to facilitate care' (2000, p. 27).

'Folk knowledge', in this case about mental health and the role of the state in its management, is developed and expressed as a 'product of an institutionalized pattern of information, processing in knowledge distribution within the group' (Clement 1982, p. 194). Clement's research locates Samoan representations of mental disorders in the social context, unsurprising perhaps for a collectivist culture. In essence, many mental disorders can be seen as descriptive sets of undesirable social behaviours as in the term *tagatavalea*, which means 'stupid or crazy person' (1982, p. 203). In contrast, Clement observes that if one's behaviour or deviance from the social norm is categorised otherwise, one is thought of as simply someone who has chosen not to act in conformance with Samoan custom and will likely be shunned, presumably in an effort to return the individuals to the social baseline. Furthermore, she finds that while Samoans viewed a hospital in many ways as a place of last resort; they did not necessarily 'expect the person to be cured' while there, only managed. This lack of confidence in the efficacy of the official mental health system persists and is seen in the folk knowledge described by Samoan participants. Despite active efforts to develop Western mental health systems and their incumbent belief structures, traditional beliefs about mental illness persist as reflected in the interviews undertaken for this study. Interestingly, there is an enduring tension between these institutions. As one respondent observed, this juxtaposition of traditional and mainstream services was

> interesting because it's completely opposite from the fact that we're supposed to be 100% Christian, because it, the whole 'witch doctor' thing, which is how other people define it, is a complete juxtaposition to what our Christian beliefs are supposed to be, so it's a very touchy and unusual topic…

The incongruence was reflected in Enoka's comments on the manner in which government mental health services were provided when she returned to Samoa in 1984. She recalled that while most people with nonviolent symptoms to their mental conditions were still cared for in the home, many with schizophrenia, drug histories or psychosis were kept at Tafaigata prison. She intimated this was due to several factors such as lack of community-based facilities to manage violent episodes, a shortage (or absence) of critical medications, and the lack of sufficient numbers of trained professionals to offer care. This situation resulted in

> the development of a community-based, family focused mental health service and it was quite difficult at the time because the psychiatrist who was working here at that particular time did not want people who were mentally ill cared for at home… I think he feared the fact that the families would not look after them when they are in their own homes, but I insisted that the culture must play a very good part in helping these people because there are no trained personnel to look after them for the 24 hours and then we should encourage the families, to look at it from the family point of you, having this person return to them and reintroduce the person who once was theirs.

[...]

[I]n 1986 the family focus, community-based mental health service was initiated by myself and the one other staff nurse who was sent to help me. It was difficult work but that laid the foundation for easing out the care of the people who were mentally ill because we were able then to have the families agree on the prospect of having these people return to them and they agreed to work with myself and the other nurse to continue every day the visits to the homes and using the cultural lens and bringing people back into their normalcy, because they weren't actually diagnosed as psychotics, or people who didn't quite fit into their family at home, and we found that this was very successful and we took it all over the country and that's how we worked up until now.

The presence of state-run institutions as a repository for the most difficult of cases dates back to the establishment of German colonial administration. In 1910, Western medical institutions in the embodiment of the hospital became a part of the fabric of Samoan life, though it would take time and extensive efforts by Westerners to persuade Samoans of their indispensability. Known at its inception in 1910 as the Apia Hospital, it institutionalised segregated care from the outset. The hospital consisted of three divisions – European, Samoan and Chinese – for housing patients. There was a centrally located operating theatre from which emanated the three divisions.

The creation of a place to bring the ill created an expectation of treatment for certain conditions. First amongst these has been mental illness. The hospital (and in many cases the prison) became a repository for individuals thought to have a Western mental illness since all known Samoan remedies had typically failed to alleviate the condition or symptoms. Since those who went there typically stayed there, this became the expectation for this place as a last resort. As discussed in earlier chapters, many Western notions of mental illness have emerged and fallen into disfavour and changed since 1920.The community treatment model is now the prevailing model and plays to Samoa's particular strengths of strong familial and community networks. Since the traditional notions of mental illness aetiologies had not been discarded, Enoka had a comparatively simpler task in enlisting families and villages in reassuming care of these individuals, together with medical outreach provided by district nurses.

5.5.1 Professional Networks as Source of Best Practices in Service Delivery

A relatively minor theme emerging from the interviews, but one worth noting in relation to the prevailing literature, involves the role of professional networks in the proliferation of mental health best practices in the region. Enoka cited as one source for this community-treatment movement information received in her capacity as member of international professional associations:

Enoka: I belong to the international mental health and psychiatric association and I write articles for the international journals and I also have friends in the mental health psychiatric field in both New Zealand and Australia who keep sending information on what goals and what's next and that sort of thing.

Interviewer: So the information that you got when you attended conferences and that which you get now through contacts, do you use it to disseminate to people here or in policy development?

Enoka: Yes, first to disseminate it to people who I know to have an interest in these kinds of things and then post it in a newsletter and also use it for discussion in probably looking at new policies, new areas in policymaking.

This cultural learning through professional networks however is an iterative process. Enoka reports a recent presentation to a meeting of 'the Samoan nurses of New Zealand who were very interested in the philosophy of mental health from Samoa' where she had been invited to share her experiences of merging Western mental health with the particularities of the Samoan cultural context. On the international level, predominant discourses such as 'rights-based' and 'neoliberal economic reforms' serve to shape the respective professions' approach to policy development and transfer efforts. On the local level, to the extent that the nation lacks its own professional schools, foreign professional education planted the seeds of prevailing legal and medical points of view on the topic (mental health).On the local professional level there was, however, the potential for hybridisation of a particular policy area between the indigenous cultural context and the prevailing institutional discourses. Therefore, the indigenous professional discursive level is where the greatest potential for policy innovation occurs.

5.6 Conclusion

In 2012, a tragic incident occurred in Samoa that highlighted the unique vulnerability of individuals with mental illness in small island states due to two key factors: poor resourcing of mental systems and susceptibility to natural disasters that result in massive system disruption or even failure. The convergence of these factors resulted in a catastrophic outcome for Hans Dalton (Gay 2018; 1News 2018). In the interests of full disclosure, I advised the government of Samoa several years after this incident on some policy reforms in the wake of this incident. The government sought to establish a more permanent and suitable mental health unit than the ramshackle, temporary structure Mr. Dalton had found himself confined within. Dalton was a Samoan New Zealander who was in Samoa visiting family. He had long suffered from schizophrenia but had lost his medication following a cyclone that ravaged the country during his stay. Mr. Dalton decompensated and became erratic and combative. Eventually the police were called and attempted to forcibly sedate him on the ride from his accommodation to the temporary mental health unit, where he was essentially locked into a small shed-sized building, secured with a padlock. These restraints proved no match for Dalton, who burst free from these futile attempts to hold him. His agitated state without his medication found him eventually transferred to Taifagata Prison where, it was thought, he could be more securely held. For Mr. Dalton, however, the prospect of further escape was to prove fleeting and within a short-time of his arrival, he was found beaten and drowned in a bucket of water in his prison cell. Initially characterised as a suicide, Dalton's physical injuries were difficult for the authorities to explain. Speculation was that Dalton had been quite disruptive and that a group or prisoners might have gained access to Dalton's cell and proceeded to kill him. The case is ongoing, including civil litigation against the Samoan government.

Incidents like this are, unfortunately, all too common throughout the world. Such incidents do, however, remind us of the preciousness of each human life and the all too tragic toll that lack of access to proper medicine and lack of insight or familiarity with a patient's unique needs and circumstances can cause bad situations to considerably deteriorate or even become fatal. Dalton's dilemma arose in a Samoa that only just a few years prior had committed to and developed its own mental health policy. A policy that was seemingly modern and had been crafted with the help of international experts. This with an overhauled mental health law with the express purpose of better enshrining human rights principles as well as Samoan cultural concepts emphasising family into the nation's mental health framework. While policy and law are certainly no immunisation from incidents such as these, such anecdotes do nonetheless suggest possible policy design and implementation failures for the underlying policies and laws.

Based on the material uncovered thus far, some preliminary observations can be made about Samoa's recent mental health policy and law development process. Firstly, the influence of professional discourses (law and medicine) on formal policy transfer is greater than the ethnicity of a particular policy actor in terms of determining policy indigeneity. Enoka merged the prevailing professional discourse of the time (community-based care) with the realities of her social and political milieu. A government with scarce resources and technical expertise is unlikely to engage in the custody and care provision for many community members. By embracing a discourse (and by implication a policy) that plays to the nation's strengths, there is little internal process tension created.

One conclusion supported by the facts presented here is that where policies do not directly impact a cultural norm or belief they are more readily adopted, but, where there is an insufficient nexus between a policy and a domestic, indigenous cultural norm, the law can become stale as the legislative agenda will be driven internally by reaction to international events (e.g. the necessity of trade or financial-norm adoption) or by domestic politics, which will invariably concern matters of Samoan social or cultural interest. Indigenous professional agents did not require official policy or law to institute fundamental mental health systems reform, only professional education and motivation to overlay psychiatric medical practice onto

Samoan culture, and societal institutions was essential (as well as an opportunity structure permitting such innovation on the practice level). While the practices themselves were late to be reflected in official policy and law, they had long been the preferred practice of the official state institutions, and therefore stood a better chance of acceptance by the population. Any suggestion, however, that the professional agents' efforts were a prerequisite for the subsequent statutory and policy changes seems dubious.

The AusAID programme (along with World Bank and WHO efforts on the international and regional level) emphasised the centrality of modern, 'best practice' being reflected in national law and policy and provided necessary momentum for the policy and law adoption. There seems to have been little concern for whether or not any prior foundation existed. While this is a stated objective of all of the international programmes and efforts reviewed here, the strategy is to first construct the institutional and structural framework and then to work on a public education campaign hung upon these legal and policy official discourses.

The policy development process itself was relatively inclusive. As it largely operated outside of the traditional Samoan political power process and outside of the traditional cultural power institutions, there were more opportunities for the inclusion of various perspectives, along with those of the professional organisations and IOs all clamouring for space in the finished document. The process saw contributions from a wide range of domestic and international stakeholders. The vetting process for the policy was much more egalitarian as well. The Ministry of Health officials consulted in this research reported seeing many stakeholders take part. The policy itself is perhaps the best presentation of a merger of discourse.

The process and presentation of the policy and the substantive areas it covers were informed by the contributions of IOs and professional actors. The policy also reflected and incorporated many Samoan cultural understandings and perspectives unique to the Samoan situation. On this policymaking level, further removed from the direct influence and control of the legal and medical professions in particular, there were many opportunities for engagement with and shaping of the Samoan mental health policy document. This document, while clearly following an ordained format and structure for what a 'good' policy should look like, succeeds at embodying ostensibly Samoan principles and insights. The policy is, in essence, an official hybridisation of international models and Samoan perspectives; similar to the unofficial changes brought to the mental health system beginning the in the mid-1980s. In the next chapter I take up Tonga's experience in developing mental health policy before returning to a fuller comparative analysis of themes identified in both cases later in the book.

References

1News. (2018, 28 September). *Family of Kiwi man killed in Samoan prison holding on to hope for justice, six years on from death.* https://www.tvnz.co.nz/one-news/new-zealand/family-kiwi-man-killed-in-samoan-prison-holding-hope-justice-six-years-death

Aiono-Le Tagaloa, F. (2003). Ola, Aitu, Mauli – the inner person. In *Tapua'i: Samoan worship*. Apia: Malua Printing Press.

Bargatzky, T. (1997). 'The Kava Ceremony is a Prophecy' An interpretation of the transition to Christianity in Samoa. In H. J. Hiery & J. M. Mackenzie (Eds.), *European impact & Pacific influence: British & German colonial policy in the Pacific Islands & the indigenous response*. London: Tauris Academic Studies in Association with the German Historical Institute.

Clement, D. (1982). Samoan Folk Knowledge of Mental Disorders, In: Marsella, A, J, White, Geoffrey M, ed, Cultural Conceptions of Mental Health & Therapy, Dordrecht: D, Reidel.

Corrin, C. J., & Paterson, D. (2011). *Introduction to South Pacific law*. London: Routledge-Cavendish.

Enoka, M. (2000). Lalagaina o le tausiga o le soifua o le mafaufau ('Weaving mental health care in Samoa'). In T. Lafotanoa (Ed.), *Measina a Samoa 2000: papers presented to the 'Measina a Samoa 2000 & Beyond' Conference, 11–14 December, Lepapaigalagala* (Vol. 1). Apia: National University of Samoa.

Enoka, M., Tenari, A., Sili, T., Peteru, L., Tago, P., & Blignault, I. (2012). Developing a culturally appropriate mental health care service for Samoa. *Asia-Pacific Psychiatry, 5*(2), 108–111.

Fadgen, T. (2019). 'Explaining policy change in Samoa's mental health system'. *Journal of Pacific Studies, 39*(1).

Fairbairn-Dunlop, P. (2000). Women's NGOs within the new governance agenda: Are they still based on alofa. In E. Huffer & A. So'o (Eds.), *Governance in Samoa Pulegai Samoa*. Canberra: Asia Pacific Press.

Field, M. (1984). *Mau: Samoa's struggle against New Zealand oppression*. Wellington: AH & AW Reed.

Fitzgerald, M., & Howard, A. (1990). Aspects of social Organization in Three Samoan Communities. *Pacific Studies, 14*, 1.

Gay, E. (2018, 13 December). *Psychiatrist a no-show at inquest into Auckland man's death in Samoan custody.* https://www.stuff.co.nz/national/crime/109316274/death-of-new-zealander-in-samoan-prison-cell-was-suspicious-former-cop-says

Government of New Zealand. (1911). Mental Defectives Act.

Government of New Zealand. (1921). Mental Defective Amendment Act 1921.

Government of New Zealand. (1961). Mental Health Amendment Act 1961.

Government of Samoa. (1961a). Mental Health Ordinance.

Government of Samoa. (1961b). *Samoa legislative assembly record of debate on mental health bill*, Apia, pp. 118–124.

Government of Samoa. (1999). *Health sector strategic plan* (pp. 1998–2003). Apia: Ministry of Health.

Government of Samoa. (2006). Parliament of Samoa Legislative Proceedings Transcript, Apia.

Government of Samoa. (2006). *Samoa parliamentary debate records*. Apia: Government of Samoa.

Government of Samoa. (2006c). *Samoa parliamentary debate records* (pp. 942–948). Apia.

Government of Samoa. (2007). Samoa Parliamentary Debate Records, Apia, (pp. 1010).

Government of Samoa. (2007a). Samoa Mental Health Act 2007, Apia.

Government of Samoa. (2007b). Samoa Mental Health Bill 2006, Explanatory Memorandum, Apia.

Hempenstall, P. (1997). The colonial imagination and the making & remaking of the Samoan people. In H. Hiery & Mackenzie (Eds.), *British & German policy in the Pacific Islands and the indigenous response* (European impact & pacific influence). London: Tauris Academic Studies in association with the German Historical Institute.

Hiery, H. J., & Mackenzie, J. M. (Eds.). (1997). *European impact & Pacific influence: British & German colonial policy in the Pacific Islands & the indigenous response*. London: Tauris Academic Studies in Association with the German Historical Institute.
Hills, R. (1993). Predicaments in Polynesia: Culture & constitutions in Western Samoa & Tonga. *Pacific Studies, 16*, 4.
Iati, I. (2000). The good governance agenda for civil society in Samoa. In H. Elise & A. So'o (Eds.), *Governance in Samoa/pulega I Samoa*. Canberra: Asia Pacific Press.
Macpherson, C., & Macpherson, L. (1990). *Samoan medical belief & practice*. Auckland: Auckland University Press.
Mageo, J. (1998). *Theorizing self in Samoa: Emotions, genders, & sexualities*. Ann Arbor: University of Michigan.
McDonald, A. (1949). *Trusteeship in the Pacific*. Sydney: Angus & Robertson.
Meleisea, M. (1987). *The making of modern Samoa: Traditional authority and colonial administration in the history of Western Samoa*.
Meleisea, M. (1992). *Change and adaptations in Western Samoa*. Christchurch: M, Meleisea.
Meti, L. (2002). *Samoa: The making of the constitution*. Lepapaigalagaloa: National University of Samoa.
New Zealand National Archives. (2011). Archives of German Samoa, Wellington (New Zealand).
Petaia, L. (2003). *Summary of recommendations, National symposium on mental health issues in Samoa*. Apia: Government of Samoa.
Peteru, C. (1996). With mad abandon, *Pacific Islands Monthly*.
Radio New Zealand International. (2012, 15 October). Survey hoped to assess mental healthcare. In: Samoa, *Radio New Zealand International.*
Samoa Act. (1921).
Samoa Government Press Secretariat. (2006). Press Release: Cabinet Approval of the Mental Health Bill 2005, Apia.
Samoa Ministry of Health Policy Team (SMHPT). (2006). *Mental health policy consultations report*. Apia: Government of Samoa.
Samoa Observer. (2005). Moves to improve mental health care, *Samoa Observer*, 05 February 2005.
Samoa Parliamentary Committee on Health and Social Services, Community & Social Development. (2006). *Samoa parliamentary committee on health & social services, internal affairs, community & social development report on mental health bill*. Apia: Government of Samoa.
Schoeffel, P. (1977). The origin of development & women' association in W, Samoa. *Journal of Pacific Studies, 6*, 1–43.
Schuster, F. (2001). Counselling against all the odds: The Samoan way. *Pacific Health Dialogue, 8*, 1.
So'o, A. (2006). More than 20 years of political stability in Samoa under the human rights protection party. In S. Firth (Ed.), *Globalisation & Governance in the Pacific Islands*. Canberra: ANU E Press.
Steinmetz, G. (2007). The devil's handwriting precoloniality and the German colonial state in Qingdao. In *Samoa, & Southwest Africa*. Chicago: University of Chicago Press.
Tamasese, K., Peteru, C., Waldegrave, C., & Bush, A. (2005). OleTaeaoAfua: the new morning, A qualitative investigation into Samoan perspectives on mental health & culturally appropriate services. *Australian & New Zealand Journal of Psychiatry*.
Victorian Health Promotion Foundation. (1999). *VicHealth mental health promotion plan, 1999–2002*. Melbourne: Victorian Health Promotion Foundation.
United Nations. (1991). *Principles for the protection of persons with Mental Illness & Improvement of mental health care (the MI principles)*. New York.
World Bank (WB). (2008). Program appraisal document on a proposed credit in the amount of SDR 1,9 million (US$3 Million Equivalent) to the Independent State of Samoa in Support of Health Sector Management Support Project, 41130-WS.

World Health Organization (WHO). (2002). *Draft executive summary of mental health promotion consultancy visit to Samoa*. Manila: WHO.
World Health Organization-Western Pacific Region. (2003). *Country cooperation strategy for Samoa,* Manila.

Chapter 6
How Has Mental Health Policy and Praxis Been Indigenized in Tonga?

This chapter explores the key historical events in Tonga's mental health policy development process. Several critical dimensions of Tonga's policy context will be examined. Firstly, I outline Tonga's key governmental and health institutions and provide a historical overview to the mental health policy setting. This section includes consideration of Tonga's indigenous governance institutions; its experience as one of the only Pacific Island nations never to be formally colonised; and it's being heavily influenced by its complicated relationship with the United Kingdom as a British protectorate. This relationship saw the introduction of numerous state structures, laws and regulations that contribute significantly to the contemporary mental health policy context. Institutions such as courts and hospitals were established with British involvement and, similar to Samoa's experience, the very notion of the state's role in confining individuals with mental illness under the guise of a medicolegal determination has its origins in these experiences. Since the United Kingdom has faded from active presence in Tonga from the 1970s onwards, other regional commonwealth powers, specifically New Zealand and Australia, have maintained a heavy development presences in Tonga.

Following consideration of these institutional aspects of Tonga's development, I next address the mental health policy context. Similar to Samoa's experience, Tonga's mental health policy transfer in its earliest forms involved essentially 'hard' policy in the form of foreign-inspired laws coming into the domestic sphere in the 1940s. Again, this early law will be seen to have continued the state institutional supremacy bound up with mental hygiene legislative initiatives elsewhere. Following this initial establishment, there was a very long period of time until the law was reformed: 50 years passed before an updated version of the Mental Health Act was adopted; this law was deemed largely unworkable by the relevant policy actors yet endured until foreign policy intervention beginning in 2000.

Mental health as policy issue will be seen to emerge again at this time as part of an overall Australian government (AusAID) funded health sector overhaul. WHO provided an Australian expert consultant to the government to redraft the Mental Health Act based on international best practices. Similar to Samoa, Tonga was

T. P. Fadgen, *Mental Health Public Policy in Global Context*,
https://doi.org/10.1007/978-981-15-6479-6_6

targeted for the piloting of a mental health policy makeover. Like Samoa, these changes will be seen to be rapidly developed but unlike Samoa the transfer of the comprehensive mental health policy and legal framework was not completed. Whilst Tonga adopted a new law, it failed to develop a formal written policy. I explore possibilities raised by respondents in this chapter as to why this occurred and will take the question up again in the following joint analytical discussion chapter. I explore the policy artefacts, supporting materials, and the perspectives of key policy actors engaged in the policy development process, including local and foreign policy actors.

As highlighted in the Samoa case study, an emphasis on only hard policy transfer would miss the importance of practice-level policy innovations occurring in Tonga for nearly 20 years. Significant 'soft' policy changes, not reflected in formal government policy, have been taken in Tonga by a lone policy actor, a government psychiatrist who is very active in the transformation of Tongan psychiatry based upon his understandings of both international best practices in his profession as well as reconciling these with his particular Tongan cultural conceptions. Changes of this nature will be observed at the practice level. Finally, I again draw attention to the importance of professional networks in proliferating these best practices on this informal policy level and for providing a possible forum for policies and practice to be repatriated, albeit with the latest iterations bearing the imprimatur of the transferee nations as well as those of the country of inception.

6.1 The Infamous Case of *R v Priven*

One of the most infamous cases in the annals of Tonga's criminal law involves mental illness and questions of criminal culpability. The case is also noteworthy for both the victim and accused were not Tongan but were instead, *palagi*, American volunteers living in Tonga and performing community-related voluntary work as part of United States government's Peace Corps programme. The case, *Rex v Priven*, has been widely regarded as the first attempt at an insanity defence (Weiss 2004). In October 1974, Dennis Priven had been accused of murdering a fellow Peace Corps volunteer, Deborah Gardner. A young lawyer who would later come to become one of Tonga's most well-known public figures, Clive Edwards, led Mr. Priven's defence before a Tongan jury. Evidence was presented of Priven's insanity in both Tongan and European terms. First, Priven's neighbour testified about Priven's bizarre behaviour in the months leading up to the murder, behaviour attributed to *tevolo*, or devils. This testimony was then buttressed by a U.S. government-funded psychiatric evaluation by a Dr. Kosta Stojanovich, based in Hawai'i. Dr. Stojanovich offered his medical opinion that Priven suffered from latent paranoid schizophrenia (Weiss 2004, p. 222).

These two prongs of the Priven defence were accompanied by Edwards's appeal to the jurors' deep Christian beliefs as well when, quoting Luke, 23: 34, he implored the jurors to "forgive the man who knows not what he does." Which gospel verse had the distinct benefit of being mirrored in the legal standard of criminal state of mind in Tonga at the time: the unit of *loto* and *'ilo* – or heart and mind – as an essential element of criminal culpability (Weiss 2004, p. 249). In the end, Edwards's holy trinity strategy to prove Priven *fakaseseke*, or mentally ill, prevailed and he was found not criminally responsible. High-level negotiations between the U.S. and Tonga's governments resulted in a manifestly unfair outcome when Priven was deported from Tonga on the understanding that he would be hospitalised until such time – many believed this to be many years at minimum – he would be found not to be not a threat to others or himself. In practice, the agreement struck between the two governments proved unenforceable and Priven was not detained upon his return to America. He eventually settled in New York City as a free man where he still resides today.

Priven's case helps to illuminate several of the themes at the heart of this book. Firstly, as this chapter discusses further below, mental health laws had been on the books in Tonga for decades prior to Priven's actions. It is curious then that in 1976 the first ever use of this defence would be made. Surely, individuals suffering from mental illness had been accused (and convicted) of criminal offences before then, so why was this the first? It is telling that this case involved foreigners and that this defence, even at the time of writing, is seldom used. As the research within this book will present, the stigma associated with such a defence is very serious indeed and unlike what might be experienced in the United States or another Western country, in Tonga the stigma extends to the defendant's *kāinga* (family) as well and there is therefore a motivation to accept culpability or conviction for an offence. For someone outside the society, the stigma was not such a relevant consideration. Although, it is worth nothing that Priven himself had initially fought the disclosure of his statements to the psychiatrist and had to be convinced to do so (Weiss 2004). In sum, the road to the mental health law reforms of the early twenty-first century was informed by these complex social and legal legacies as well as the interactions between Tongan cultural norms and practices with those of the Europeans with whom so much of the government, legal and policy contexts came to reflect.

6.2 Institutional Overview: Indigenous and Introduced

The road to a hybridised system of governance with indigenous belief systems and introduced governmental institutions developed over more than two centuries. By the time of European contact, Tonga alreeady possessed a highly developed hierarchical social and political system with extensive kinship groupings and allegiances that all played a part in periodic struggles for supremacy. This developed a class structure with a highly centralised chief structure (Lawson 1996). European contact with Tonga officially began with Abel Tasman and Thomas Cook and brought with it new technologies, including arms, which were increasingly employed in internal power struggles and disputes. The discord increasingly took on the character of sectarian conflicts with different missionary factions aligned with various local power brokers. These conflicts also had a political dimension and ultimately ended in 1852 with the establishment of the monarchy and landed nobility (Lawson 1996, p. 88). Taufa'ahau, the Ha'apai paramount chief, later crowned King George Tupou I, established the Tupou dynasty that still rules Tonga today. The monarchy was established with the close support and advice of Wesleyan Missionaries. Perhaps equally important within the European scramble for Pacific colonies, Tupou I was successful in gaining international recognition of the legitimacy of his rule.

Christianity continues to be an important part of Tongan identity. The spiritual and political influence of Christianity writ large on Tonga's social institutions was not, however, considered to be an example of mere acquiescence in the face of European might. As Lawson notes,

> the introduction of the European religion to Tonga was not simply a one-way process of acculturation whereby Christianity was implanted in Tonga and remained entirely European in form and content … Christianity itself underwent changes … traditional melodies were added into the practice … histrionics of Tongan oratory … (1996, p. 90).

The influence of European political discourses was hardly far from the core of Tongan public affairs at this time. One such example is the emancipation edict of 1862, which 'freed commoners from the effective serfdom and is referred to as the Tongan Magna Carta' (Lawson 1996 p. 91) and the 1875 Constitution that was heavily influenced by another English-inspired, Polynesian constitution in Hawai'i and the British Constitution.

The laws developed at this time served to combine uniquely Tongan attributes derived from their authoritarian system of governance and English jurisprudence (Ntumy and Angelo 1993). Powels and Pulea (1988) argue that the ascendancy of traditional Tongan political and cultural norms together with the Enlightenment and Christian notions rooted in the self as individual served effectively to undermine traditional cultural jurisprudential concepts of reciprocity and the 'primacy' of the family network. Moreover, as Marcus (1980) notes, the body of Tongan tradition under challenge today is an amalgam of earlier Tongan culture with a particular version of *papalangi* culture. It has been described as a 'compromise culture' that is defended as *anga faka Tonga* (the Tongan way).

For instance, Philips (2004) reviews the records of Tongan magistrate courts and argues that in these venues, crimes are framed in both modern legal terms and distinctly neotraditional Tongan moral terms. The magistrate courts are the lowest tier of the court system in Tonga; the officials as well as the litigants are Tongan and all proceedings are conducted in Tongan. In contrast, the judges in the higher-level Supreme Court are British and the procedures are bilingual in Tongan and English; the Supreme Court chief judge has long been a British jurist. In Tongan criminal procedures and proceedings, Philips finds that magistrates typically 'alternate between more British influenced legal framings of crime, and more Tongan based moral framings of crimes and the sequential structures of courtroom discourse' (2004, p. 233). She notes the use of *anga faka Tonga* as a frame of reference for interpreting wrongful acts in these proceedings. Whereas the formal framing rhetoric of law is universalistic, Tongan moralising (and thereby interpreting) in the middle of procedure is not. As Philips argues, this merging of concepts serves to incorporate social roles and relationships essential to Tongan understandings of social action and what those roles are shift from case to case.

Similar to Clement's (1982) arguments about the social moderating role played by the assigning of identities based on either exhibiting desirable or undesirable social traits, Philips (2004) suggests that when court personnel raise particular identities and apply them to parties involved in a crime, they are indicating what is bad about the crime as the violation of behaviour expectations associated with those identities (2004, p. 241).Furthermore, the Tongan courts are 'ideologically diverse', resulting from '[p]ressure on the Tongan nation state from the West to become more Western in its legal practices is part of the Tongan development since the 1800s' (2004, p. 242).As such, the local magistrate courts managing more mundane or lower-level crime and civil offences persist in reflecting the values closest to the community, but these 'neotraditional Tongan ways of doing things that one finds in the magistrate courts are erased, at the higher court level' (2004, p. 242).As presented above, the interjection of British jurists dating from about the time of the Treaty of Friendship in 1900 – a British instrument designed to preserve internal order over financial and other matters – caused the divergence in court practice and symbolises Tongan's 'willingness and ability as a nation state to deal with the Western nations through legal practices that derive from those nations' (2004, pp. 24243).

With only minor changes, the core constitutional framework remained relatively unchanged from its inception in the mid-nineteenth century until 2010. The Legislative Assembly, or Fale Alea, is unicameral and had until very recently consisted of three sections. The ministers and governors (3) appointed by the King, 9 representatives of the hereditary nobles elected by their number, and 9 representatives of the people elected on a universal franchise (Campbell 1992a). The Legislative Assembly, even though stacked in favour of the monarch, was a relatively weak political body empowered to suggest Bills whereas discretion as to what should actually come to be enacted rested with the King's Privy Council (Campbell 1992a). Moreover, constitutional amendments had to be passed in two consecutive sessions of the legislative assembly. As illustrative of the significant obstacle this measure posed, Tonga's parliament unsuccessfully sought on several occasions during the 1990s to either reform aspects of the constitution or to send the matter out for external review (Campbell 2005; James 2002). Recent electoral changes resulted in a 26-seat chamber consisting of 9 seats for representatives of the nobility and 17 'people's representatives' elected to four-year terms. The 2010 elections ushered in significant change, with the Democratic Party of the Friendly Isles (a successor organisation to the Human Rights and Democracy Movement) netting 12 of 17 available commoner seats in the 26-member body.

6.2.1 Tonga as British Protectorate

Towards the end of the nineteenth century, whilst Samoa was partitioned between the United States and Germany, Great Britain retained 'control' over Tonga. Britain maintained the appearance of Tongan independence until internal political instability (manifested in conflict between rival church groups) erupted in 1887. This ultimately resulted in Britain and Tonga signing the Treaty of Friendship in 1900 (Lawson 1996). While the year incidentally coincided with both Germany's and America's formal steps to consolidate control over their Samoan possessions, the Treaty of Friendship established the British 'protectorate' of Tonga. But, as Lawson observes, this treaty, when read together with the later Supplementary Agreement of 1905, served to effectively supplant Tongan sovereignty by placing all foreign relations as well as domestic fiscal matters under British oversight and control. This system of ostensibly shared sovereignty endured until 1970 when the Treaty of Friendship and Supplementary Agreement were revoked (Lawson 1996).

The absence of formal colonisation, however, remains a source of immense pride for Tongans, as does their place as the only remaining constitutional monarchy in the Southern Pacific. The Constitution has been a special element of pride since its adoption in 1875 (making it one of the oldest in the world) when it first entrenched the current form of government and was, in the view of many commentators, instrumental in preventing formal colonisation (Lātūkefu 1975; Lawson 1996). The form of government established by the Constitution was one with formal hereditary nobility, consisting of numerous chiefly titleholders who were promised these offices in exchange for their enduring support of the succession of the Tupou dynasty. In addition, the form of government adopted was also modelled on that of England, especially in light of the chief adviser to the King being an English missionary by the name of Shirley Baker. The legislative and executive branches were in the form of Parliament and Cabinet, albeit with tighter control exercised by the Tongan King and his privy council. The arrangement proved very successful and endured nearly unchanged until a prodemocracy movement emerged in 1993 and pushed for significant reforms in response to several high-profile instances of public malfeasance by the government of the day as well as within the royal family. This prodemocracy movement would, however, require more than 15 years to achieve meaningful political reforms.

The historian Colin Newbury has documented a longstanding Tongan political interest in Western policy who writes of King Tupou I's 1853 visit to Sydney in order to observe a foreign government at work (2003, p. 246). Furthermore, the King engaged in correspondence with the governor of New Zealand, Sir George Grey, and accepted guidance from the former Hawaiian commissioner to Polynesia, Charles St. Julien. Following this period of observation and learning, the King embraced the counsel of Baker, a Wesleyan Methodist missionary in Tonga (2003, p. 246). The law code resulting of this partnership, which emerged in 1862, ended serfdom, imposed an annual tax on all inhabitants, and established a formal land allotment scheme. The particularly strong form of monarchical rule has elsewhere been derided as the creation of 'a constitution under a monarch' (2003, p. 247). In addition to collaborating on this foundation political and legal text, the pair also created the Free Wesleyan Church of Tonga, free from the edicts of the Sydney Free Wesleyan congregation. This partnership is often credited with establishing Tonga's effectiveness in staving off formal colonisation by a European power.

Tonga, while never formally colonised, was forced to accept the aforementioned Treaty of Friendship with Great Britain. An envoy of the British high commissioner in 1900 secured concessions over control of Tonga's foreign affairs and in certain internal affairs – particularly those concerning foreign citizens and subjects. When Tupou balked at this encroachment, the envoy 'declared a formal protector by proclamation until the treaty was ratified on the sixteenth of February, 1901' (Newbury 2003, p. 251). These domestic controls were significant. The position of chief justice, for instance, has traditionally (including for the period examined in this book) been held by a British jurist. As Newbury concludes, Tonga's development since European contact has been one of selecting or permitting the transfer of certain values (and not others) and that personality played a critical role in the success (or failure) of each. Clearly throughout Tonga's historical battle to adopt some aspects of imported values and technology and reject others, personalities were often as important as changes in principles. One such personality was Baker, who successfully complemented King Tupou's vision for Tonga. Their partnership led to the adoption of several European government institutions and jurisprudential precepts that have had a profound impact on Tonga's subsequent development. We will soon examine the role personality has played in Tonga's incomplete adoption of a mental health policy during the early 2000s.

6.2.2 *Traditional and Introduced Governance Structures*

The historian Sione Latukefu has written extensively on wrote much on Tonga's history and the influence of British jurisprudence (Latukefu 1997). Tongan society traditionally used oral transmission of knowledge and formal rules of conduct or laws. The oral traditions and structure were supported in the day-to-day institutions of Tongan governance structures manifested in its hereditary chief-based political system, which would serve as the foundation to the dual institutions of monarchy and nobility in the nineteenth century (1997, p. 178). The authority of the chief, believed to be derived from the dual notions of *mana* and *tapu* (or supernatural origins and 'customary prohibitions') was both to land (*tofi'a*) and the villagers themselves (*kainga*). This authority is understood as more pervasive and authoritarian than similar structures found in Samoa. With the divine origins of the ruler's authority and the authoritarian manner in which this authority was exercised, there was neither a notion of 'liberty or social equality' nor any 'idea of social justice for commoners who were the majority of the population' (1997, p. 180). Likewise, given the construction of power deriving not from the commoner but from the divine, there was also no concept of political 'accountability'; a theme which would be asserted in the later years of the twentieth century.

The maintenance of traditional Tongan institutions benefited from the British colonial policy of the time that insisted upon the least amount of intrusion in a country without adequate potential of financial return and instead 'encouraged indigenous government supported and guided by missionaries and responsible settlers'

(Latukefu 1997, p. 181). These initial codes prohibited 'murder, theft, adultery, fornication, and the retailing of ardent spirits' whilst institutionalising certain Christian rituals and 'industrious habits, proper cultivation of the land, and design ways to prevent pigs from destroying crops' (1997, p. 182). Outside of the traditional village dispute resolution system, an independent judiciary was established to handle more serious offences. The liberal European principles of 'liberty, equality, social justice and accountability' were all enshrined in these successive law codes including 'freedom of worship, speech, the press and assembly, the right to petition the King and parliament' (1997, p. 182). Moreover, legal authorities in New Zealand were consulted when law codes were drawn up and the laws of New South Wales were referred to in was preparing the constitution.

6.2.3 Governance: Enduring International Role as Legacy of British Protectorate

Scarr et al. (1998) note that the centrality of foreign involvement in Tonga shifted after the 1970 rescission of the Treaty of Friendship with Britain, primarily to Australia. This new relationship saw the development of the South Pacific Regional Trade and Economic Corporation Agreement (SPARTECA) that included Australia, Fiji, Tonga and others that gave Australian privileged access to Tongan production. The present relationship is marked by extensive development assistance and defence cooperation programmes, as well as the heavy flow of human capital between the two countries, despite this agreement failing to provide an actual large external market for Tongan goods (Scarr et al. 1998, p. 66).In addition to the maintenance of strong clergy ties between the two nations, there were also strong educational connections in the form of in-service educator trainings for secondary teachers provided by Australia (1998, pp. 7071).Similar to the Samoan experience, there was a steady stream of emigration not only to Australia but to New Zealand and the United States. As Scarr et al. note, the migrant experiences of both pluralism and multiculturalism in these adopted nations has led to increasing levels of information-sharing between the diaspora, particularly with their villages back in Tonga (1998, p. 73).

Tonga's main trading partners are its main aid donors Australia and New Zealand. In a history of aid to Tonga, Campbell (1992b) notes its origins in the British Colonial Development Act 1929 and its successor the Colonial Development and Welfare Act 1940, which led to aid packages to Tonga beginning in the 1960s. Secondly, Campbell notes the Canberra Agreement (1944) between Australia and New Zealand, which had two main objectives: security and development. The second prong of the Canberra Agreement came to fruition in many Pacific Islands following World War II with massive public expenditures (by colonisers and United Nations [UN]trustees) for such public facilities as hospitals, schools, roads, harbour works, airfields, electricity supplies, radio communications, and agricultural research and development (Campbell 1992b). For instance, in the 1960s Tonga received considerable received foreign aid from the World Health Organization (WHO) for an environmental sanitation project (Campbell 1992b).

The Asian Development Bank (ADB) continues to be one of the largest aid (loans and technical assistance) providers to Tonga. According to recent statistics, Tonga has received US$57.79 million in loans and a further US$17.05 million in technical assistance since it joined ADB in 1972 (ADB 2011a). The picture of Tonga's fiscal picture provided by ADB is not a rosy one. A very slight positive growth was projected of 0.5 per cent for 2011 based primarily on 'donor-funded infrastructure activities' and a significant increase in government spending (nearly 15 per cent) was designed to 'support aggregate demand through an increase in wages and salaries'. This projection is 'primarily based on commitment for further budget support from donors' (ADB 2011b).

ADB's (2011b) prognosis is that while revenue projections remain weak, the only hope of improvement, in the medium-term, is through the 'continued implementation of its public sector reforms (with its associated) improved efficiency and greater private sector participation' (2011b, p. 2).While, in ADB's view progress towards an increased living standard has been slow to materialise, this has largely been due to 'past policy and governance environments that discouraged private sector investment, and the crowding-out effects of a relatively large public sector' (2011b, p. 2). In addition, ADB notes that despite considerable financial support by itself and other 'bilateral aid agencies' to assist these reforms, the results have been 'disappointing', which they attribute to a lack, prior to 2002, of sufficient 'political will'. These incremental reforms were capped with the 2007 agreement between Tonga, ADB, New Zealand and Australia entitled 'Declaration on Aid Effectiveness between the Government of Tonga and Development Partners' which obliged the parties to 'apply the principles of the Paris Declaration on Aid Effectiveness'.

Government and political reforms in Tonga have been inextricably linked with aid and concerns over foreign aid dependency. Bilateral aid donors, most centrally Australia and New Zealand, have advanced public sector reforms in Tonga on two fronts, according to Campbell (2005). First, the reforms advanced the New Public Management objective of public sector efficiency by insisting on a reduction in both size and scale of government. Second, the donors created educational and training opportunities for civil servants (Campbell 2005). As discussed below, these themes would become central to recent reforms of Tonga's public health sector.

6.3 Tonga's Mental Health System History and Overview

One high-ranking government official, a member of the Mental Health Advisory Committee established under the Mental Health Act 2001 (discussed below) discussed mental health in Tonga as being.

> dealt with initially, of course, at home in the community, so it is normally the parents, grandparents, aunties and uncles or siblings. And as per normal, small communities tend to stigmatise mentally disabled, and so carers often marginalise them.

This quote illustrates the profound centrality of Tongan social patterns at the centre of well-being (Ka'ili 2017). After the home and community attempts, the next step for individuals with a mental illness in Tonga is within Tonga's mental health system, which essentially orbits around the nation's sole psychiatrist, a Tongan, Dr. Mapa Puloka. Dr. Puloka oversees the national mental health unit and small staff located at the nation's main hospital in Nuku'alofa. As in other jurisdictions, other common state actors often implicated in mental health symptom management include the prosecutors, courts and prison system. Tonga's health system ostensibly began with the erection of Tonga's first hospitals in the major island groups in 1909 (Campbell 1992a, b, p. 118). The government ministry dedicated to health would however not emerge until a decade later following the Spanish Influenza pandemic of 1918 (Poltorak 2002, p. 207). The general wards of Tonga's Vaiola Hospital would serve as a primary point of official contact for less acute mental health concerns until 1977, when the establishment of the country's first psychiatric unit occurred (2002, p. 207).

Tonga's Police and Prisons Reports, beginning in 1950, provide valuable information on the development of the mental health system, despite sizeable gaps in availability for sets of years in the 1980s and some years of the 1990s. The first mention of mental health (or rather illness) was in the very first of these reports in 1950, which refers to the 'Lunatic Asylum' and records data under this heading. The asylum records began with a census of ten 'lunatics'. These early reports were very brief, averaging little over five pages per annum for combined prisons and police information. In fact, until 1959 the only information given about this population was its size; in that year a trend of irregular commenting on the conditions began. This report was also the first to note the need for a building to separate the male and female 'lunatics' from other inmates. Presumably, violent offenders and individuals with mental illness were simply housed together until these changes could be made. This arrangement of housing individuals with mental illness together with inmates was recognised as undesirable from nearly the very beginning of recordkeeping on the asylum project in Tonga. The 1960 report notes that plans had been drawn up for separate quarters, but a decision on moving forward was required as soon as possible; both the 1961 and 1962 reports note the project's approval, but that 'urgently required' construction had yet to begin. The 1963 report reiterates this need with the comment that especially male patients need to 'be kept separate from other prisoners' (Tonga Police and Prisons Department [TPFPD] 1963, p. 7). This report notes approval of both project and building plans, but construction has still not begun. The 1964 report strikes a more certain tone, noting that its population, now numbering ten (five male, five female) would soon have 'separate quarters away from prison compound for both men and women' that would 'be erected in the following year, as the [current] environment is not conducive to their illness' (TPPD 1964, 9).

In a further related development, the 1965 report includes for the first time a section titled 'The State of Crime' and consisting of a narrative account, or explanation to the reader, of the particular characteristics of crime in the kingdom. This development is closely linked to the touted creation of a new statistics unit introduced in the 'Criminal Records' section, which would result in the inclusion of much longer and fuller quantitative-based explanations of crime. The report makes no mention of 'lunatics'. The 1966 report was the first to link increasing crime rates to 'population pressures and economic side effects' (TPPD 1966, p. 17).Further, the report notes 'the natural population increase and drift from outer islands to the amenities of Tongatapu gave rise to the greatest police problems … leading to upward trend in crime' (1966, p. 9).The 1967 report is interesting for disclosing the involvement of a foreign police adviser, one Mr. H.C. Gay, CPM, whose tenure would run from 19,651,967 (TPPD 1967, p. 2); this began a longstanding practice that would end in 1975.

Once again, urbanisation was lamented as a cause of the kingdom's rising crime. The population expansion, shortage of land and unemployment created social pressures which inevitably 'had their effect on trends in crime' (TPPD 1967, p. 10). A nearly 70 per cent increase in Nuku'alofa's population from 19,571,967 was noted as central to this trend by Tongan police (1967, p. 11).The 1968 report reveals a staggering increase in the rate of crime of nearly 18per cent, which is attributed to 'social and economic' factors. This report uses new language in terms of the 'mental patients' population and notes the Prisons Act 1923 and system rules delineated in 1947 were by then outdated and in need of urgent reorientation to 'modern opinion'. In the case of 'mental patients', as they are now labelled, the report notes that the.

> department is charged with care for all certifiable mental patients, a situation which the prison administration is reviewing in the light of modern practice. The ideal situation would be for the medical department to take full responsibility for all patients, with the prison supplying the appropriate building for the mentally insane and violent criminals only. This problem is a priority in 1969 (TPPD 1968, p. 23).

The 1970 report modifies this sentiment only by stating that while the Prisons Department is charged with care of certifiable mental patients and that care is subject to the supervision of a medical practitioner (TPPD 1970, p. 8). It is not until 1976 that the 'near completion' of a psychiatric ward at Vaiola Hospital was suggested. The 1977 report comments that the ward was now overdue. Then, in 1978, without much fanfare, a notation appears notifying the reader that the care of mental patients is 'no longer part of prison administration' and is instead handled by the Ministry of Health.

Later, in 1982, the presence of certain types of individuals with mental illness – the 'more violent patients'– is confirmed in the prison for 'security reasons', including one man held since 1972 at the Crown's direction after being found not criminally responsible for a murder due to his 'insanity'. There seemed to be some back and forth again in 1993 following implementation of the Mental Health Act 1992 (Government of Tonga 1992) with the report for that year noting that 'all patients were removed to the psychiatric ward at Vaiola in 1993 in accordance with the Mental Health Act', but again, the prison would house the violent patients per order of the Privy Council (No. 82, 27 April 1993).

Besides the specific mental health system implications of these reports – those specifically pertaining to the construction of institutions and practices designed to separate the general public from the mentally ill – the reports illuminate the development of thinking in Tonga officialdom both on the proper roles of professionals and the state in handling the mental patient and in terms of explaining or at least framing some of the significant social problems facing Tonga over the decades covered by these reports. For instance, the 1992 Police and Prisons Report notes that 'like all systems, there are failures, and causes have been attributed mainly to some form of mental abnormality which is properly the province of medicine and related sciences' (TPPD 1992, p. 181).Earlier in the same report, the presence of 'anxiety neurosis in young adults makes them susceptible to delinquency due to internal migration and shock of adaptation [urbanisation]' is observed (1992, p. 26).This exact language is found in numerous reports going back many years. Similarly, the 1989 report focuses on female crime and notes urbanisation as a contributing factor in the social decline. The growth of the urban centres of Nukualofa, Pangai and Neiafu has caused.

> a new way of life [to] develop[], quite different from that found in villages. This is characterized by an emphasis on material goods … the increasing demand for prestige, ownership of fashionable clothes, western style parties … and general wasteful living. (TPPD 1989, p. 31).

The same report finds, however, that drugs, often associated with a decline in traditional civic structures and increasing urbanisation as well as being linked to mental health matters, were not found to be a serious problem (1989, p. 44).

The Youth Mental Health in Tonga (2009) report notes that the increase in mental health public education efforts of recent years had yielded a common appreciation for the distinction between mental illness as disease and mental health as a state of being (Guttenbeil-Likiliki 2009, p. 21). The report also notes that prior to the 1940s no services at all were available to individuals with mental illness. In 1948 the Ministry of Health started to confine individuals suspected of having a mental illness, with the more agitated being confined in the national prison at Hu'atolitoli (Government of Tonga 1948). This practice persisted until 1978 when the Psychiatric Unit was established for these high-risk individuals within the health system and these individuals were sent from the prisons to the newly established unit. The Lunatic Act 1948 persisted, however, until the Mental Health Act 1992 updated the law to change terminology and to include drug addictions within the scope of state treatment efforts. Despite the updated law, medical and legal practitioners interviewed for this study viewed this law as an enigma that was largely unworkable from its inception: in fact no one could quite explain why it had been adopted at all (see also Poltorak 2002, p. 208). Notwithstanding this development, in the years that followed the 1992 Act, a Mental Health Welfare Officer post was established to liaise between the Ministry of Health and Tongan communities. A 1996 health survey was conducted and indicated the strong enduring practice for Tongans to first seek the assistance of traditional healers for many medical and particularly mental health concerns. In 1999 a psychiatric social worker position was created within the Ministry of Health. Shortly thereafter, Tonga embraced the 2001 statutory updates to the Mental Health Act, as discussed below.

In 2003 the new Mental Health Act 2001 came into force. Once again bureaucratic delays hindered its full implementation: in October 2007 the Act was only being implemented in Tongatapu since outer islands have no properly designated medical practitioners per the Act's requirements. The Act established a Mental Health Tribunal that is to include legal, lay and medical members as well as a Mental Health Advisory Committee to the National Health Development Committee. Before considering the Act, however, the role of civil society in the mental health system will be considered.

6.4 International and Regional Organisational Influences on Mental Health System Reform

As set forth above, Tonga has been a long-time recipient of financial and technical assistance from Australia, New Zealand, the United Kingdom, Japan, China, the United States and other countries. In addition, it has received grants, loans, and technical assistance from ADB and other international agencies for all manner of structural and development reform, including for its health system. According to an ADB publication, Pacific Choice: A New Vision for the Health Sector in Tonga (Tu'itahi 2008), the ADB's commitment has been consistent with the Paris Declaration on Aid Effectiveness and the Pacific Principles on Aid Effectiveness. ADB cites the efforts of other donor agencies –AusAID, NZAID, the UN Development Programme (UNDP), World Bank – as embracing similar capacity development (Tu'itahi 2008).The perceived aid programme shortcomings spawned 'approaches that are more systematic and integrated, and which focus more on developing country ownership and achievement of sustainable results' (Tu'itahi 2008, p. v). To that end, ADB's Pacific Department commissioned a regional study in 2007 that was rooted in 20 case studies from 12 countries prepared by 'Pacific Island consultants' and covering a wide range programmatic experiences including 'health and legal sector reform' (ADB 2007).

Tonga's health sector reforms began in January 1997 when the Government of Tonga (GoT) requested AusAID and the Ministry of Health to 'develop plans for an extensive program of support' (Tu'itahi 2008, p. 1).In the following month, a project identification team was in Tonga which recommended AusAID support a project that would 'improv[e] planning, management, and resource utilisation in the Ministry of Health'(Tu'itahi 2008, p. 1). Similar to Samoa's experience, Tonga has been undergoing the same epidemiological transition: as communicable diseases were brought under control, lifestyle disease (diabetes, obesity, cardiovascular disease and neoplasm (cancer) rose. The first phase of AusAID's project would find the 'core problem' to be lack of proper 'planning, management and coordination' and suggested that a properly functioning management system would contribute to improved planning, human resource management, training and communications.

The Ministry of Health suffered from problems common to the region and needed to address staff shortages, especially key medical staff, training and development of staff, procurement of essential equipment, drugs, maintenance, and repair of existing facilities, or provide much needed additional facilities; there was also a shortage of management capacity. The Ministry of Health had historically heavy relied upon donor and other external funding sources. Its major external donors have been New Zealand, Australia, Japan and WHO. With this money, however, Tonga has been successful in maintaining a 'reasonable level of health services' so that 'Tongans [now] enjoy a standard of health comparable to countries of similar per capita income' (ADB 2007).

Once the initial assessment was completed, a formal Memorandum of Understanding was signed between the Governments of Tonga and Australia setting forth the Tonga Health Sector Management and Planning Project with the overall goal 'to significantly improve the planning, management and delivery of health services of the Government of Tonga' (Governments of Australia & Tonga [GoAT] 1999). The project would be done in three phases. Phase I took place between February 1999 and February 2001 and involved an 'intensive diagnosis of capacity'. Phase II was designed to build on the Phase 1 diagnostics and Phase III – from September 2003 to August 2004 – focused on sustainability and coordination of achievements from the earlier phases as well as developing a model and guidelines that other government agencies could use. Phase III was extended and a completion phase was added focusing on sustainability. The project adopted a collaborative approach with close links between the project team and ministry staff. At the same time, cooperation parameters as well as stakeholder roles were clearly defined. This framework was intended to enable 'ministry staff to propose, negotiate, and ultimately define the key directions and focus of the project themselves' (GoAT 1999). The project involved highly interactive meetings, consultations and discussions and was referred to as a process of 'developing Tongan solutions to Tongan problems' (GoAT 1999). The reform process was headed by Hon. Viliami Ta'u Tangi, a surgeon appointed Minster of Health in March 1999. ADB (2007, p. 6) cited the minister assuming his duties early in the project cycle, his relative youth and attitude of openness to reform, and his willingness to put his office's resources behind the recommendations as key factors in the project's success. In addition, the pairing of this relatively youthful minister with a contemporary on the civil servant side in the person of the Director of Health was viewed as another good omen for the success of the reform process.

As discussed in Chap. 4 revealed that the Pacific Islands Mental Health Network (PIMHnet) has been a critical Pacific regional organisation active in mental health policy proliferation. PIMHnet, echoing the words of other NGOs active in Tonga, lamented the scarcity of funding for mental health issues given the predominance of NCD funding in the health field. The organisation lamented the focal shift in international funders, particularly in New Zealand where the organisation is based, away from 'poverty' as the main theme to 'sustainable development'. The effect of such a change required greater sophistication in the framing of aid and grant applications. While Samoa was held out as a model of partnership with the organisation, obstacles unique to Tonga were considered as the primary reasons that Tonga had not yet developed a policy. A representative of PIMHnet suggested.

> Yes, now Tonga has had quite a different relationship. We had a workshop in Tonga, we had a meeting in Tonga, we have given them, they've attended the workshop on how to develop policy, and we've had issues with Tonga in regard to the national focal contact being accessible and available. This is crucial because if the focal contact is off island for long periods of time, they don't take ownership of the work then we can't force ourselves on them, so we've worked with them at the pace they've wanted to work at. They've had a few key things to work with. I was about to go there when they had the ferry disaster then the tsunami, I say, they know we're willing to come in to support them and they just need to give us the dates. That's hard because you can't force them, you can't write it for them. They need to actually use this; it isn't something that just sits on a shelf.

From the Tongan perspective, the absence of a national focal contact was seen merely as a scheduling difficulty that would soon be remedied. But the absence of a central highly placed political insider during a key policy change moment would seem to be a significant factor in Tonga's incomplete adoption of a mental health policy. At the same time, the insistence on a local focal person for statutory development does not seem to have been a high priority. While local individuals reported being talked to by the foreign consultant about the law development in its embryonic development, drafting and editing until translation into Tongan seems to have been a predominantly foreign occupation.

In addition to PIMHnet's involvement, WHO contributed to these reforms, although to a lesser extent than AusAID and ADB. Yet, the consultant who drafted the Tongan Mental Health Act was in the employ of WHO, as opposed the AusAID-funded consultant in Samoa. A WHO respondent felt that in regard to mental health in Tonga,

> …I'd say it's not at all a major priority, I'd say it's probably an issue, probably a difficult issue as in a small country where you've got someone with mental illness it's a shame to a family, something people talk about, Tonga being a small country, everyone knows what's going on. There's not a lot of open advocacy on mental health, as far as I can see, it's been kept relatively quiet.

This connected with the overall sense that NCDs remained the top health priority in Tonga and there was little association of the persisting mental health burden with the increasing NCD burden. To that end, the WHO representative reported that.

> My first meeting with the Minister of Health … he said "we need assistance with NCDs"… [w]e also provide capacity development in terms of fellowships and provide a wide range of fellowships for doctors, nurses, health care technicians, etcetera, some short term some long term. When you look at a breakdown of our budget, most of it goes to building local capacity, followed by NCDs….

The sense was that mental health was neither being vigorously pursued by the Ministry of Health nor insisted upon by Geneva as a matter requiring sustained attention beyond the particular agenda of any particular ministry of health. As such, while the legislative reforms have occurred, the implementation of other aspects of mental health system development, such as community education to increase understanding of the complexities of mental ill-health and wellness as part of a stigma-reduction (and human rights protection platform) has failed to materialise.

6.5 Mental Health in Tonga: Perceptions of Homelessness, Domestic Violence and Suicide

As was found in respondent comments in Samoa, for most Tongan civil society organisations mental health was a tangential concern that was relevant to their primary responsibilities. These core responsibilities include domestic violence, drug abuse, or the concerns about deportees in Tonga. One domestic violence NGO representative opined that.

> I think mental health plays a huge role in domestic violence … [m]ental health pays a role in how you cope with these daily stresses and if you don't have the support base in the people around you it can lead on to something more serious, more damaging, it can lead to mental illness so mental health is very important.

This understanding was reflected in a comprehensive strategy to approaching policy development in key areas to the organisation. The domestic violence advocacy organisation consulted in this study saw its role in the policymaking process as showing.

> … why it is important that we promote and put our resources in to push the mental health issue forward because it can have such a damaging effect on women and children survivors. For instance our incest survivor cases, these are girls who have gone through years of sexual abuse. Helping them maintain their mental health helping them cope is so critical, the last thing we want to see is them having temporary or permanent mental illness … give case studies and talk about client stories, highlight the loop holes and the gaps where services are not available, you know, probably contribute to the myths that we continue to hear that maybe she is losing her nutters as she's just walked out of the house, she's shut her bedroom door and shut everyone out, you know, those little scenarios that have built up a lot of myths in our society, and then traditional healers are called to shake her out of her mindset.

NGOs, such as this domestic violence entity, had been inextricably linked to foreign aid and development policies and have had to adjust to changing times. This particular NGO existed at one time as part of the government, and while it provided consistent and regular funding and a guaranteed job for its employees, it had limited its advocacy activities due to its place as part of the apparatus of government. NZAID originally provided this funding but pulled out when priorities shifted from 2009. Since 2009, the organisation has subsisted on private funds from Mamma Cash in the Netherlands as well as AusAID funds. In addition, in order to fund more of its preferred activities to the community (e.g. safehouses for battered women) private donations of goods are relied upon.

Other concerns, such as suicide prevention entities, were also closely allied with other mental health civil society organisations. Tonga Lifeline is the most prominent of these and is under the direction of a local pastor who has worked for many years on these matters. He felt that the central role played by churches in service delivery to be.

> an element of pastoral care on the level of caring because everyone in the community or in the villages or islands here in Tonga is having a church and the church is belonging, under the umbrella of religious leaders and our traditional counsellors here in Tonga are the

> Ministers, Pastors of the local churches, what we are trying with Dr. Puloka is just to equip them with some technical skills on the basic levels just to know the first stages of the mental health problems.

While he had been working on these concerns for many years and Lifeline itself had been setup in Tonga in 1981, it was a 2005 regional meeting called by WHO that led to data creation there. He recalled this meeting as.

> the first time for us to consider that suicide is an issue here in Tonga but before that it wasn't an issue it was recorded but we did not do anything for suicide but since that time we came back and developed a network on suicide and started working on suicides and that's my closest link with the mental health issue.

The 2005 meeting and the international attention it generated, in his view, moved the issue of suicide from purely a church recognised issue in Tonga to the government agenda. He noted that the hotline received between 40–80 calls a month and nearly the same number of walk-ins. The increased emphasis had been occasioned by an international study undertaken in Tonga in conjunction with both WHO and Griffith University in Australia that was designed to assist states with developing a 'strategy to develop a preventive outreach to the community'.

In addition, this respondent referenced further partnerships with University of Adelaide and many local government entities. He acknowledged that the importance of these international partners and the network created in Manila as a result of the conference there was critical in establishing suicide prevention on the political agenda in Tonga. The conference was crucial in his view in expanding the focus of his organisation. One area of expanded interest is that of Tongan deportees being forcibly repatriated to Tonga from Australia, New Zealand and the United States, typically for a criminal conviction that has violated their immigration status. While the topic is beyond the scope of the present study, many of these deportees arrive with significant mental health conditions that pose a significant burden to the local mental health system and their presence was suggested in several interviews as a significant policy concern.

6.6 Tonga's Civil Society and the Mental Health System: Domestic Violence, Suicide Prevention and Disability Associations

There is an emerging NGO sector increasingly taking on a role in service delivery and policy advocacy in Tonga. One main concern raised by these actors was the still foreign nature of seeking counselling from secular counsellors outside of church and family. As one prominent NGO policy actor commented,

> counselling is a very new, Western concept to many Tongans. We've had to do a lot of awareness to encourage women to come in and talk to complete strangers about what is going on at home … so talking about mental health again, postnatal depression, Tongans believe this is a Palagi thing, how can you get depressed after having a baby unless you have 'aitu or mentally ill. Nothing about why is she depressed? What are the contributing factors to this? It is very myth based.

At the same time, NGOs tended not to view their role optimistically, at least in terms of service provision. One respondent lamented:

> Well, there is actually no service provider that states that they provide mental health counselling or services. For example, the services that we provide, we like to think makes some contribution to that to help women with depression at home due to physical or mental abuse or financial stresses … but there is no provider providing specific care.

In addition, NGOs noted the relatively minor importance given to mental health issues by the budgetary process. One respondent stated that 'I know for a fact that mental health and even the psychiatric ward received the lowest portion of the health budget in past years as it just wasn't prioritised. Noncommunicable diseases has been prioritised…' At the same time, homegrown NGOs have emerged in an attempt to shift these domestic health policy preferences. One of the more interesting recent developments in Tonga's NGO sector has been the establishment of the Tonga Mental Health and Disabilities Association in September 2010. The organisation emerged after a decade of advocacy for such a group by Dr. Puloka. One of the organisation's founders observed that the membership consists primarily of family members of those with mental illness but lacking in knowledge about the nature of the illnesses, prognosis and treatment. The initial efforts are to get the group established locally and there were no significant external links at the time of interview. The group's sole outside contact was with a New Zealand organisation that deals with Pacific Islander mental health concerns in New Zealand and thus has significant experience in this regard. The organisation was planning to start with some fundamental functions such as organising care for individuals in the mental health unit by providing supplemental food and clothing to the patients. They are preoccupied with 'the basics at this point before thinking about policy'. Despite the lack of policy focus at this point in time, circumstances seem to warrant attention. As this respondent said,

> when we went in as an association and viewed the conditions at the hospital we were very concerned. They are designed for 20 patients but is currently holding 57 and some of the male patients are sleeping outside. So I think it is important that they fill positions provided for under the Act.

The explanation for the state of matters within the mental health system is linked to the nation's politics. The lack of individual advocacy in Tonga was cited as being a possible contributing factor for this and was linked to a culture within which.

> doctors are highly regarded. We always look to them as being helpers so I think Tongan's are very reluctant to question why something has happened… Tongans are very reluctant to take [an issue] to court [because] the professionals they see as very important. I think it is also institutional, we don't have clear guidelines in the legislation or in the procedure about how we can complain. Most people think they only way they could complain is to the Minister and this is seen as too much to do.

At the same time, Tonga's civil society stakeholders tend to view the political reforms positively in the hopes of establishing a clear policy serving to guide the Ministry of Health and to provide information to the public, as well as provide clearer guidance for lodging complaints. As one respondent speaking on the importance of policy within the new governmental context pointed out,

> [w]e now have a new government in place that will change every 4 years, so having a policy in place will help to each new administration but also for directing the legislations well so that if we have legislation that is falling behind in terms of practices and processes, then it can be changed more easily if the policy is heading in a different direction.

Other civil society organisations in Tonga, with broader scopes, reported being engaged in mental health issues, internally. All credited Dr. Puloka as the driving force behind their engagement and more than one likened his role as that of an 'eyeopener' to the issues of mental health in the social context.

Tonga Community Development Trust (TCDT) is a local NGO working on all manner of community development matters including health, water, voting and human rights and environmental issues. In 2009 they completed a project funded by NZAID to prepare a situational analysis of Tonga's youth mental health. The organisation produced an analysis with Dr. Puloka's full support but it has not been endorsed by the Minister of Health. This failure to endorse the report meant that it was not promoted as a government project. One commentator notes that this lack of support might have stemmed from the fact that.

> when the report came out there were still a lot of political issues and during the political reform here in Tonga, he wasn't sure if it was a good thing to endorse it or not [...] we did a lot of awareness raising with youth, different youth groups throughout Tonga, we did some workshops here in Hapa'i, Vav'au, trying to develop a better understanding of some of the cause of mental illness and to advocate for the importance of mental health....

More general civil society organisations such as TCDT are market-driven. In a competitive market for funder dollars, NGOs (and their agendas) must follow the money. As such, where money is made available for youth mental health, TCDT devotes appropriate resources to the application for said funds. It is critical that there be grant writers and other local experts on hand to provide some institutional support for such initiatives, as Dr. Puloka provided for TCDT. The problem seems to be that with a diverse set of priorities that are both board-driven and contingent on international fund availability, the market and hence products are dictated by the supply; in this setting where funds are made available for mental health, efforts are put in applying for them. TCDT reported seeing only one viable funding possibility come through in the years since its youth report and there was insufficient lead-time to assemble a proposal.

6.7 Tonga's Mental Health Law

Tonga's legislative history on mental health began with the Lunatics Detention Act of 1948 (No. 9) which defined a 'lunatic' as an 'idiot and any other person of unsound mind' but defined neither of these terms in the law. This law appears to have been based on a Fijian Lunatic's Act of the era, itself based upon British mental health law. In essence, the Act permitted the detention of one deemed a 'lunatic' in any 'place of detention', defined as 'any house or building', as designated by the

Privy Council. There was no requirement that this be either the prison or hospital, though the prison became designated as the nation's asylum. This law persisted until 1992, when the Mental Health Act of that year repealed the singular 'lunatic' designation with three terms: 'mental disorder', which was understood as 'mental illness, arrested or incomplete development of the mind, psychopathic disorder and any other disorder or disability of the mind'; 'mental handicap', defined as 'a state of arrested or incomplete development of mind which can render a person incapable of independent living'; and 'mental illness', defined as a 'psychiatric disorder which substantially disturbs a person's thinking, feeling, or behaviour and impairs the person's ability to function' (Mental Health Act [MHA] 1992, s. 2). In addition, the Act introduced the notions of 'alcoholic' and 'drug addict' as included dependents on these substances. The Act was a curiosity in the sense that, as reflected in this research as well as Poltorak's (2002), both lawyers and medical personnel found the Act utterly unworkable and the degree of consultation between these professionals and the law's drafters seems limited.

By 2000, an opportunity for reform of the law arose with the health sector reform programme initiated in partnership with AusAID and the presence of an Australian legal consultant with experience on such matters (Fadgen 2015). Records of the Parliamentary consideration of Tonga's Mental Health Act 2001 contain only a very limited, but revealing, discussion of the proposal (GoT 2003). The Minister of Health was present to address questions and Dr. Puloka reported being on-hand, outside of the chamber, in case he was needed to address any specific points raised by the members; he wasn't called. The Minister of Health presented the law as necessary to permit voluntary treatment of individuals since all previous laws only envisioned involuntary, custodial treatment. An issue was raised by Samiu Vaipulu, Tonga's Deputy Prime Minister at the time of writing, regarding a 'doctor working in this area', who must be assumed to be Dr. Puloka since there were no other doctors working in mental health at this time. Vaipulu said that this doctor was alleged to inappropriately use his authority by threatening to detain people with whom he is unhappy under the guise of a mental disturbance (GoT 2003). The Minister of Health responded that one of the purposes of the new law is to more actively bring the judiciary into the involuntary commitment process to ensure effective review of medical determinations in this regard. Consensus was soon reached, however, around the notion that in emergency situations, those in which there is a public behaviour that might cause harm to members of the public, the doctor should retain (as he does under the 2001 Act) the authority to immediately detain an individual. Interestingly, the parliamentarians make reference to a specific individual known throughout Tonga to travel when his mental condition sufficiently deteriorates, to travel from Ha'apai to Tongatapu and behave erratically (see also Poltorak 2002).

Tonga's legislative changes in the area of mental health occurred within the health sector reforms in 2000, culminating in the Mental Health Act (2001) ultimately adopted in 2003. AusAID had been enlisted to assist (in both dollars and expertise) with the overall health sector reforms involving management and human resource reforms as well as registration provisions for doctors and pharmacists. As had been the case in Samoa, Tonga was provided an Australian legal consultant via WHO to provide the legal drafting for the respective Acts. The drafts were done in conjunction with local officials or experts. Dr. Puloka reported that the Australian consultant.

> …was a specialist in health legislation and mental health, she came and we did a lot of talking. She came many times; she came for mental health and came for the others [proposed health legislation] as well. But she consulted me a lot of time….
>
> […]
>
> So we were involved in the sharing of information with [the consultant] and I understand that although she drafted the law, it was based largely on an existing law form Australia and while I do not have a copy of it but that is what I understand. You understand that in the past here in Tonga other Ministries, as no one is the expert, they often followed laws from New Zealand or some place and just change some details and make it the official document for Tonga. That has been the common practice. Now there is a greater desire to inform the public now when making an official document.

This consultant, even though working as part of the AusAID reforms, is believed to have been funded by WHO. In addition, the product she produced underwent considerable editing by the then Chief Judge in Tonga, a British judge who had worked in Tonga and other islands for many years. One respondent reported that perhaps 40per cent of the original draft was cut by the then Chief Justice Gordon Ward and other members of the Law Reform Committee.

The result of these efforts, the Mental Health Act 2001 (Government of Tonga 2001), defined 'mental disorder' as a 'clinical condition in which a person manifests abnormal behaviour that does not meet the criteria for mental illness in this Act but the person is dangerous to himself or to others' (Government of Tonga 2001, s. 3). 'Mental illness' is in turn defined as 'a condition which seriously impairs, either temporarily or permanently, the mental functioning of a person in one or more of the areas of thought, mood, volition, perception, orientation or memory and is characterized by the presence of at least one of the following symptoms: delusions; hallucinations; serious disorder of the content or form of thought; or of mood; or sustained or repeated irrational behaviour which indicates the presence of at least one of those behaviours' (Government of Tonga 2001, s. 3).

As can instantly be seen, the definitions adopted here are more nuanced and explicit than the 1992 Act. Similarly, the specific separate categories for drug and alcohol addictions were removed. The law, however, failed to incorporate many of the formal rights protections later found in Samoa's mental health law, based on both Australian law but also those reflecting the MI Principles. For instance, one of the identified source laws for Tonga's Act was the Victorian Mental Health 1986, which, in common with the Samoan Act, made explicit policy exclusions from the definition of mental illness for conditions such as acting immorally, for promiscuity, failing to promote or exhibit preferred political beliefs, or the consumption of drugs or alcohol. These provisions are firmly in both the Victorian law as well as the MI Principles yet are conspicuously absent in the 2001 Tongan Mental Health Act. It seems unlikely that a consultant brought in by WHO would purposely exclude these provisions. Instead it is far more likely the provisions were removed by the Law

Reform Committee headed by the then Chief Justice. Unfortunately, the dearth of available commentary on the legislative process as well as the unavailability of key participants in this reform process leaves any possible answer to this question speculative.

6.8 The Absence of a Mental Health Policy and Public Education Efforts

Given the preference for establishing a policy that would later inform the law changes, one might ask why in Tonga, given the 1992 Act was at least a much more modern law, a policy was not first developed. Dr. Puloka was also unsure why this had occurred.

> Puloka: That's one thing (laughs) when I heard the law I thought the cart comes before the horse. This is not just in mental health; in other Ministries too it's the same I think too. That's the way it works here. The Act comes first before the policy. When the Act came I was surprised and I felt the policy should come first and the law later.
>
> INTERVIEWER:How has this worked, having the law first?
>
> Puloka: I found now that the difference between policy and law because the policy needs workshops, technical people, and there needs to be a lot of money and that's why when I mentioned before that Tonga usually makes policy by copying overseas, New Zealand law, they do it without consultants, they just modify it to make it fit Tonga and it involved not a lot of work.

In fact, in 2004 a policy workshop was held in Tonga and both international consultants and domestic policy actors attended. The session had all the elements of the Samoan conference held in 2003 but did not result in the creation of a policy and was originated by PIMHnet to serve precisely the same purpose. There were perhaps several reasons for the lack of success in Tonga's case. The most critical difference is that the leader of this cohort, Dr. Puloka, had left for several months overseas and was not present to push the process along and there was not as much in the way of administrative or policy support staff in Tonga as in Samoa to assist. At the time, the officials engaged in Tonga's state-based mental health system numbered two: a psychiatrist and a clinical social worker who works with Dr. Puloka. Dr. Puloka attributed the failure to develop a policy to a lack of local policy expertise as well as 'infrastructure and money', and because mental health was not made a priority by the then government.

Interestingly, however, lacking a policy (or significant budgetary allocations) hasn't prevented Dr. Puloka from undertaking the community education component found in many other regional policy documents. In fact, this education component is a core aspect of Dr. Puloka's work:

> I try to change people's perception. Writing about possession as mental illness in 1997–1998 I made many TV programs that really had an impact on people we tell about how we were able to find out it was later in those years we had a lot of phone calls after we talk about anxiety disorders, depression, psychosis, people hearing voices, also higher members of society. It really had an impact on people, so there has been a change in the perception of mental health. So I would say that mental health is becoming, they do understand more about mental health issues now. In other words, people are now looking at mental health in and of itself rather than having something to do with spirit or something else although it is not yet to an acceptable level to me but it is something that is changing.... I even wrote one article in the paper every week for 1 year and I have about 45 articles and probably have more than 1000 now, in Tongan. The English words people don't understand so I explain in Tongan and the culture and it improves the understandings.

Moreover, Dr. Puloka makes television appearances and hosts an occasional talk-back radio programme with the express purpose of raising public awareness of mental illness. He also actively translates medical terminology into Tongan. He mentioned many of social ills as symptoms of the mental health challenges in Tonga including alcohol and drugs, as well as domestic violence as both symptom and cause of mental ill health. In addition, in conjunction with the Seattle Theological College, he has taught a segment of a local curriculum on mental health and disorders in local churches. Despite these efforts, all respondents felt that mental health as reflected in policy, law or official practice was not well understood by the population and that traditional understandings persisted. The Mental Health Act 2001 was felt to be positive in that it created a complaint process for those subject to an order and ensured dignity and access to justice.

Dr. Puloka reported the importance of access to international resources in framing his understanding of mental health policy and law, particularly the WHO guidance package for legislation. He also reported information available through the Australian and New Zealand College of Psychiatry was of use but to a lesser extent. Attendance at international conferences was not instrumental mostly due to his inability to secure funds enabling him to attend the conferences. Dr. Puloka was hopeful, as were so many other respondents in this study, that the political changes brought about by the democracy movement would have a positive effect on raising mental health's lowly agenda position. He felt that in order for it to move up the agenda, however, he would still require a 'champion':

> If you come to a brick wall, identify a champion to advocate for you. My advocate now is a politician. He is a bit aggressive this one, and I like aggressive people to do this. Aggressive to do something that will benefit the people.

There was a recognition that having a reasonably current law is one thing but having institutional support for mental health as a valid area for the Ministry of Health's work was another and, notwithstanding the international support available to nurture a mental health system, in many ways Tonga's has had to develop as an intricate set of professional practices embedded within the Tongan cultural context outside of the official law and formal policy process.

6.9 Conclusion

Contemporary mental health principles, such as respect and dignity for the individual, reducing stigma associated with a mental illness, and community care have been subjects of both local and informal initiatives. In fact, these efforts had been underway before mental health had been prioritised on the international level. The formalisation of these principles, however, involved the presence of local professional-experts to 'contextualise' the international renditions of 'best practice' into the local. Tonga's legal framework, in contrast, did not necessitate local professional experts but required the availability of international experts to provide the necessary official 'confidence' in the proposed reforms necessary to see their adoption.

The absence of a written policy document in Tonga can be understood as a function of the absence of a local bureaucratic champion during the critical policy opportunity provided by international funding and motivation to develop and implement these policies. In fact, the political upheaval in Tonga, which may have triggered the key mental health advocate's absence for the critical period in question, might be more of a critical factor in Tonga's incomplete adoption of a mental health policy. If the former Minister of Health, who was observed by foreigners to be a willing and enthusiastic partner in health sector reforms, was equally viewed by indigenous mental health advocates and civil society stakeholders as the major impediment to the government not embracing the youth mental health report findings, then it is unlikely he would have supported a government mental health policy that would have largely embraced many of the same principles and findings of that report.

In essence, the political conflict in Tonga between the democracy advocates and the more conservative elements of society served to complicate the more comprehensive development of a mental health policy by driving a wedge (or further separating the divide) between mental health's main advocate and the Minister of Health who had to endorse such initiatives. This may explain why there was near consensus amongst respondents that, with a new Minister coming in to office at the time of this research, a mental health policy might at last be forthcoming. This is not to say, however, that the former Minister was purposefully impeding a mental health policy for the whole of Tonga because of a purely personal or political dispute with the opposition. It seems more likely that the political infighting in such a small community served to create incentives for the local mental health chief advocate to depart, which happened to coincide with the regional push for policy development.

Tonga's legal framework, in contrast, has long been inextricably linked to the legal practitioners and jurists, many of whom were British, Australian and New Zealand expatriates; the local practitioners and judges were all trained in one of these three nation's law schools. In other words, there has been low connectivity between these laws and the community because they were hardly ever utilised or encountered by large numbers of people beyond the bench and bar and the medical professionals whose evidence was necessary to issue confinement orders. In fact, Dr. Puloka reiterated one of his priorities in the recent Mental Health Act was to further restrict the type of legal practitioner capable of working on mental health as one holding a law degree and not a local practitioner who had become qualified through apprenticeship. This step, whilst assuring a degree of professional intimacy with the law and legal thinking, serves to further entrench mental health determinations within the narrow confines of a technical, legal determination made by 'experts'. Moving the mental health issue up the policy agenda, however, requires broader community buy-in, a reality fast approaching, it would seem, based on the emergence of advocacy organisations and the spread of mental health and wellness ideas and concepts into other policy realms such as domestic violence, drugs and alcohol, and the increasing importance of the politically sensitive deportee question.

Finally, it is worth noting the juxtaposition of the Mental Health Act 2001 with the Acts preceding it and immediately following it in the official Legislation of Tonga: an act regulating eye surgeries and the act addressing the kingdom's rubbish. Placing mental health between these two acts effectively provides us with a useful metaphor for analysing the function of a mental health system. Dr. Puloka lamented how mental health had always been a low priority and the facility he now oversees had been placed next to the open septic tanks of the hospital; the individuals in his facility were the most underserved of all the medical cases. Mental health laws have been placed between laws that regulate corneal transplants(operations that help someone to see) and laws that regulate how Tongan's manage refuse. As Dr. Puloka explained, he sees his mission as a champion for those afflicted with mental illness, to not only treat them but to educate the population as to the true nature of these diseases in hopes of eliminating the stigma. Having seen the truth of these conditions, according to his training and experience, Dr. Puloka hopes to stimulate a discussion on how best to manage, treat and care for those once considered 'waste' by the social system (Fadgen 2016). His mission, as he sees it, is to have the public consider how best to redeem individuals afflicted with mental disorder and to, in a sense, recycle their lives, to make them function in society as contributing members of the social fabric of Tongan society. Indeed, the placement of mental health along with these other acts may have been accidental but it has proven prophetic for those few individuals engaged in mental health advocacy in Tonga.

We will turn now to a combined discussion of Tonga's and Samoa's mental health system development over the past decade and the factors that account for the adoption of an updated mental health law in both countries, which might also explain why of the two, Tonga failed to adopt a mental health policy, despite having a similarly placed indigenous mental health professional in place.

References

Asian Development Bank. (2007). *Pacific Subregion Development Effectiveness Brief*, Manila: Asian Development Bank.
Asian Development Bank. (2011a). *Development effectiveness brief Tonga sustaining a strong culture while building the future*. Manila: ADB.
Asian Development Bank. (2011b). *Asian Development Bank & Tonga FACT SHEET, Manila.*
Campbell, I. C. (1992a). The emergence of parliamentary politics in Tonga. *Pacific Studies, 15*(1).
Campbell, I. C. (1992b). A historical perspective on aid & dependency: The example of Tonga. *Pacific Studies, 15*(3).
Campbell, I. C. (2005). The quest for constitutional reform in Tonga. *The Journal of Pacific History, 40*(1), 91–104.
Clement, D. (1982). Samoan folk knowledge of mental disorders. In A. Marsella, J. White, & M. Geoffrey (Eds.), *Cultural conceptions of mental health & therapy*. Dordrecht: D. Reidel.
Fadgen, T. (2015). International and regional influences on Tonga's Mental Health Act' 21. *Canterbury L.Rev, 145.*
Fadgen, T. (2016). Constructing madness: Exercising legal and cultural power in Tonga. In S. Marusek (Ed.), *Book Chapter: Synesthetic legalities: Sensory dimensions of law and jurisprudence*. Routledge.
Government of Australia and Government of Tonga. (1999). *Memorandum of understanding on health sector reform initiative*. Nuku'alofa.
Government of Tonga. (1948). *Lunatics Detention Act.*
Government of Tonga. (1992). *Mental Health Act.*
Government of Tonga. (2001). *Mental Health Act.*
Government of Tonga. (2003). *Record of parliamentary debate on Mental Health Act 2001.* Parliament of Tonga: Nuku'alofa.
Government of Tonga Police Fire Services & Prisons Department (TPFPD). (1950–1992). *Tonga Police Force, Tonga Fire Services, & Prisons Department annual report*. Tonga Police Force: Nuku'alofa.
Guttenbeil-Likiliki, O. (2009). *Youth & mental health in Tonga: A situational analysis*. Suva: Foundation of the Peoples of the South Pacific International.
James, K. (2002). The Recent Elections in Tonga: Democratic Supporters Win but Does Democracy Follow? *The Journal of Pacific History, 37*(3), 313–322.
Ka'ili, T. (2017). *Marking indigeneity: The Tongan art of socio-spatial relations*. Tucson: University of Arizona Press.
Lātūkefu, S. (1975). *The Tongan constitution: A brief history to celebrate its centenary*. Nuku'alofa: Tonga Traditions Committee.
Lātūkefu, S. (1997). The impact of the British on the Tongan traditional concept of justice & law. In: H. Hiery, J. Mackenzie, (Ed.), *European impact & Pacific influence: British & German colonial policy in the Pacific Islands & the Indigenous response*. New York: Tauris Academic Studies.
Lawson, S. (1996). *Tradition versus democracy in the South Pacific: Fiji. Tonga & Western Samoa.* Melbourne: Cambridge University Press.
Marcus, G. (1980). *The nobility & the chiefly tradition in the modern Kingdom of Tonga.* Wellington: Polynesian Society.
Newbury, C. (2003). *Patrons, clients & empire: Chieftaincy & Over-rule in Asia, Africa, & the Pacific*. Oxford: Oxford University Press.
Ntumy, M., & Angelo, A. (1993). *South Pacific Islands legal systems*. Honolulu: University of Hawaii.
Philips, S. (2004). The organization of ideological diversity in discourse: Modern & neotraditional visions of the Tongan State. *American Ethnologist, 31*(2), 231–250.
Poltorak, M. (2002). *Aspersions of agency ghosts, love & sickness in Tonga*. PhD book, University College London.

Powles, C. G., & Pulea, M. (1988). *Pacific courts & legal systems*. Suva: University of the South Pacific.

Scarr, D., Gunson, N., & Terrell, J. (Eds.). (1998). *Echoes of the Pacific War*. Canberra: Target Oceania.

Tu'itahi, K. (2008). *A new vision for the health sector in Tonga: Change & capacity development strategies*. Manila: Asian Development Bank.

Weiss, P. (2004). *American taboo: A murder in the peace corps*. Pymble/New York: Harper Collins.

Chapter 7
What Insights Can Be Gained from Mental Health Policy Change in Samoa and Tonga?

This chapter has four main aims. Firstly, I will consider whether there were different types of policy transferred as part of the mental health policy transfers discussed in the two previous chapters. Secondly, I identify the different types of actors engaged in different types of policy transfer and how they were involved. Thirdly, I explore the different roles that these actors played in localising transferred policies. Fourthly, I consider variation in the degree of localisation depending on the policy type and actors involved in transfer. There were two related questions which emerged from the research assembled here: firstly, whether the mental health policy transfers in Samoa and Tonga were similar or different. Secondly, I will address whether any of the actors involved in the examined transfer could be considered 'policy entrepreneurs'. I provide general conclusions from the preceding chapters concerning the understanding of mental health by policy actors in Samoa and Tonga. These actors' discussion of the different types of 'policy' implicated in the mental health system is then considered. The policy typology I develop from these responses and elaborate on below has been organised into three divisions: formal (laws); quasi-formal (policy statements, instruments); and informal (government actor practices in mental health service delivery).

Following this preliminary discussion, this chapter will reach several conclusions about mental health policy transfer and localisation in Samoa and Tonga. I set forth five specific conclusions in this part. Firstly, I establish the justification that policy transfer has, in fact, occurred in Samoa and Tonga due to the absence of an independent domestic explanation which could adequately account for each nation's decision to engage in mental health policy reform when each did. Instead, formal and quasi-formal transfers occurred due to international policy agendas that included mental health policy reform. Secondly, I contextualise the formal, quasi-formal and informal tiers of policy transfer. In each of these subsections I advance arguments concerning the conditions under which each type of transfer occurred and the actors engaged in each level. Each instance of formal transfer examined in this book involved very little indigenous policy input. Instead, foreign policy experts were heavily relied upon to craft suitable mental health laws for each country. Moreover,

T. P. Fadgen, *Mental Health Public Policy in Global Context*,
https://doi.org/10.1007/978-981-15-6479-6_7

both Samoa and Tonga are unitary states with Westminster-style parliaments with relatively high party discipline, making serious opposition to government proffered legislation highly unlikely. In the latest iteration of formal policy transfer in Samoa and Tonga, policy actors perceived these laws to more closely align with indigenous values even though they were not crafted by indigenous actors. This is because the adopted laws were part of the overall health reforms implemented through domestic political processes.

Quasi-formal transfers, as a middle category of policy transfer, tended to be centrally derived and controlled yet involved community consultations on official drafts. Since this tier of transfer directly implicated community input, conditions of relative political stability were necessary for successful transfer. Political instability, as occurred in Tonga during the relevant years of reform, resulted in unsuccessful quasi-formal policy transfer. Informal policy transfer, evidenced by government actors implementing changes to practice or service delivery without resorting to or even necessarily pursuing either formal or quasi-formal policy changes, required the presence of an interested, indigenous, professionally trained leader with high social status in order to occur. In addition, the actors here both exhibited a high degree of enthusiasm for their reform efforts, were motivated by personal feelings about proper treatment regimes, and were prepared to take risks to advance their vision. Finally, this level of transfer was highly hybridised between official psychological or psychiatric best practices and the actors' individual constructions of their respective cultural contexts. Unlike formal and quasi-formal policy transfers, informal transfers were purely agent-driven.

This chapter will conclude by identifying important insights for policy researchers interested in understanding specific policy transfer episodes. Firstly, as noted above, policy transfer is a useful framework, but disaggregating policy into formal, quasi-formal and informal policy types would add significant nuance to policy transfer, localisation and translation. Secondly, a close examination of the types of actors involved in policy transfer, localisation and translation activities and an exploration of their assumptions concerning the particular policy contexts within which they are working will provide useful information for understanding policy transfer success and failure. Moreover, such an examination will provide valuable insights into the form and substance of policies and laws that have been transferred. Lastly, considering the unique role of domestic, cultural insiders and their contributions to policy transfer, localisation and translation, across all three levels of policy is vital to determining the sufficiency of local ownership of the policy process. These actors, which I have labelled culture entrepreneurs, are likely active wherever public policies are being introduced as part of international development processes or as part of bilateral and multilateral organisations are mediating a policy change process. Again, as the cases and previous scholarship considered throughout this book have clearly demonstrated, success in policy transfer is not limited to adoption of a policy or law but in its successful implementation. Successful implementation is most likely to occur when policies are sufficiently localised and translated to meet local needs.

7.1 Defining and Locating Mental Health in Samoa and Tonga

The WHO was found to be the primary international actor engaged in the international mental health policy context. Nearly all respondents defined 'mental health' as some derivative of the World Health Organization (WHO) definition as a 'state of wellbeing' for self-actualisation and possessing the necessary skills to cope with the 'stressors' common in the contemporary world. The definition was always an individual one: the individual should have the ability to confront the modern world, and the individual should have the capabilities to be a productive, engaged citizen. All respondents contrasted this with the Samoan and Tongan understanding of 'mental health' as rooted in the collective context of family and community, often observing that individuals are rarely considered and that the health of the group is paramount. Mental illness, by extension, is the inability to manage these factors and because of that the suffering of a period of deviant behaviour (e.g. depression might result in withdrawing from the family, sleeping for long periods of time, etc., or manifest in violence or addictions). As outlined above, the commonly held explanations for these conditions amongst both publics are often ascribed to the work of spirits, particularly deceased family members. Moreover, all respondents shared a common understanding of the definition of mental health and illness and also universally found the public to hold on to traditional beliefs and not defining mental health in the same manner; a disconnect between policy, policymaker and public.

7.1.1 Identification of Mental Health and Illness as Socially Situated Phenomenon: Common Themes

There were four central themes and two ancillary themes identified in the interviews conducted for this book related to the issue of mental health in Samoa and Tonga. Firstly, respondents noted the persistence amongst each nation's population of traditional indigenous belief structures regarding mental health and that using the state-based psychiatric services was normally a last resort. Secondly, and related to the first theme, respondents reported the continued centrality of traditional medicine and healers in the mental health system and that securing their involvement in official state-based health systems has been met with mixed results. Thirdly, respondents acknowledged a strong association of mental illness with social ills such as suicide, homelessness, drug and alcohol abuse, and domestic violence. This phenomenon coincides with predominant beliefs on the relationship between mental disorder and these social problems throughout the world. Fourthly, respondents referenced the enduring nature of the dire social stigma in nearly all facets of social, community and economic existence. Related to this theme was recognition of the insidious discrimination accompanying a mental health diagnosis, primarily for those utilising state-based psychiatric services. There were also two ancillary themes related to the mental health sector and aftermath of the policy reform initiatives. There was nearly uniform scepticism that the policies would ever be fully implemented due to scarce resources, both financial and in terms of requisite professional expertise. A notable countertheme to this general wariness was found in the promise seen in the emergent nongovernmental sectors in both countries. I address these themes in more detail below.

Government officials and NGO representatives held essentially similar understandings of the mental health systems. What is interesting, however, is that NGO representatives mention government more prominently in their discussions of mental health overall. This is likely due to the centrality of the public mental health sectors in both countries in terms of programs and services. Moreover, both groups tended to emphasise the state's role relative to the management of mental illness as opposed to mental health promotion. Following, Fennell (1999), these findings suggest the both populations tended to emphasise negative controls upon the state vis-à-vis individuals proposed for involuntary treatment rather than the international prerogative of the affirmative duty of the state to create a context within which the individual can most likely attain an overall state of wellbeing.

As a general matter, this book affirms previous studies' findings (see e.g. Clement 1982; Poltorak 2007) of enduring indigenous mental health beliefs and practices amongst Samoans and Tongans. Additionally, this study finds that the persistent traditional belief structures, which are held by many amongst the general populations of both countries, are fundamentally different than those held by the policymakers and reflected in the laws, policies and practices in both countries. This study also notes the widely held perception of policy actors, both foreign and domestic, of this divergent belief structure around mental illness. Norris et al. (2009) offers a recent report into the cross-national qualitative study of Samoan treatment-seeking practices in both Samoa and New Zealand, and notes the phenomenon of a widespread sense that mental illness or disorder properly belongs to the category of 'Samoan illness' as opposed to *Palagi* (Western) illness (see also Agnew et al. 2000). This book confirms this general point and finds the delineation between Samoan and European conditions is perceived by relevant policy actors in both Samoa and Tonga.

Samoan policy actors perceived that their population, while not rejecting Western medicine, particularly with regard to mental health, based their categorisation of an illness as Samoan or Western on how it responds to treatment. Mental illnesses are not often 'cured' like an infection but are instead subject to symptom management. As such, many traditional remedies such as massage and gentleness with the afflicted work to alleviate symptoms and to restore the individual's behaviour to a culturally acceptable baseline. The most critical insight offered by Norris et al. (2009), however, is their finding of the importance of including the family in the treatment planning, given the central role of 'family beliefs and positions and family influences on individuals' which will vary by illness (see also Sobralske 2006, p. 1473; Puloka 1997).

There were differing opinions on the proper role of traditional healers in the mental health system. Most respondents saw them as rather unsophisticated on such matters, as being both unregulated and uncertain in number and methods. Many felt the healers should be brought into the official system and thus regulated whilst others felt that the medical system should learn from some of the more perceived successful practices in which these practitioners engage (e.g. massage, oils, and use of a calm and welcoming demeanour). Similarly, given the central place of the church in Tongan communities, it might come as no surprise that the pastors were thought critical to an effective mental health system in Tonga. Dr. Mapa Puloka sought to educate the pastors and ministers on symptom recognition and when to refer individuals on to the psychiatrist for treatment.

All respondents linked mental ill health with other social ills, mostly based on anecdote or personal experience. For instance, a Tongan suicide prevention NGO representative saw his agency's involvement with an overall mental health strategy as due to his understanding that underlying mental health conditions, such as depression, can often lead to a suicide attempt. As such, he found common cause with Dr. Puloka's agenda. Other common social factors include alcohol and drug abuse; the decline in traditional family and community-based life; the presence and experience of deportees from Australia, New Zealand and the United States; domestic violence and child abuse; homelessness and women's health (e.g. postnatal depression).

A further common theme both in the international literature and in the comments of respondents in both Samoa and Tonga is the related issues of stigma and discrimination. Dr. Puloka acknowledged that since individuals are usually only referred to his unit after all traditional attempts to intervene in the mental condition have been exhausted, they are often subject to the worst stigma and discrimination. This, in part, explains why people are still hesitant to bring a family member in for evaluation, preferring a string of traditional healers that might or might not heal or exacerbate the condition. The stigma associated with traditional remedies is much less severe and permanent than a hospital admission. Public education is likely the only remedy to such endemic beliefs, which might partly explain Dr. Puloka's many efforts to raise the profile of mental health throughout Tonga as well as his creative efforts to localise the foreign concepts and terminology of mental health and illness. Moreover, the efforts to reduce stigma and discrimination will likely involve the government's eventual embrace of the Youth Mental Health Report and the promulgation of a policy and support of Dr. Puloka's efforts if there is any hope of reducing the stigma associated with use of the medical system for such maladies.

The emergence of a nongovernment sector to offer treatment, temporary housing and support to individuals in both Samoa and Tonga was also commented upon as a recent and critical development in each nation's mental health system. Perhaps unsurprisingly, the individuals active in these efforts are arriving (or returning) from abroad, particularly New Zealand. Wilson (2000), writing on New Zealand's mental health system, notes a trend over the late 1990s towards privatisation of mental health services, in line with broader government reforms. As a complement, a private sector of providers has emerged to take advantage of government (and international donor) funded service programmes. Following a similar pattern is the recent founding of groups such as Goshen Trust by a Samoan New Zealander who worked in similar capacities in New Zealand. It was only in the mid 1990s that New Zealand undertook the task of setting goals and strategies designed to streamline and improve service and reduce discrimination and stigma, and to develop related policies and programmes under the large umbrella of mental health, including alcohol and drug policy. In both Samoa and Tonga, suicide and domestic violence support and advocacy NGOs were firmly established in civil society and were considered well-respected leaders within the NGO community. These actors endured without any formal policy framework yet were founded and supported by foreign civil society sponsored projects. Both nations have long had dedicated NGOs on this issue who provide crisis support and limited, focused counselling.

Respondents from both countries provided strikingly consistent accounts for locating mental health within the particular social contexts in both countries. The respondents supported, for instance, the preference for community treatment and the need to avoid institutionalisation, reflecting both international best practice and traditional notions of an appropriate locus of mental health care. At the same time, the tension existing between traditional constructions of mental illness and science-based ones was universally recognised. These observations led many respondents to note the importance of increasing community mental health literacy through community education initiatives. Moreover, nearly all respondents continued to see a place for traditional healers in mental health service delivery. The need for a viable NGO sector to assist in service delivery, despite most health services in both countries being central government responsibilities, was common amongst most study respondents. All actors from government, traditional and NGO fora were thought to be essential in changing the general stigma attached to mental illness in both cultures and the resulting discrimination experienced by individuals labelled as such. Related to this, respondents commonly associated mental illness with social problems such as suicide, drug and alcohol abuse, and domestic violence. Finally, many respondents remained dubious on the prospects for successful implementation of the new laws and policies due to inadequate resources, yet a consensus emerged on the necessity of such follow-through to address these numerous concerns. With this shared demographic, cultural and thematic context established, I next turn to consideration of similarities within each nation's mental health policy contexts involving the type of policy changes pursued concerning mental health.

7.2 Three Levels of Policy Change: Formal, Quasi-Formal and Informal

Given the inclusive definition of 'policy' with which I began this book as a category embodying legal structures, written policy instruments and government practices, we can analyse a range of transferred items in the cases in this study. I find it helpful to separate these observed mental health policy changes into three distinct policy levels. Firstly, at the 'formal' policy level, artefacts tended to be prescriptive and involve professional construction of a 'problem' (e.g. as a legal or medical matter) and the state apparatus in delivering curative or custodial care (e.g. laws designating certain bureaucracies responsible for mental health). Secondly, at the 'quasi-formal' policy level, artefacts tended to be aspirational and involve policy instruments developed through collaborative processes. In Samoa, the one case adopting a policy at this level, official professional actors crafted policy instruments, but other stakeholders as well as the wider community were consulted and input sought for policy development. There are noticeable cleavages between government, traditional, and exogenous actors in governance structure at this policy level. Finally, 'informal' level attributes tended to be normative and include practices by professional government actors (such as doctors and nurses) in delivering mental health care to the population that merge traditional mental health concepts and beliefs, medical discourse and social context into a unique service paradigm. This policy level relies on professional agents as drivers of discourse based on moral or other non-compulsory motivation to act. This level also includes traditional constructions of mental ill-health aetiologies and appropriate treatment paradigms. I expand upon these categories below.

The thematic analysis was also used in this book to identify evidence of 'localisation' of mental health policy. The term 'localisation' was not itself used by any of the respondents to this research. Instead, terms such as: 'context' ('contextualise'); 'situation' ('situational'); 'Tongan' or 'Samoan' (as in making a law fit the 'Samoan context'); 'culture' ('cultural'); and 'spiritual' were used to explain the process of changing a foreign model to suit local needs. Through an identification of these words, documents could be coded to locate the specific contexts within which they were used. It soon became possible to distinguish between levels of policy transfer by identifying when these concepts were employed: there was a discrete statutory process pursued for law, another slightly less formalised process for policy instruments and finally an informal actor-driven process for localising practice-level changes. For instance, contextualising proposed legal changes for the 'Samoan context' will be seen to involve using the 'Samoan context' as a filter to remove areas of model legislation deemed 'inappropriate' to the 'Samoan context'. In contrast, at the practice level, a significant degree of localisation will be observed where key actors engaged in service delivery shifts used the culture to broaden the universe of participants (e.g. engaging traditional healers in mental health services).

7.2.1 *Formal and Quasi-Formal Policy Transfer*

In both countries formal policy transfer had occurred at various points in their respective histories in the form of several law reforms in both countries. These reforms, however, seldom occurred without foreign government, NGO or other direct support, which was most often significant in nature. Samoa's mental health law was a colonial legacy until the 2007 Mental Health Act was adopted. Provision was first made in the Samoa Act (NZ) 1920 permitting involuntary institutionalisation, written and adopted in Wellington to be used by colonial administrators. This was followed by the Mental Health Ordinance 1961 as part of several law reforms leading up to independence, again drafted by foreign bureaucrats and adopted by the pre-independence legislative assembly acting under the close scrutiny of Australian and New Zealand constitutional experts. There was no further foreign or domestic action on mental health system reform until the early 2000s. These years brought the health system to the fore as the subject of a massive reform effort spearheaded by the Australian Agency for International Development (AusAID) together with World Bank and with technical support of WHO as well as other assorted regional and international aid agencies. Only then and once again only under the direction of a foreign mental health legal expert from Australia was the mental health law reformed and a new one, based largely on Australian state law, adopted and implemented in Samoa and Tonga. This generally follows Tuohy's (1999) institutional argument regarding health system reforms across the Organisation for Economic Cooperation and Development (OECD) as well as Rochefort's (1997) arguments that general health sector reforms most often are the best predictor of mental health system reforms, as set forth in Chap. 2.

Unlike Tonga's experience, Samoa contemporaneously adopted a mental health policy. While this process was crafted to permit significant local input into the policy instrument, it was again drafted with the strong guiding hands of the international community and Samoa's development partners. While, as previously suggested and expanded upon further below, the effective informal policy of community-based care was founded on the understanding of the Samoan context – with its own assumptions about the proper place for care and treatment (not in hospital but in the home and village) – held by the Samoan psychiatric nurse Matamua Iokapeta Sina Enoka (Enoka), the formal policy came to embody these very same principles while conforming to international templates of a 'proper' policy as provided to the local policy committee and advanced by its internationally supplied expert consultants. While it can be argued perhaps that law reform constitutes significant change since it typically involves institutional creation or modification, the necessity of the formal written policy is somewhat questionable. Moreover, there is little evidence that the formal written policy informed the law drafting process in any significant way. In fact, it appears, based on the data, that the two were being crafted on parallel tracks. The drafter of the law essentially had carte blanche to craft the law, subject to the law-making and vetting process through the Attorney General, Cabinet and Parliament. In the end, the policy served the function of being a formal embodiment ostensibly on the government's position on mental health and perhaps little else. Service delivery had been, and continues to be, handled at a lower level and essentially along the same track as it had been since the 1980s and the introduction of Enoka's practice-level reforms.

Again, Tonga provides contrast. At the time of writing, Tonga had not developed a mental health policy. International and regional supports were available for developing a policy yet were not utilised. This research suggests competing explanations for this incomplete transfer. In interviews included in the previous chapter, the nation's psychiatrist often wondered how Tonga could adopt a law without a guiding policy to inform the process and eventual product? As we saw in Samoa, there is no guarantee that the existence of a policy would have had much influence on the finished product. As in Samoa, Tonga was provided a foreign legal consultant to draft a new mental health law. Again, a law was produced based largely on Australian state law and was subjected to the domestic law vetting process including what was reported to be significant revision by the then Chief Justice (a British citizen), seeking to make the expert's draft fit the 'Tongan context'.

A regional mental health intergovernmental organisation (IGO), however, suggested that the absence of a local policy leader on mental health during critical times over the past decade was the central factor contributing to Tonga's failure to develop a mental health policy. The law is, by all accounts, functioning and widely accepted as a good tool for managing mental ill health. This application of law, primarily concerned with managing mental illness as opposed to encouraging mental health, is one limitation of prioritising mental health law as opposed to policy: the work of a mental health system is broader than simply establishing the proper rules whereby one's liberty can be constrained for the public good. Policies also tend to embody more holistic constructions of mental health; defining it as something broader, encompassing an individual's right to it as well as the community's formal understanding of what it means to be a complete person: one who has the capabilities necessary to live a full and happy life in the community. Since there is an informal consensus on this amongst stakeholders, again based both on the international posture for mental health and the Tongan notions of family and community, there is simply no great urge to spend time and money on formally embodying these principles in a written government policy.

I argue, however, that it is probable, given the critical years of health sector reform in Tonga coinciding in large part with the political and constitutional upheaval, that there was little political will to hold a nationwide, public policy vetting process at that time. In other words, development partners insisted that a policy process be open and encourage both stakeholder and community participation in it, unlike statutory drafting under foreign stewardship. Since it was entirely probable such a process would further the political reform efforts of opponents to the conservative regime, the process was simply not actively pursued by the Government of Tonga. Instead, the reform-minded Minister of Health apparently sought to split the difference: law reforms involving foreign consultants, bureaucrats and elites would achieve a significant advance for the Tongan mental health system but the public and potentially politically volatile populist policy process had to be avoided. Several years on from the crisis the impetus for policy reform has passed. The health sector reforms are largely complete and the actors have moved on to other priorities. Developing a policy is still on Dr. Puloka's to-do list, however, along with his continuing efforts to champion the cause of medical mental health concepts understood in Tongan terms and managing the day-to-day operation of a sizeable mental health unit for a nation of its size. In short, without the urging of an international or regional partner willing to take the lead in such a process, there are simply other and more pressing matters to attend to, making policy adoption, at least in the near term, unlikely.

Following Dolowitz and Marsh (2000), this study finds that, at least in regards to formal policy transfer, the process was found to be only minimally iterative and the localisation of these foreign-derived laws was similarly minimal. Foreign professionals/experts were instrumental in legislative design and drafting but indigenous professionals were not significantly involved in the legislative drafting process. This was not perceived, however, by either the foreign or indigenous professionals to be of great moment. Incidentally, Dolowitz and Marsh (2000) have suggested that this sense of 'success' in policy transfer indicated by transfer actors is one possible hallmark of transfer success. This finding leads to the suggestion that, when coupled with prior instances noted throughout the book, notably the Samoan constitutional conventions, an institutionalised practice of deference is developed; local policy leaders are likely to defer to outside 'experts' when it comes to imparting professional best practices and/or knowledge for implementation in the Samoan and Tongan contexts, even where the task might have been adequately achieved through local professional expertise. Professionals are trained to be self-reliant except perhaps on those occasions where a fellow professional of greater expertise within the given field is available. This deference has itself become part of the mental health system as a historical institution, serving to constrain the relevant policy actors' action potential.

Both countries endured stagnant formal mental health policies for long periods of time due to limited available resources to adequately address mental health. In addition, as has been argued in this book, earlier solutions had been introduced from imported arcane legislative pronouncements and foreign institutional infrastructure. Innovative institutional policymaking capacity was lacking due to each country's institutional legacies as policy importers. While recognising the need for health sector reform, officials from both countries awaited the availability of expert guidance and structural funding from development partners to undertake policy reform efforts.

International actors, including, primarily WHO, provided mental health policy expertise together with guarantees of substantial foreign financial support in order to update domestic mental health policy. Again, the recognition of the need for reform was a local decision, and the resources for effectuating change consistent with international best practices was the context within which the necessary linkages between agents and international and domestic institutional structures would take place. The AusAID programme (along with World Bank and WHO efforts on the international and regional level through the Pacific Islands Mental Health Network [PIMHnet]), had emphasised the centrality of modern best practices being reflected in national law and policy and provided necessary momentum for the policy and law adoption.

Taking each nation's mental health policy history as illustrative of the broader trends in mental health, the 1920 Samoa Act (NZ) and 1948 Lunatics Detention Act (Tonga) provisions relating to mental health were meant to provide government authorities broad authority to maintain order. Samoa's 1961 Mental Health Ordinance was part of an effort to transfer as much power form New Zealand's mandate government to the new Samoan government within the decolonisation context of the time and under the supervision of foreign constitutional, legal and political experts. Tonga's Lunatics Act persisted throughout this period despite its inappropriateness being reflected in numerous official police and prisons reports lamenting the practice of confining individuals with mental illness within the prison.

Samoa's 2007 Mental Health Act was again drafted by a foreign legal professional based on his expertise as a former judge and attorney specialising in disability and mental health law and drew heavily upon South Australia and Victoria state laws of the time (which have undergone [Victoria] or are undergoing [South Australia] significant overhauls themselves since Samoa's Act was adopted). The most notable difference between the laws is found between the substantially similar Australian and Samoan and Tongan laws' consideration of non-process 'rights' and the international guidance materials. The international materials offer a comprehensive rights emphasis whereas the domestic laws focus primarily on the notion of informed consent. The textual analysis tends to confirm the interviewees impressions that the laws were essentially derived from Australian sources.

The former Samoan Attorney General (as well as every other respondent in this study) agreed that the 1961 ordinance was untenable and deferred to the foreign expert for the crafting of a law that would reflect international best practice. These attitudes, when coupled with the presence of a foreign (Australian) psychiatrist, ultimately led to implementation. Tonga experienced a strikingly similar pattern to its 2001 mental health law overhaul. An Australian legal consultant employed by WHO was provided to the Government of Tonga proceeded to craft a mental health law based closely on similar Australian mental health laws of the time. There is suggestion, however, of a significant pairing down of this imported legal framework by a Tongan official. That 'Tongan' official, however, was an English Chief Justice of the local judiciary. The final products are substantially similar in their preference for voluntary treatment in the least restrictive environment, most often the community, whilst seeking to ensure judicial constraints on the confinement process. The embedded nature of these foreign legal professionals within Samoa and Tongan government institutions further implicates Dolowitz and Marsh's (2000) observation that circumstances, such as these, tend to blur the line between voluntary and coercive policy transfer. Given the perception of these actors both as 'foreign' and as holding official status within the domestic policymaking apparatus created a complex perception amongst interview respondents who saw the laws as foreign derived yet locally-vetted.

As pointed out earlier, South Australia's Mental Health Act (1993) and Victoria's Mental Health Act (1986) had been identified by key policy actors as sources for subsequent Samoan and Tongan legislative proposals and were included in the sample of documentary sources analysed for this book. Both Acts refer to a 'person' and 'patient' in terms of the affected class of individuals. 'Treatment' is a similarly frequent focus of both Acts. Victoria's makes more specific reference to 'hospital', 'medical', 'psychiatrist', 'patient' and involuntary admissions. South Australia's

Act refers more broadly to 'practitioner' indicating a broadening of the class of individuals competent to make preliminary mental health custody determinations. Neither Act refers to 'disorder' or 'illness' with any prominence.

Samoa and Tonga's Acts were similarly analysed. Samoa's is the most recent Act passed in 2007. This law uses the person-first language championed by disability advocates the world-over such as when it indicates the scope of the Act applying to 'persons with a mental disorder'. This law also avoids use of the term 'patient', maintaining the focus on the human individual. Similarly, Samoa's law does not mention 'psychiatrists' instead referring to 'professionals' duly authorised to make mental health diagnoses, again reflecting the reality that on any given day in Samoa one would not find a psychiatrist but also reflects the trend found in South Australia's earlier Act recognising the task-sharing within the mental health sphere generally to include individuals who are psychologists, clinical social workers or psychiatric nurse practitioners, all having attained a high level of specialised skill in the area of mental health. In addition, Samoa's Act contains specific prohibitions on certain behaviours and attributes serving as the basis for a mental illness such as political affiliation or for merely exhibiting socially unacceptable behaviours.

Tonga's law reflects more of the older generation of law. Notably, Tonga's law does not contain this general exclusion of certain behaviours common in liberal democracies such as voicing an opinion contrary to a dominant political party. In addition, Tonga's mental health law makes specific reference to the position of 'psychiatrist' and his (or her) function in 'involuntary' admission to a 'facility' for individuals with a mental illness, who then are labelled 'patients' under the Act. This language, on balance, reflects more closely Victoria's Mental Health Act dating to 1986. The *MI Principles*, adopted in 1991, do not seem to be reflected in Tonga's law. The Act, however, contains substantial process protections as advanced in the MI Principles. Tonga's Act contains provision for a Mental Health Tribunal to review admissions determinations, while maintaining judicial review of civil commitments, a Mental Health Advisory Committee, consisting of community members, individuals with mental illness and their families, and other key mental health actors. This Committee is designed to advise the Minister of Health on matters pertaining to the mental health system. Finally, the law also continues the institution of 'visitor'. A 'visitor' is an independent community watchdog with the power to inspect the mental health facilities. Each of these institutions is intended to balance the individual and community concerns against determinations made by the designated health practitioners.

While these mental health laws were almost entirely based upon two Australian state laws (Victoria and South Australia) they nonetheless constituted a significant upgrade to the then existing statutory framework. At the same time, however, within a few years of these enactments both Australian source laws underwent significant community review and revision. For example, a review of the 1986 Victoria Mental Health Act (MHA) was launched in May 2008, little over 1 year on from Samoa's adopting much of it and little more than five after Tonga's Act was ultimately enacted. Stating the need for review, the State Government of Victoria revealed that

> The MHA is the oldest mental health law in Australia and it has not been comprehensively reviewed since the mid-1990's. Apart from modernizing the MHA, the review aimed to make the MHA more consistent with the Victorian Charter of Human Rights and Responsibilities and the International Convention of Persons with Disabilities. (State Government of Victoria 2010: p. v; underlined emphasis added)

Given this, Tonga's and Samoa's reformed laws did not fully reflect the latest international mental health best practices of the time. In addition to building and perpetuating a dependence on foreign expertise in this area, the transferred laws continue to fall short of the most current position of the policy area. For instance, the MHA overhaul was motivated by a presumption that individuals with mental disorder should be supported in making independent decisions and only where a determination has been made to the contrary should the state be involved in individual autonomy. This principle is consistently embodied in provisions such as in formally recognising advance statements by individuals when they had legal capacity about their wishes should that capacity cease for any reason, including directing care options. In sum, the extensive international texts supporting a rights-based mental health system for the world were instrumental in moving the issue of mental health onto the international policy agenda but were not found to significantly inform Samoa or Tonga's formal policy context. Further, when policy actors crafted a legal framework for Samoa and Tonga and required source material to guide them, they did not use these international resources. Instead, the evidence presented here suggests that the foreign legal practitioners utilised domestic laws with which they were intimately familiar from their home jurisdictions.

For instance, and as evidence of this, the South Australia Mental Health Act 2009 included provisions to work collaboratively with traditional healers. This inclusive theme within primary care settings is common in the international mental health development literature and both Samoan and Tongan respondents observed the presence of (and at least initial preference for) traditional healers in the indigenous mental health system. This language was not included in either nation's Mental Health Act, however, and only sparingly referred to in Samoa's policy document. It is fair to note that these proposed changes were not part of the relied-upon Australian legal frameworks at the time, but they are not new. The ICRPD has been widely used by mental health advocates throughout the Western world for many years and, while both Samoa and Tonga lack comprehensive human rights legislation, Samoa does have a Constitution containing a Bill of Rights that could have formed the basis for crafting a mental health act that reflected second (or third) generation rights as embodied in the Victoria MHA.

Statements of Rights in older laws tended to provide only the requirement that natural justice principles be communicated to the individual. Newer versions of both Australian state laws include 'Guiding Principles' and 'Objectives' sections, formerly found only in policy statements. Most notably, the new laws build on the least restrictive environment requirement of second generation mental health laws and seek to include family and carers in the circle of treatment regimes. This is a notable omission in Samoa's Mental Health Act given that both indigenous and international actors alike repeatedly cite family as a key strength of Samoa's and

Tonga's systems. It is highly likely that given some of the Samoan contextual limitations that were raised by the drafter of the Act, there was a sense that since the community possessed low mental health literacy there was not much to be gained by including this provision, hence a simpler law. The problem this omission presents, however, is that the competing aims of simplicity and community education here are in conflict. Greater inclusion and information provided to families would likely enhance the community's understanding of mental health and leaving this aim out of the law, while making it simpler, fails to assist the achievement of this competing and broader policy interest.

7.2.2 Informal Policy Transfer

The informal transfers effectively delivered the values of the modern mental health system undergirding Samoa's formal policy and law and in Tonga's ongoing reform efforts. The informal transfers involved medical professional policy entrepreneurs: a psychiatric nurse in Samoa and a psychiatrist in Tonga. In both cases, long before formal transfer was undertaken, these actors sought to move the policy through practice-level service delivery from an institutional context to a more community-based one, though with varying degrees of success. Both actors confronted similar institutional opportunities within their respective health systems and related bureaucracies, such as a relative lack of domestic political constraints on their efforts to innovate, though there were some notable differences. This aspect of the policy transfer process speaks directly to Dolowitz and Marsh's (2000) observation that the scope of transfer often depends on the extent and degree to which different actors become involved in the process and at which point.

In Samoa, the psychiatric nurse worked under the direction of a foreign psychiatrist and reported some hesitation on his part to permit a shift from institutional to community treatment. This shift in the locus of care would result in less central control over the direct monitoring of prescribed treatment regimes and similar institutional hesitancy found in the literature about deinstitutionalisation in nearly every other country to undergo this transition in service-delivery paradigms. Eventually, the psychiatrist capitulated due to the nurse's persistence and her insider status and shifted the locus of care to the community. This was a reflection of her training in the emerging best practice converging with her deep understanding of the particular Samoan cultural milieu.

The shift was enabled not only by the psychiatrist, but by the ostensibly permissive institutional and bureaucratic culture within the Ministry of Health. Since the changes proposed did not add any apparent cost to the budget, and in fact, were offered as cost savings measures with the shifting of patients from the hospital to the family home, there was little reason for intervention by the bureaucratic hierarchy as suggested by respondents in this study as well as the experiences of other countries with similar deinstitutionalisation processes. As such, the combination of a persuadable psychiatrist and the apparent tacit consent of Ministry bureaucrats, the psychiatric nurse as policy entrepreneur was able to accomplish informal policy transfer of a Western-informed, community-based mental health service nearly 20 years before the nation adopted a formal, written national mental health policy and accepted law reforms in this area both under the aegis of international agencies and bilateral development relationships.

In Tonga, by contrast, the main policy actor has been a Tongan psychiatrist. While he confronted institutional obstacles of his own, as a medical doctor and head of the psychiatric unit he was able to more authoritatively determine the direction of service delivery and the posture to be taken by the Ministry of Health. It is, however, for this very reason that the reforms in Tonga have been somewhat different and there has been less of a shift away from the institutional setting. This psychiatrist, however, acted not only as a doctor with the beliefs incumbent upon his position, such as his responsibility to the patient's wellbeing, but also as an administrator or bureaucrat in regards to the operating of the Mental Health Unit. As such, the convergence of these two roles created an institutional arrangement whereby his bureaucratic clout was merged not only with his public profile shaped through his dedicated efforts to translate modern mental health and psychiatric terminology into Tongan terms and concepts but also with his identity as a political reformer. As such, he found himself in frequent disagreement with the then Minister of Health, himself reform-minded yet representing the more conservative, status quo elements of the Tongan political elite. While he was widely recognised as the nation's mental health expert, the larger political dynamic surrounding his reforms served as institutional obstacles to significant formal policy reforms. This is evidenced by at least one critical instance where the aforementioned Youth Mental Health Report, which was produced by a local civil society organisation was nonetheless quashed by the then Minister of Health for reasons never fully explained to the relevant actors yet widely believed to be due, at least in part, to the adversarial relationship between the psychiatrist and the Minister.

In sum, the informal policy reforms in Tonga were of a qualitatively different nature to Samoa's in that while the rhetoric of community-based treatment clearly marked a convergence of Western best practices and Tongan traditional concepts and institutions of the family, mental health practice under the tight control of the nation's sole psychiatrist still centred on an institutional paradigm whereby the Mental Health Unit is very much at the heart of the mental health service delivery regime. The main policy actor in Tonga confronted a more rigid bureaucratic hierarchy but was still granted significant leeway due to his very public efforts around mental health that placed him front and centre of any and all national mental health discussions.

These findings suggest that at the level of formal mental health policy instruments (e.g. law) significant change occurs in Samoa and Tonga only with the intervention of foreign legal experts. Although great pains were taken to 'contextualise' the respective laws and formal policies, there are no significant indigenous population-derived deviations in the final official products from the templates offered by the international experts. Shifts in informal practices (e.g. practice in service delivery), however, occurred in both countries through the convergence of foreign best practices and the presence of an interested foreign-trained professional actor in the policy-receiving country, whereby indigenous practices become hybridised as both a medicolegal and indigenous construction of mental health (e.g. family-based treatment in the village is both therapeutic and consistent with Samoan/Tongan cultural values).

In Samoa and Tonga the Western medical/human rights discourses on mental illness are highly institutionalised in a formal sense (law, government policy, dedicated public health employees and programmes, both medical and penal), while the traditional understandings of mental health and treatment are also highly institutionalised in an informal sense (family and village ways of dealing with a mentally ill [understood in traditional terms] community member, traditional healers and practices). These two institutions typically do not come into conflict with each other because the central government's coercive control tools are not widely used in the mental health context. Instead, the traditional governance and indigenous health structures are used at the village level and these fit comfortably within the traditional discursive institutional construction of mental health.

Following and building on Dolowitz and Marsh (2000) and Evans (2004, 2009), I argue that a more nuanced application of policy-oriented learning typology is necessary to fully explain complex (multi-layered) policy transfers such as those considered in this book. In both Samoa and Tonga, mental health policy was transferred as part of a long-term process involving each country's health systems writ large. The typology resulted in slightly fewer absolute categories of transfer applied to the type of transfer in question (formal, quasi-formal or informal transfers).Significant localisation was found in both nations' informal transfers where individual agency was at its highest. This ability to narrowly tailor a foreign model decreases as the formality of the transfer product increases, so at the level of law transfer both countries' laws were essentially copied from source laws in Australia. Emulation is found in the Samoa's mental health policy instrument. As observed above, the discourses surrounding this type of policy formulation were more participatory and deliberative and involved formal procedures and a formal foreign template but were subjected to significant stakeholder input.

Moreover, again following Dolowitz and Marsh's (2000) consideration of degree of voluntariness in transfer and employing Evans's (2004, 2009) processes of transfer categorisation scheme I argue the categorisation of voluntariness requires further elaboration. Evans and Davies (1999) draw a distinction between the process of voluntary and coercive policy transfer: internal circumstances trigger a voluntarist approach whereas external regime-formation pull factors, which might include IOs as agents of the normative process seeking out nonconforming states and targeting them through regional organisations or other international level venues for demand-creating measures, such as the threats of failure to grant loans for development without adoption of neoliberal market reforms.

Ultimately, both Samoa and Tonga had the choice of whether or not to receive aid in order to reform their respective health systems. As such, aid often comes with strings attached and Samoa and Tonga are no strangers to foreign aid resources and their many conditions. At the same time, the specific policy transfer actors involved on the international level went to great lengths to present their ultimate crafting of the proposed laws as rooted in the cultural context in each country. I am inclined to believe that in order for a transfer to be described as truly voluntary there must be an internal policy search of available models and a selection from those available with only limited technical advice, if any, from outside actors. If, however, a domestic problem recognition and search process is undertaken that ultimately recommends borrowing in toto from abroad with foreign assistance, then this would perhaps constitute a voluntary transfer.

In both Samoa and Tonga, however, the transfers could perhaps best be described as 'negotiated' but not in the sense that they were negotiated by two equal parties acting at arm's length. Negotiated transfers, in a truly rational sense, might be said to have occurred with the informal transfers embodied in the experiences of Enoka and Dr. Puloka. Both professional medical actors were trained in foreign medical models yet transferred these practices into Samoa and Tonga respectively through a process of internally negotiating between foreign and indigenous paradigms. The foreign models were passive in the sense that no force or law backed them up. They were simply lessons learned through training and professional networks that were then employed to create a uniquely culturally informed mental health service delivery model in Samoa and for recasting foreign psychiatric concepts into traditionally understood notions of madness in Tonga. There is evidence, however, that at least with regard to Samoa's quasi-formal process, indigenous policy actors have instituted ongoing evaluation mechanisms to review the implemented policy. This finding is suggestive of Tews's (2009) comment that in addition to appropriateness as a transfer criterion, local recognition of the policy suggestive of policy learning (either in terms of form or substance) should be found.

The formal law transfers, in contrast, were somewhere between negotiated and direct coercive transfers. Samoa and Tonga voluntarily accepted foreign funds to achieve a domestic political objective of health sector reform and voluntarily implemented the 'borrowed' policies and laws. In both countries, however, the adopted statutory reforms lacked any significant indigenous input into the substance of the reforms. This lack of meaningful engagement is a hallmark of coercion since the substance conformed to templates of 'acceptable' law and policy substance. So, while no one coerced Samoa or Tonga to undertake health system reform or to accept international aid for doing so, once the decision was made, in most aspects of the adopted reforms anyway, the die had been cast as to what the reforms would actually look like.

7.3 Transfer Agents: International and Bilateral Organisations and Indigenous Policy Entrepreneurs

As argued in Chap. 3, in order to distinguish the active policy transfer process from the passive convergence studies perspective, Dolowitz and Marsh (2000) (offering a transfer motivation spectrum) and Evans (2009) who argues for a multistage process in which first, the researcher should (1) identify the agent(s) of transfer; (2) distinguish the brought resources; (3) specify the role agents and resources play in the transfer; and (4) determine the nature of the transfer that the agents are seeking to make. From here, the process of transfer must be analysed within a three-dimensional frame which encompasses global, internal and transnational levels, the macro-state level and interorganisational level. In both Samoa and Tonga there is no question that formal and quasi-formal transfers involved significant foreign stewardship. Once World Bank and AusAID offered to finance health sector reforms in both countries, local political buy-in was essentially assured and within the context of mental health examined here, there were willing indigenous partners to work as local change agents in the reform process. These domestic political actors had the political power to implement changes that the policy actors – professional actors working within each country developed. The international and bilateral organisations brought financial resources as well as expert knowledge to the fore.

Indigenous policy actors were bifurcated between those who were relatively unsophisticated in the mental health field yet politically empowered and the trained mental health professionals possessing expert knowledge within their respective professions, be it nursing or psychiatry, as well as insider status in regard to the cultural context within which these policies and laws would be implemented. There was a shared desire to see a formal written policy and law changes by all of these actors as evidenced in the voluminous interviews and textual sources analysed for this book. This desire assured a shared objective and outcome. However, in Tonga's case, I argue domestic political concerns prevented the more participatory component of mental health policy formation from occurring since this would have involved significant community engagement during relative political instability brought upon by a desire for democratic reforms during the relevant policy window provided by the health sector reform initiatives.

7.3.1 International and Bilateral Organisations

The critical contribution of IOs and actors was widely recognised in the interviews. There was recognition that the most current law was the product of such actors including WHO, World Bank, AusAID and the New Zealand Aid Programme (NZAID). This also highlights the importance of foreign 'partners' such as Australia, New Zealand and, traditionally, Great Britain in the Tongan policy context. There was an overall impression that the mental health incidence was on the rise due to economic difficulties and the changes in Samoa and Tonga, such as increasing urban populations and disruption to traditional family and village life.

The central importance of overseas actors and their considerable funding in formal and quasi-formal agenda-setting cannot be overstated. At the same time, this research suggests that it would be just as easy to overstate the impact of international actors in the informal policy transfer process. International agencies and their foreign experts exerted great effort to delineate the best practices for Samoa's and Tonga's health systems. These practices were a reflection of their own philosophies and involved controlling mental illness whilst balancing it with individual human rights. At the same time, there was very little effort put forward to understand or decipher indigenous constructions of mental health, particularly with respect to the possibly dichotomous collectivist dimensions of it referred to above. It might well be that indigenous constructions of mental ill-health, particularly those rooted in the supernatural, are deemed irrational and simply incapable of being incorporated into a practice-based policy framework. While the Samoan and Tongan aetiologies themselves might be deemed irrational and incapable of incorporation, the treatment methods used by traditional healers might yet offer insight into the development of the mental health systems and programmes yet to come.

The evidence uncovered here suggests that where 'task-sharing' is already entrenched, such as in Samoa, the eventual adoption of a comprehensive mental health policy was possible; but where there has been task-consolidation in the person of a psychiatrist, such as in Tonga, it was not. Furthermore, there is evidence that this task-sharing approach has benefits in terms of service delivery and that in regions having policy-expert scarcity, this effort to share responsibility for certain types of work could benefit other related areas of service provision, including the crucial public education component of the mental health policies.

An additional structural problem faced by individuals with mental illness and their advocates is that mental health care initiatives are seldom donor priorities (Hunt and Mesquita 2006). Hunt and Mesquita offer suggestions to overcome this, including suggesting donors see the funding of such projects as 'the development of appropriate community based care and support services, supporting advocacy by persons with mental disabilities, their families and representative organisations and providing policy and technical expertise' as being in 'accordance with their responsibility of international assistance and cooperation' (2006, pp. 223–25). Moreover, they argue that safeguards should be built into existing and future funding initiatives seeking the principle of equality in service provision or policy development.

At the same time, the benefits of readymade policy solutions and expert assistance in drafting are not without their drawbacks. Building on Kwon's (2009) and Tews's (2009) similar observations that a top-down formal policy adoption approach is preferred by policy actors in an effort to reduce the development gap between technologically advanced nations and developing ones, this book argues that the institutional path dependency created by successive waves of modernisation schemes offered by development partners and aid agencies has served to effectively limit the ability (or willingness) of domestic policy actors in the developing context to innovate when confronted with domestic policy dilemmas. In both Samoa and

Tonga, for reasons of previous institutionalisation, the locus of intervention has relocated from traditional governance institutions to official, centralised and bureaucratic ones, acting, in this case, at the direction of foreign development partners. Mental health systems were, at key moments in the institutional transfer events from Germany and New Zealand to Samoa and the United Kingdom to Tonga, bound up with the health care apparatus generally. As such, even while the predominant mental health paradigm moved from institutional to community-based treatment regimes, officially Samoa's and Tonga's systems remained centralised, despite both nations' abundant natural resource of strong family and community structures more conducive to the community-based treatment paradigm. Only through the efforts of institutional insiders in both countries was the persistence of these outdated institutional modes of service delivery ended and only then because they too were couched in the language of formal best practices as evidenced in international models for the implementation of modern mental health policies.

7.3.2 Indigenous Professionals and Informal Policy Transfer

Medical professionals perceived as leaders within the mental health policy space were clearly identified and consistently mentioned across both countries. Enoka was mentioned in nearly every Samoan interview in this study as one of the main driving forces behind Samoa's current mental health system and its community-based treatment focus. As addressed in Chap. 5, Enoka is a Samoan psychiatric nurse who received specialised professional training in New Zealand and returned to Samoa where the Ministry of Health employed her. Upon her return to Samoa in the mid-1980s, she led an effort to modernise the mental health service delivery model based on her training and in line with her interpretation of Samoan cultural attitudes on appropriate mental health treatment. She was recognised as a leader in the area of mental health generally but also in the particulars of the particular Samoan mental health context. Enoka engaged in academic writing and teaching in the area of mental health and trained a cohort of mental health nurses, many of whom remained and form the core of Samoa's mental health system to this day. Unlike the bureaucratic obstacles confronting Dr. Puloka in Tonga, Enoka took advantage of the presence of a foreign psychiatrist as head of Samoa's mental health unit, who reluctantly permitted her to pursue her community-based treatment approach. Her service delivery model was able to operate within the existing mental health structure and apparently required no greater funding appropriation in order to be implemented. This undoubtedly facilitated the transition of treatment on an inpatient basis to the community-based model prevalent today. Importantly, in both cases these policy innovations never directly implicated political actors. As noted above, Enoka was able to implement a community care model in Samoa in a manner that did not disrupt the existing institutional arrangements within the Ministry of Health. In Tonga, Puloka did confront institutional obstacles along the way but these were not of an overtly political nature. The relative flexibility within each bureaucratic structure was likely due to the fact that mental health has not been an area of important political concern. This low profile is likely due to mental health institutions essentially existing as subdivision of the broader health sector. This status caused mental health to endure in the policy background. Because of this, mental health policy actors were able to operate beneath the political processes to effectively change the trajectory of state mental health services.

Enoka argued that hospital-based care caused a loss of identity for the Samoan. Some policy actors viewed the hospital as a 'dumping ground' for the most difficult of mental health cases. This moral and cultural appeal was however accompanied by an economic argument. Enoka cleverly argued that the community treatment approach would have cost-cutting effects since it would shift the individual back to the home together with the costs of care, such as food and hospital staff and resources. In both a practical and economic innovation, Enoka worked to include *fofo* (traditional healers) in the process of symptom identification and treatment. She did this simply because she understood that this is what the people used for 'healing in the Samoan way'. Enoka, working in collaboration with the University of Technology Sydney's WHO Collaborating Centre, made nursing central to successful mental health care in the Samoan context. With this assistance, Enoka developed a psychiatric nursing curriculum at the National University of Samoa. Enoka's training of numerous community mental health nurses has aided in mental health practice being mainstreamed. As one respondent declared, nurses essentially 'run the show' in mental health. Other health policy actors echoed this since it is 'nurses (who) actually do the service delivery because they usually go out to the people'. In sum, community treatment and nursing's role in it are at the centre of the Samoan mental health treatment paradigm due to Enoka's effective and passionate advocacy.

Tongan respondents similarly referred to the central role of Dr. Puloka in the mental health system. He was described not only as the psychiatrist but also as the main organiser, agitator and advocate for nearly every conceivable dimension of mental health. He is a pioneer, in a sense, pushing the boundaries of indigenous understandings of mental health and illness from his place as an indigenous psychiatrist, fluent in both medical science and cultural understandings of mental health. In this, he serves in a unique capacity. He is interpreting, translating and educating all facets of Tongan society via his interpretations of the proper place of psychiatry in the medical system and society at large. His radio, television and print activities were all well known by the study participants and evidenced as indicating his superior place in the system itself. It seemed, however, that his position of high status and his own recognition of his unique and transformative role would likely unsettle superiors and there was an undercurrent of tension between the doctor and the former Minister of Health. This friction seems to have played a part in the prevention of even further advances in the institutionalisation of the mental health system along international aspirational lines.

Related to this subject is the difficulty confronted by Dr. Puloka in his quest to see international mental health concepts translated into Tongan and used by Tongans. This is not an uncommon occurrence in developing countries, however. As Sourangshu Acharyya remarks, most psychiatrists working in developing nations are 'mainly, if not wholly trained, by Western psychiatrists … The psychiatric elite of the Commonwealth has been trained by British psychiatrists in Britain' (1996, p. 339). Dr. Puloka was himself trained in Fiji and New Zealand, which both follow the British medical education model. This fact has a profound impact on all aspects of the mental health systems of these countries and also serves to make difficult innovation in terms of 'new ways or methods of examining psychiatric disorders within their own cultures' (1996, p. 339). This issue arose in several interviews for this study. On the one hand, Tonga's psychiatrist is innovating by translating Western psychiatric terminology into Tongan and attempting to raise the profile of psychiatry and mental health there in the process. In Samoa, the absence of a psychiatrist (setting aside the presence of a retired Australian psychiatrist, who, while recognised as critical to the system, is understood to be there on a part-time, temporary basis) has been suggested as leaving the mental health system rudderless, particularly since mental health systems persist in having the specialist psychiatrist at the top of the institutional hierarchy.

Acharyya's observation is a critical one, however, and implicates similar arguments advanced by Tuhiwai-Smith (2012) in her *Decolonizing Methodologies*, which, apart from its wider message on the proper context for doing 'research' in former colonies or in settler societies, argues that scholars and professionals trained abroad and often incorporated into regional metropolitan cultures of New Zealand and Australia. Moreover, the role of these 'native intellectuals' requires they move across these institutional and professional boundaries of their indigenous cultures and the professional associations of their specialities. Mental health, as a field of study, again implicates a fascinating crossroads in Samoa and Tonga. As Tuhiwai-Smith argues, one of the last remaining fields of 'resistance for indigenous peoples' is their 'spirituality' broadly understood as 'values, attitudes, concepts and language' embedded in spiritual beliefs might offer the 'clearest contrast' between the West and populations such as those in Samoa and Tonga (2012, p. 77–78). Given the particular spiritual dimension found in both Samoan and Tongan mental health aetiologies, this research has sought to examine individual actors and their perceptions of the intersection of mental health policy and indigenous beliefs and practices surrounding mental disorder.

In examining this relationship between these policy actors and the institutions within which they work, this research has taken into account Evans and Davies's (1999) observation that the relationship between state structures and agency remains underdeveloped. Similarly, Dolowitz and Marsh's recent observation that 'when and where an agent becomes involved in the policymaking process can tell us a great deal about his or her motivations for offering transferred information' (2012, p. 341). Here, the specific relationship between relevant state health, political and bureaucratic structures was examined as well as the agency of individual health actors in the policy transfer process.

Following Kingdon (1995) and Mintrom (2000) who argued that policy entrepreneurs are judged successful when they both develop the ideas serving as the basis for policy innovation and take action to see the policy change, this book advances the argument that by privileging formal policy adoption as evidence of transfer success, the researcher risks overlooking the critical contributions played by entrepreneurs who influence informal practice-level matters. Here, I have presented two profile sketches of the entrepreneurs at the centre of mental health policy transfers in Samoa and Tonga which I argue expand the existing construction of a policy entrepreneur as well as the motivating factors for being entrepreneurial. In fact, in the cases examined here it is not apparent that either actor became an entrepreneur to actually affect formal public policy. Instead, both actors reported having a moral basis for acting rooted in their particular cultural upbringing. Both actors reflected a commitment to their respective professions and the best practices advanced by those professions as well as a yearning to see those practices reflect their understandings of the best indigenous cultural practices.

Furthermore, while Mintrom and Veragi (1996) noted the importance of entrepreneurial framing issues so as to appeal to diverse interests in order to successfully build coalitions, this research suggests that in both Samoa and Tonga this step was not critical to the law-making process, as evidenced by the law drafting process and parliamentary records in each case. The policy drafting process in Samoa, however, suggests that while not critical, the Samoan cultural context as defined by the stakeholders was important in defining the application or fit for the new policy. Similarly, Dr. Puloka's efforts in Tonga are important steps in securing eventual public support for a new mental health policy based on the recasting of medical terms into traditional Tongan concepts.

As neither of the central mental health actors in Samoa and Tonga strictly fit the rather narrow categorical construction of 'policy entrepreneur' in the existing literature, they do satisfy many of the core characteristics of such identified by scholars such as Kingdon and Mintrom (see also Lightfoot 2002), including possession of the innovative and practical spirit embodied in the traditional entrepreneur role. I therefore propose a new category of entrepreneur that I have tentatively labelled 'culture entrepreneur'. What I mean by this category is similar to what I take Kingdon and others to mean in the traditional policy entrepreneur context. Previous presentation of the policy entrepreneur involved the reintroduction of human agency into institutional contexts. Since the entrepreneur is successful when key events create opportunities for change, the change itself requires human agency in order to come about. Culture entrepreneurs, while also operating within existing institutional contexts, might not be the actual policy change agents or even the ones proposing such changes be made to quasi-formal or formal policy frameworks. Instead, acting across these institutions, these actors seek to bring culture back (or perhaps introduce cultural contexts) into the inherited or borrowed institutions themselves. These actors are nonetheless 'entrepreneurs' in the sense that they have taken an innovative step to reform an area of state action (mental health service delivery).

Another observation gained through examining the attributes of each entrepreneur identified in this book can be used to explain why the informal, practice-level changes in Samoa and Tonga differed, despite sharing so many common origins. Samoa's change was effectuated by a psychiatric nurse whose aim was to reduce centralised health delivery and the role of the institutional model. This change necessarily required a reduction in the concentration of medical authority in the position of psychiatrist and his relinquishing some authority over daily inpatient management. At the same time this increased the institutional authority and prestige of this nurse in particular and nursing generally. Conversely, Tonga's central mental health policy entrepreneur began from basically the same cultural and moral critiques concerning the shortcomings of borrowed mental health institutions yet forged a system very much in line with a medical doctor's approach. He sought to formalise the traditional Tongan mental health language around existing medical mental health diagnostic categories. In addition, he encouraged community treatment, family and consumer advocacy, and many other progressive, rights-based initiatives consistent with international best practices in this regard, whilst also increasing the size and role of the Mental Health Unit and the number of individuals treated there. These agents are thus seen to embody several overlapping institutional identities (e.g. medical actor identities, bureaucratic actors, insiders within their respective cultures) through which they mediated informal policy change at the practice level and achieved input into their respective policy processes.

These profiles allow for the identification of common culture entrepreneur attributes from which a preliminary profile might be sketched: both possessed specialised, technical knowledge (as medical professionals); both were cultural insiders (being from Samoa and Tonga, having lived most of their lives in their respective country); both were embedded in the local cultural and professional communities to which they belonged and possessed a certain modicum of status within their respective communities; both embodied a profound moral sense about the proper (cultural) manner in which to care for individuals suffering from a mental illness that was inextricably bound to the particular cultural context of each country; and both undertook efforts to influence the informal practice frameworks in their respective countries by implementing practice-level changes in the absence quasi-formal policy instruments and in the presence of obsolete formal institutional structures.

Historical institutionalism offers perhaps the best explanation of how 'culture' came back into the mental health policies of Samoa and Tonga. Mental health policy changes, as part of the larger state health institutional structures, required shifts in these larger state health structures – 'policy episodes' in Tuohy's (1999) analysis – to create an opportunity for the emergent policies to reflect indigenous values. This, however, was not solely due to local activist or policy entrepreneurship; rather the changes occurred because of the attributes of the policy transfer process itself. The transfer processes were marked by local stewardship of the policymaking process (for quasi-formal policy).Where a state succeeded in such transfer as occurred in Samoa, the written policy instrument included elements of the local culture as recognised by policy process participants, such as the inclusion of the spiritual element to recognise the holism underlying Samoan philosophy on identity. Similarly, however, where the transfer process did not require local stewardship, such as in the formal policy transfers, the resulting legislation was not crafted by indigenous policy actors and scarcely reflects a uniquely indigenous identity. Instead, the local 'contexts' were used by foreign policy consultants as a filter to remove perceived ill-fitting policy attributes from the proposed legislation. Thus, this begs the ultimate question of whether the institutions can be said to have changed.

This book suggests the answer to this question is no, they cannot. The institutions in question in Samoa and Tonga are larger than the laws and policies or hospitals, prisons or other formal state apparatus. Institutions include practices and behaviour patterns developed over time. Reliance upon foreign policy agendas in order to effectuate change has long been a defining attribute of the policy process in Samoa and Tonga and this book demonstrates a continuation of this practice. The singular change is not one of rhetoric, since, as demonstrated particularly in the case of Samoa, successive foreign actors beginning with German colonial administrators have pledged only to assist Samoa in its own governance. Instead, the key change is one of practice: development partners took a relatively laissez-faire approach to quasi-formal policy and insisted this must be locally led. Since they withheld official stewardship over this process, local actors stepped in (in Samoa) to see a policy adopted that sought to incorporate ostensibly Samoan cultural values concerning the appropriateness of community-based care as intrinsic with the Samoan sense of self containing spiritual, mental and physical dimensions as well as the inextricable relationship between self and community. In Tonga, similar themes were unearthed yet these quasi-formal changes were not developed due to the absence of the critical mental health policy actor during relevant policy episodes and the political hesitancy to engage in a community-based policy vetting process.

7.4 Conditions Peculiar to Samoa: Framing the 'Samoan Context'

As established above, a foreign lawyer and medical doctor drove Samoa's mental health law reform. There was, however, opportunity for interchange and feedback into the Mental Health Act 2007 and most respondents were satisfied with the end product, which they perceived to contain elements particular to the 'Samoan context'. The various mental health laws adopted in Samoa have been to varying degrees, reflective of the predominant professional attitudes of their respective times. The Mental Health Ordinance 1961 was prepared under the guidance of foreign expert consultants and was essentially adopted to transfer an existing government power from one legal entity (mandate government) to the sovereign authority of a free Samoa. Even though this ordinance failed to reflect the most current legal standards present in New Zealand, it accomplished the role of placeholder legislation that did not diminish state power with regard to mental health matters. The 2007 Act, again crafted by foreign hands, was an effort to update the much outdated ordinance. In the latest iteration of the Act, the dual discourses of individual rights and responsibility-sharing between traditional medical professionals (medical doctors) and paraprofessionals (nurses and counsellors) are added to the presumption of state responsibility on matters of control and care of individuals with mental illness.

The relevant actors in 1961 were the foreign 'experts' in charge of drafting the ordinance as successor to the Samoa Act 1920 and the indigenous Legislative

Assembly representatives adopting the proposal. The object of this transfer seemed to reflect policy instruments or administrative techniques on a practical level but also serve to transfer certain ideas, attitudes and concepts embedded within the law and reflected in the debates over the provision. The instruments and techniques related to state control over the individual and the manner in which legitimate custody and control is obtained. At the same time, it continued the notion of central state authority over the individual in situations of mental illness by subjecting this category of unusual or harmful behaviours to the jurisdiction of state authority along with the professional institutions of medicine and law. There is no discernible reflection or reference in this law of any particular 'Samoan context', which incidentally seems to maintain the particular attitude of universality in regards to medically managing mental health the policy instrument sought to remove.

The various constructions of the 'Samoan context' by key policy actors (see Table 7.1) served as a device for providing the necessary social context for the 2007 Act. Unlike the 1961 process, considerable attention was put into making the 2007 Act a homegrown one, reflecting the 'Samoan context' albeit one reflected in official, professional understandings. Again, as has been demonstrated in the Samoa Act 1920 and the 1961 ordinance, I argue that one would not find any ostensibly 'Samoan' aspect of the 2007 Act. Instead, the 'Samoan context' or at least the construction of it in the eyes of the Act's chief architect, better helps us to explain what is omitted from this law. The various constructions of the 'Samoan context' are summarised in Table 7.1. The drafters used their conception of the 'Samoan context' as one of scarcity in terms both of resources and knowledge on mental health requiring shared responsibilities between professionals and non-professionals, and

Table 7.1 The 'Samoan context' as understood by policy actors

WHO Consultant	"[D]eterminants of mental health relevant to the Samoan context include: income, housing, education; changes in Samoan life and culture (intergenerational gaps, differing expectations of parents and children and eroding traditional authority norms); changes in physical activity and dietary patterns; increasing influence of media and from relatives living abroad in Australia and New Zealand; a perceived increase in individualism and inequality; the influence of underage drinking, marijuana use and teenage pregnancy and suicide were also cited as key concerns." (Unpublished WHO Consultant's Report 2002, pp. 67)
AusAID Consultant	"[There is] a general reluctance in Samoa (as elsewhere) to openly deal with mental health; a distrust of health care and hospitals; limited resources; need to empower nondoctor health carers and family; need to avoid court based system due to lack of resources and reluctance to use courts; small geographic area and population facilitating the ability of individuals to see nondoctors in the first instance; and need to keep the system as uncomplicated as possible due to very limited resources." (Interview with the Author).
Psychiatric Nurse	"Mental illness is culturally defined and as such 'knowledge of the beliefs, customs and how to use these as effective tools for implementation of health care is transferable to other cultures',(which leads her to the conclusion that given the social context in Samoa), 'the approach to care in the Samoa society is not the use of institutionalisation or removal form society but the use of society family and the strength of Samoan culture to facilitate care." (Interview with the Author).

for the law to be as 'uncomplicated' as possible. One result of this approach was that the drafting of a simplified law stripped of core best practices integrating both family and individual into the treatment process marginalised the central strength of the 'Samoan context'. This decision undermined the community education aim found in the policy but is arguably consistent with the framer's view of the 'Samoan context.'

Similarly, while there seemed to be a recognition that the 1961 ordinance was outdated and flawed, this research reveals a troubling aspect of this area of policy change: mere recognition of a policy area in need of reform is not enough to effectuate that change. Samoan policymakers and bureaucrats developed a form of dependency on international policy expertise as surrogates for advancing what they perceive to be necessary policy revisions or developments. Evidence of this is in the bare mention of a Samoan legislative proposal dating back to 1995 (recall, this was at a time of other major institutional reforms in Samoa, most notably universal franchise) entitled the 'Health of the People's Bill', which sought to overhaul the health sector at that time. Policymakers balked at the proposal after it was described in an interview by one indigenous policy actor as 'too ambitious'. Instead, once the AusAID-sponsored health sector reforms were initiated a few years later, a foreign consultant arrived and crafted separate Bills (those passed along with the Mental Health Act) aimed to achieve similar reforms. Even though most of the proposals provided are obvious adaptations of existing foreign law, policy and practice, there seems to be an enduring belief that indigenous policymakers and bureaucrats are unable to forge policy and law that would adequately reflect international best practice.

This situation was not due to a lack of funding since foreign actors persist in providing experts; it is rather that the constant, sustained availability of these funds and the expertise that tends to arrive with them has created an expectation that they will exist in perpetuity. This is strong evidence of path dependency at the heart of the historical institutionalism literature. Here, the 'institution' created is one of dependence on foreign policy and legal experts in forging a formal policy. Therefore, while change is within the ken of various Samoan policymakers and bureaucrats the preference is to do what comes naturally and await the eclipse between the international agenda and the domestic one, thereby reducing the relative costs involved in the process.

In essence, what is reflected is the presence of distinct understandings around mental health shared by most respondents: there was wide acknowledgement of changes to the official mental health services practice from one based on custodial care to one which was community-based beginning in the 1980s.At the same time, respondents' understandings as represented in their definitions of mental health and the purpose of mental health treatment in Samoa reflect an adoption of the WHO definition of mental health, one which is a more holistic, comprehensive understanding of mental health, as opposed to either the traditional, cultural formulation of it or a medical or legal definition.

7.5 Factors Peculiar to Tonga: Political Instability During Health Sector Reforms

The political implications of this analysis suggest that in the two cases examined the governments reformed their mental health systems not because they confronted changing local economic patterns or a social movement, exerting political pressure; nor were the courts instrumental in bringing about change; nor indeed was the media agitating by taking up the plight of the mentally ill, all factors present elsewhere in the policy development in this area. Instead, the reforms were triggered by the ascendancy of the international neoliberal economic order, influencing policies and practices all the way down to the judgments of Samoan and Tongan 'normalcy'. In a sense, social movements, human rights campaigns, the psychiatric profession's evolution, and court decisions common in North American and Europe all had significant influence on the subsequent policy options available to Samoa and Tonga. The existence of these exogenous factors – and not the independent efforts of any local actor – eventually shaped the 'best practices' advanced by experts and their written legal frameworks and policy templates. Political will, as exerted by WHO, ultimately exploited the health sector reforms of the World Bank and AusAID to export law by way of South Australia and Victoria to Samoa and Tonga.

There were, however, special political considerations in Tonga which likely contributed to the government's unsuccessful adoption of a mental health policy. The continuing constitutional unrest during the early 2000s and the effect of the prodemocracy movement on the organisation of government were unique to Tonga. Nearly all Tongan respondents noted that the prior, more conservative government was generally unsupportive, or at least lukewarm to the full implementation of mental health reforms. This, to a certain extent, might have had something to do with the personalities and the mental health topic being so closely aligned with an apparent bureaucratic foe. Since the constitutional changes of 2010 and the recent elections, however, a new government has been formed and a new Health Minister selected.

The Tongan respondents seemed uniformly hopeful that these changes would at the very least open up the possibility of even further changes to the mental health system, including the formal adoption of the Youth Mental Health Report and the production of a nationwide mental health policy document. It is worth noting, however, that only one respondent was directly critical of the former Minister of Health, indeed, in most of the literature produced by international actors at the outset of the health sector reforms the former Minister was referred to as 'young', extremely progressive, and motivated for significant reforms; his reputation as an advocate for the health of Tongans seems unchallenged. This former Minister was heralded for his professional experience as a trained and practicing surgeon, which was viewed as a great asset to his stewardship. The general dissatisfaction with more authoritarian styles of leadership amongst many Tongans, however, might have helped shape an impression amongst local respondents for this book (most of whom were active in civil society), that the former Minister was uncompromising and had a propensity to micromanage, much to the dismay of other local stakeholders.

7.6 Conclusion

At various points throughout this book, including at the beginning of this chapter, I have restated my four primary research questions and the two related queries. I now summarise the four primary conclusions reached in this book followed by a summary of the two ancillary points. Firstly, there are three different categories of policy identified in this book: formal policy (laws); quasi-formal policy (written government policies documents); and informal policy (government practices). Moreover, all policy layers were transferred at different times. Formal and quasi-formal policy transfer required some form of punctuation within the political or health system in order to bring about change whereas informal policy change took a more incrementalist, agent-driven path to change. Secondly, different types of actors were engaged in different types of policy transfer depending on the transfer level. Formal policy transfer tends to be effectuated by policy elites (lawyers) drafting laws vetted primarily by other lawyers in the transferor jurisdiction. Quasi-formal transfers tended to involve international policy stewards who offer process and content advice yet insist on local leadership of process and local input into boilerplate policy content. Informal transfers tend to involve only indigenous professional actors who acted as culture entrepreneurs merging cultural concepts with medical best practice. Thirdly, these different policy levels also demonstrated different degrees of localisation. Formal transfers were found to be the least localised and the one instance of quasi-formal transfer in Samoa is best described as embodying a moderate degree of localisation. Informal transfers, given their high dependence on local, indigenous professional policy actors to be implemented, represented the highest degree of localisation. Fourthly, different actors played different roles in localising transferred policies with international actors most actively engaged in formal policy transfer (drafting legislation), moderately involved at the quasi-formal policy level (providing structural support for mental health policy development) and virtually non-existent at the level of informal policy transfer. Indigenous actors tended to mirror these patterns being most engaged at the informal level where they were essentially free to navigate their own bureaucracies to effectuate change, moderately involved in policy development at the quasi-formal level and least engaged in the formal policy transfers.

Furthermore, my ancillary questions asked how Samoa and Tonga's mental health policy transfers compare to one another and whether any of the actors involved in transfer could be considered 'policy entrepreneurs'. I argue that despite international efforts to see the transfers succeed in both places, the transfers were different. Critically, they differ in that Samoa completed transfer of all three policy tiers whilst Tonga's transfer was incomplete in that quasi-formal transfer failed. I conclude Tonga's failure was due to two central elements. Firstly, the international development partner insistence that any quasi-formal policy process be locally led while admirable was not similarly insisted upon in formal policy transfer. This demand required the presence of an important, motivated actor within Tonga who would be able to steward the policy development process along independent of direct international engagement. It was well-known that there was only one individual within Tonga capable of filling this role and that any absence of this individual would likely lead to a failure to develop the policy. Secondly, and related to the first point, the concentration of bureaucratic power and leadership within the mental health system in the nation's sole psychiatrist who had experienced personal conflict with the Minister of Health and was attempting to engage the public in a participatory policy process during a period of political instability likely led to the failure to successfully transfer quasi-formal mental health policy to Tonga. Samoa, in contrast, was politically unified and motivated to achieve health sector reform in compliance with development partner prerogatives.

I also conclude that the indigenous policy actors engaged in localisation served a substantially similar purpose as policy entrepreneurs identified in the relevant literature. Firstly, actors in Samoa and Tonga were similar to the entrepreneurs identified in the policy entrepreneur literature in that they took risks to achieve their objectives. Unlike the risk envisioned in existing literature, however, these actors risked social status in the pursuit of their policy objectives. Similarly, these actors were highly motivated to achieve their policy objectives. Their motivations were not necessarily to achieve law change; rather they were in response to a common moral calling to serve their community in a manner consistent with professional obligations and cultural norms. Both agents were also highly active and engaged in pursuit of their goals.

These agents served a unique role, however. They both walked into mental health systems that were perceived as out of step with their interpretation of their respective cultures and sought to bring their cultures back into the mental health treatment paradigm. The merger of professional treatment practices with indigenous interpretations was a common event yet the form these changes took differed. In Samoa, the community treatment paradigm was implemented with vigour; in Tonga the community treatment paradigm was important but institutionalisation was also increased. I argue this was a result of the type of professional actor engaged in each localisation. In Samoa, a psychiatric nurse was operating under a psychiatrist and was attempting to move treatment from the facility to the community. In Tonga, by contrast, a psychiatrist controlled the mental health system and sought to consolidate it and control the process in its entirety. As a doctor who had intended to be a surgeon, this doctor was more comfortable in an inpatient treatment setting in order to establish the prescribed treatment regimen. This resulted in a higher emphasis on use of civil commitments and institutional-centred mental health treatment.

In sum, the difference between the formal and informal policy transfers showed little variation between the two cases. Foreign legal experts effectuated formal transfers with only modest indigenous involvement in them. Additionally, and following Tuohy's insights on institutional change, in both cases examined here, each government operated under a Westminster-style parliamentary structure with a highly centralised, disciplined party system making adoption of government legislation nearly certain. Similarly, the presence of interested, enthusiastic indigenous professional policy actors in both places brokered informal transfers. These actors also required relatively fluid bureaucratic structures within which they could manoeuvre. This fluidity might be due to mental health policy's lack of official prioritisation by policy elites in both Samoa and Tonga over the past 60 years.

Divergence was, however, seen at the level of quasi-formal transfer. Specifically, Samoa adopted a mental health policy during the critical years of health reform whilst Tonga failed to do so. Being more participatory in nature, this divergence was ostensibly due to the presence of an actively engaged indigenous actor and the presence of government support of the policy. The reason for Samoa's success and Tonga's incomplete transfer, however, seems to flow from the ideas underlying the quasi-formal policy transfer process. International actors insisted that a written 'policy' instrument be locally driven and led. This was possible in Samoa due to the presence of higher numbers of local mental health actors during the years of opportunity able to marshal this participatory process along, together with a stable political system and a government in support of the health sector reform initiative.

In Tonga, however, there was only one such recognised national focal actor, an increasingly unstable political system, and an ongoing constitutional crisis, making government support of a participatory policy process unlikely. Had the policy simply been vetted at the ministerial level and promulgated, as the respective Mental Health Acts had been, and based on the same international templates Samoa's policy had been based upon, it is highly probable that Tonga, too, would now have a written mental health policy. Instead, since the international actors supporting such efforts insisted on the participatory approach to policy development, transfer on this level failed in Tonga.

References

Acharyya, S. (1996). Practicing cultural psychiatry: The doctor's dilemma. In T. Heller (Ed.), *Mental health matters*. New York: Palgrave Macmillan.

Agnew, F., Pulotu-Ednemann, F., Robinson, G., Suaali-Sauni, T., Warren, H., Wheeler, A., Erick, M., Hingano, T., & Schmidt-Sopoaga, H. (2000). *Pacific models of mental health service delivery in New Zealand ('PMMHSD') project*. Auckland: Health Research Council of New Zealand.

Clement, D. (1982). Samoan folk knowledge of mental disorders. In A. J. Marsella & G. M. White (Eds.), *Cultural conceptions of mental health & therapy*. Dordrecht: D Reidel.

Dolowitz, D., & Marsh, D. (2000). Learning from abroad: The role of policy transfer in contemporary policy-making. *Governance: An International Journal of Policy & Administration, 13*(1), 5–24.

Dolowitz, D., & Marsh, D. (2012). The future of policy transfer research. *Political Studies, 10*, 339–345.

Evans, M. (2004). *Policy transfer in global perspective*. Hants: Ashgate.

Evans, M. (2009). Policy transfer in critical perspective. *Policy Studies, 30*(3), 243–268.

Evans, M., & Davies, J. (1999). Understanding policy transfer: A multi-level, multi-disciplinary perspective. *Public Administration, 77*(2), 361–385.

Fennell, P. (1999). The Third Way in Mental Health Policy: Negative Rights, Positive Rights, & the Convention. *Journal of Law & Society, 26*(1), 103–127.

Government of Samoa. (1961). Mental Health Ordinance.

Government of Samoa. (2007). Samoa Mental Health Act 2007, Apia.

Government of South Australia. (1993). South Australia Mental Health Act.

Hunt, P., & Mesquita, J. (2006). Mental disabilities & the human right to the highest attainable standard of health. *Human Rights Quarterly, 28*(2), 332–356.

Kingdon, J. (1995). *Agendas, alternatives & public policies*. New York: Longman.

Kwon, H.-J. (2009). Policy learning & transfer: The experience of the developmental state in East Asia. *Policy & Politics, 37*(3), 409–421.

Lightfoot, E. (2002). A comparative study of social policy transfer. *The Social Policy Journal, 1*(4), 5–22.

Mintrom, M. (2000). *Policy entrepreneurs & school choice*. Washington, DC: Georgetown University Press.

Mintrom, M., & Vergari, S. (1996). Advocacy coalitions, policy entrepreneurs, & policy change. *Policy Studies Journal, 24*(3), 420–434.

Norris, P., Fa'alau, F., Va'ai, C., Churchward, M., & Arroll, B. (2009). Navigating between illness paradigms: Treatment seeking by Samoan people in Samoa & New Zealand. *Qualitative Health Research, 19*(10), 1466–1475.

Poltorak, M. (2007). Nemesis, speaking, & Tauhi Vaha'a: interdisciplinarity & the truth of 'mental illness' in Vava'u, Tonga. *The Contemporary Pacific, 19*(1).

Puloka, M. (1997). A commonsense perspective on Tongan folk healing. *International Journal of Mental Health, 26*(3), 69–93.

Rochefort, D. (1997). *From poorhouses to homelessness: Policy analysis & mental health care*. Westport: Auburn House.

Smith, L. T. (2012). *Decolonizing methodologies: Research and indigenous peoples*. London/New York: Zed Books Ltd.

Sobralske, M. (2006). OlakinoMaika'i: Health care in Pacific Island culture. *Journal of the American Academy of Nurse Practitioners, 18*, 81–82.

Tews, K. (2009). From law-making to policy making, the environmental dimension of the EU accession process – Challenges, risks & chances for SEE countries. *Environmental Policy & Convergence, 19*, 130–139.

Tuohy, C. H. (1999). *Accidental logics: The dynamics of change in the health care arena in the United States, Britain, and Canada*. New York: Oxford University Press.

Victoria Mental Health Act 1986.

Victorian Government Mental Health Drugs & Regions Division. (2010). *Exposure draft mental health bill 2010: Explanatory guide*. Melbourne: Victorian Government.

Victorian Health Promotion Foundation. (1999). *VicHealth mental health promotion plan, 1999–2002*. Melbourne: Victorian Health Promotion Foundation.

Wilson, J. (2000). Mental health services in New Zealand. *International Journal of Law and Psychiatry, 23*(3–4), 215–228.

Chapter 8
Postscript

Samoa and Tonga both pursued health sector reforms during the early 2000s. Both nations had access to similar international funding and expert personnel. Samoa successfully implemented both mental health law and policy whereas Tonga succeeded in only implementing legislative reform. The critical difference is the internal political division in Tonga versus the relative political stability in Samoa. The divisions in Tonga led to incongruence on the peripheral issue of mental health, which had become inextricably linked to the personality of its chief advocate and policy agent. This led the then Minister of Heath to turn away from formally embracing policy development on mental health issues and likely contributed to the chief psychiatrist's decision to accept an overseas placement and be absent from Tonga for key periods of external policy development resource availability. As such, successful policy transfer of peripheral policy concerns, such as mental health, required several elements in order to fully succeed in such a small context. Firstly, successful transfer required domestic political will and consensus including the presence of a local, indigenous and knowledgeable policy actor who is recognised as a leader in the particular policy field. This actor must also have the necessary political capital to organise the resources necessary for the multistage policy vetting process that must pull together numerous civil society stakeholders. Finally the availability of both aid and expert human capital from international and/or bilateral partners in order to provide technical documents, drafting or other policy consultation as well as to shepherd the process from inception through to adoption must be made available.

The policy opportunity created for mental health system reform through health sector reforms in Samoa and Tonga required the presence of an indigenous policy leader to shepherd the policy development process but not for the law-making process. This is because statutory innovations were led by foreign legal drafters with limited input from local stakeholders whereas the more intensive and localised nature of the policy process necessitated the sustained presence of a locally recognised policy focal/leader for the more gradual process of establishing a formal, written policy. Hence, Samoa successfully implemented both a mental health policy and

T. P. Fadgen, *Mental Health Public Policy in Global Context*,
https://doi.org/10.1007/978-981-15-6479-6_8

Act due to the availability of bilateral and multilateral resources for overall health sector reform and the presence of a psychiatrist and – more importantly – local personnel recognised as mental health leaders in the community. Tonga, in contrast, succeeded in developing a mental health law but not a policy due to two central factors. First, there was continuing political discord that divided the key personalities on mental health and general health, with the Minister representing the more conservative political elements operating within a reformist political context. This led to a reluctance to embrace or support the mental health policy implementation process despite the presence of the international resources to see the process through.

The existence of health systems reform and mental health on their respective agendas didn't bring about change in any meaningful sense in either Samoa or Tonga but it did serve as the catalyst for formal policy transfer. In Tonga, the main mental health policy actor mentioned at different points in the interviews that he remembered finding it odd that the foreign experts insisted on law reform before policy adoption, saying he felt that it amounted to 'putting the cart before the horse'. No one seemed to have that sense of achievement that tends to accompany major legislative enactments following a prolonged battle for change. This seems to be because the policies were essentially adopted because they were asked to adopt them and not because there had been widespread domestic agitation for legislative reforms. This isn't to suggest an absence of desire for such things or even possibly a need for them. These findings suggest that in areas not of central concern to government, like mental health, policy shifts that, in essence, reduce costs (such as moving away from an institutional to community setting and shifting care from formal medical professionals to family caregivers), are less likely to attract formal, institutional opposition.

What is revealing about the attitudes and comments of most of the stakeholders in both Samoa and Tonga is that the formal 'policy' instruments were far less instrumental in bringing substantive change to either nation's mental health system. In both cases, interested indigenous professional actors, after having received a foreign education, returned to their country of origin and confronted institutional arrangements that were unacceptable to their moral sense of right and their knowledge of cultural best practices as insiders. Moreover, formal policies seem to be prepared more for the foreign audience of funders and other international organisations (IOs) themselves.

The more complete picture painted by this book suggests that this omission is a serious shortcoming and likely perpetuates the image of many developing countries as essentially incapable of effectuating such change without direct, foreign intervention to right these inadequate or wholly absent practices. This could not have been farther from the reality in either nation. There does appear to be, for various reasons beyond the scope of enquiry here, questions as to why governments might be hesitant to take on such rigorous policy development undertakings on their own accord. One claim advanced here is that this is an example of path dependency due to the historical dependency of colony or client and the metropolitan power now acting in concert under the aegis of several IOs including the World Bank (WB) and the World Health Organization (WHO), as well as their traditional development partners in New Zealand and Australia. Actors on the ground, such as the medical professionals in Samoa and Tonga, witnessed the failures of the formal past practices and sought change from their professional networks as to best current practice. Since there are not significant institutional barriers to instituting changes, so long as budgets were not increased, change was possible. These leaders also incorporated the ideological shift behind these changes not only in the Western-inspired notion of human rights but more importantly in their particular understandings of their respective cultures, arguing eloquently how the institutional paradigm was anathema to Samoan and Tongan culture.

If an objective of these international human rights-inspired policy agendas is to make lasting change to the domestic policymaking capacity as well as the actual policies themselves, then providing foreign models, expertise and funding without more in the form of policy development capacity building, has been demonstrated through this study to have missed the mark. Reconciling the desire on the part of international agencies to see immediate, demonstrable change as reflected in formal institutional arrangements with the parallel goal of achieving 'sustainability' must be achieved if remote, homogenous populations are ever to grapple with their own perceived or actual public policy problems in future.

In sum, successful policy transfer of matters, which do not have widespread public buy-in and tend to be very personality-driven at the elite level, requires both the external availability of expertise and resources to develop significant, formal policy instruments. This law normalisation is more easily achieved since the instruments itself, the laws, are used by a very small number of specialised elites and can thus be vetted in very tightly controlled, small circles of policy actors. Furthermore, mental health systems are subordinate systems within the predominant health system. The actors within these subsystems do not often have as much prestige relative to other health system actors. As such, mental health systems are seldom the focal point of the global and, as a result, the developing nation agenda. Mental health policy entrepreneurs seem to require the opening of a macrolevel window of opportunity to achieve significant reforms. This apparent institutional inability to act when circumstances would otherwise dictate leaves Samoa's and Tonga's policy environments more reactionary or malleable to foreign development agendas. This extends across policy areas and is a longstanding issue.

Tellingly, Tonga's 1963 Police and Prisons Report lamented

> the tendency of aid donors to give the Kingdom what they feel Tonga ought to have, which is often related to their own development, rather than what Tonga wants is excessively restrictive... and there seems little likelihood of those attitudes changing ... a firm stand must be taken in rejecting imposed aid and implying acceptance of help from completely new sources which have the effect of inducing a change of heart and direction. (Tonga Police Fire Services & Prisons Department 1963, p. 8)

Unless the significant international development presence becomes one of active engagement through a partnership of both objectives and methods, the apparent lack of institutional confidence in policymaking elites in places like Samoa and Tonga, as outlined in this book, is likely to endure. It is not due to a lack of ability, sophistication, creativity or wisdom that changes were not made independent of international intervention – rather that the past practices and patterns of interaction have themselves become institutionalised and their inertial manifestations path dependent. In other words, whenever significant aspects of the 'modernisation' project arise, the availability of lawyers, foreign expert consultants, and donor funds creates strong incentives for a developing state to act. These states act to demonstrate their commitment to modernisation and it makes sense from a purely rational perspective: an offer is made to fund, either completely or substantially, reforms that are meant to improve the long-term fiscal health of the borrowing nation.

As Kwon (2009) and Tews (2009) argue, however, the fundamental dilemma posed by such a policymaking paradigm is that it tends to cause stagnation in the domestic policy agenda whereby peripheral policy areas, such as has been seen in mental health, have periods of change followed by long periods of 'stability' (or more likely in our context, the changes merely fade into the background as a nonfactor). The pattern that emerges is one where the change-trigger is never one caused by an endogenous shock; it is only brought about where the international policy agenda drives a particular policy outcome. Hence, despite decades of indigenous mental health innovation in Samoa and Tonga pursued by indigenous, professional policy actors, formal policy and law reforms did not take place until neoliberal institutional reforms to each nation's health sector created an opportunity for change.

Moreover, the governments of Samoa and Tonga have proceeded deliberately when it comes to formally adopting international instruments related to disability that would perhaps create greater momentum for broader policy and social change. While both governments have signed on to the Convention on the Rights of Persons with Disabilities (CRPD), only Samoa has ratified the convention and this only in 2016. In 2017, Tonga held a national Mental Health Symposium headed-up by a Dr. Leonaitasi Hoponoa, now the President of Tonga's new Mental Health Association. This forum reiterated the general view that Tonga's government does not prioritise mental health in the Kingdom. This is reflected in the lack of a dedicated mental health policy and strategy and less than robust support for the Kingdom's mental health system. Meanwhile, Samoa is not fairing much better. Whilst Samoa has ratified the CRPD, a major potential step forward for individuals with disabilities, the disability community's recent hopes of seeing the Mental Health Act amended amended to broaden and update its protections were unsuccessful. This despite calls from the nation's Ombudsman and the United Nations to undertake these revisions to the Act. Yet, there are encouraging signs that emerge out of these recent events. Firstly, advocacy for change is far more localised than in the past. While some institutional resistance to change endures, these might be considered to be political in nature, much as disability and mental health issues tend to be in nearly any other context. This means that the situation is ripe for domestic interest groups and advocacy coalitions to work with institutional champions, such as Ministries of Health, Ombudsmen and International Organisation partners to bring about reforms that make these policies and laws more alive and responsive to public opinion. This would be a vast improvement over the past 100 years of experience has outlined in this book where legislative and policy changes tended to only occur due to some exogenous shock (e.g. colonisation/foreign influence, decolonisation, part of neoliberal policy diffusion).

These observations continue to raise questions about the sustainability theme at the heart of contemporary development agendas since if policy change is really only effectuated when the international policy agenda elevates a particular cause and global actors are willing to finance the reforms, the only thing being sustained is the underlying modernisation project itself. If, however, the principles underlying such rhetoric are to have true currency, then what is required is a sustained, cross-cultural dialogue. The Samoan and Tongan 'contexts' shouldn't be used simply to remove central aspects of Western laws and policies to account for the perceived limitations of the recipient nation. Instead, the skills, expertise and understanding of local professionals, policymakers and stakeholders should be used to clearly establish and inform the values any policy instrument might contain and promote. International actors must recognise that they do not have perfect understanding and perhaps cannot have such an understanding of these social and cultural contexts. Sustainability should mean, at a minimum, that the laws and policies that develop or do not develop in these states must be their own and be informed by their own understandings of themselves and of their needs, while founded upon an enduring indigenous policy process.

Reflecting upon this, our perspective might be deepened to recognise that the purpose of research of this nature is not to discover some external 'reality'; it is rather to have an opportunity for reflection on our own nature. Constructing the 'Samoan context' or the process of converting psychiatric notions into Tongan and adapting modern psychiatry to the cultural context of a traditional collectivist society was, as the many instances of transfer that have come before them, not a one-way motion. Indeed, the longevity of institutions of all sorts in both countries can be attributed to their adaptability and that of the respective populations. Foreign expert consultants constructed a notion of the Samoan and Tongan contexts based on their individual interpretations of Samoan and Tongan reality and used these notions to pare away what they deemed to be needless appendages of model laws. Indigenous practitioners, in contrast, used their professional and cultural-insider status to broaden the Western notions bound up with mental illness. In both Samoa and Tonga, Western psychiatry was recast to serve indigenous values of community and family-based interventions.

The policy transfers discussed in this book tended to follow a familiar pattern: foreign laws brought in to suit external notions of appropriateness gather dust as they fall into disuse and become dismissed as the laws of a metropolitan power. Practitioners or policymakers did not make linkages between fundamental rights and the impact of laws from eras prior to these rights being valued and enforced. Institutions that bring together the best aspects of the foreign with the indigenous, such as Lands and Titles Courts, endure. These succeeded in that they were used and trusted by wide pluralities in both countries. In these most recent mental health policy transfers, key insiders, who were included in the policy and law development process, laying the foundations on an informal basis, have advanced the objective of crafting a sustainable health regulatory regime to the point where these measures might possibly not only endure, but also overcome the institutional confines of the past.

References

Kwon, H-J. (2009). Policy learning & transfer: the experience of the developmental state in East Asia. *Policy & Politics, 37*(3), 409–421.

Tews, K. (2009). From law-taking to policy-making. The environmental dimension of the EU accession process – challenges, risks and chances for the SEE countries. *Env. Pol. Gov.*, 19: 130–139. doi:10.1002/eet.498.

Tonga Police Fire Services & Prisons Department, 1950–1992. (1963). *Tonga Police Force, Tonga Fire Services, & Prisons Department Annual Reports*. Nuku'alofa: Tonga Police Force.

Appendix 1: Timeline of Key UN General Assembly Measures, WHO Initiatives and International Conventions related to Mental Health

1. 1965 – International Convention on the Elimination of All Forms of Discrimination, Article 5(e)(iv)
2. 1975 – Declaration on the Rights of Disabled Persons
3. 1976 – International Covenant on Economic, Social and Cultural Rights (ICESCR), Article 12
4. 1976 – International Covenant on Civil and Political Rights (ICCPR), Art. 7
5. 1979 – Convention on the Elimination of All Forms of Discrimination against Women, Articles 11.1(f) and 12
6. 1981 – International Year of the Disabled Person
7. 1982 – World Programme of Action Concerning Disabled Persons
8. 1984 – UN Convention against Torture and Other Cruel, Inhuman or Degrading Treatment or Punishment, Art 16
9. 1984 – Siracusa Principles on the Limitation and Derogation of Provisions in the International Covenant on Civil and Political Rights
10. 1983-1992 – UN Decade of Disabled Persons
11. 1989 – Convention on the Rights of the Child
12. 1990 – Declaration of Caracas
13. 1991 – Principles for the Protection of Persons with Mental Illness
14. 1993 – Standard Rules on the Equalization of Opportunities for Persons with Disabilities
15. 1994 – Salamanca Statement and framework for Action on Special Needs Education
16. 1996 – Declaration of Madrid
17. 1996 – WHO Technical Standards (Mental Health Care Law: 10 Basic Principles & Guidelines for the Promotion of Human Rights of Persons with Mental Disorders)
18. 2001 – Mental Health as theme of World Health Day
19. 2001 – Mental Health as subject of World Health Report
20. 2002 – WHO Western Pacific Region creates a 'Regional Strategy' for addressing mental illness in the region

T. P. Fadgen, *Mental Health Public Policy in Global Context*,
https://doi.org/10.1007/978-981-15-6479-6

21. 2005 – 'Situational Analysis of Mental Health Needs and Resources in Pacific Island Countries' is published by WHO and the University of Auckland
22. 2008 – Convention on the Rights of Persons with Disabilities and Optional Protocol comes into effect

Glossary

SAMOAN	ENGLISH
aiga	family
aitu	spirits
ali'i sili	parliament of district representatives
fa'amatai	house of matai (traditional governance structure)
fa'aSamoa	the 'Samoan' way
fono	council
fono a le nu'u	village council
Komiti Tumama	women's committee
matai	chief/titled person
nu'u	village
pulenu'u	village mayors/police authorities
ta'imua	advisory group of representatives of the leading titles

TONGAN	ENGLISH
anga faka Tonga	the Tongan way
'api	home
'atamaifaingata'a'ia	mental illness
'avanga	acute short sickness due to possession
fono	village meetings
kāinga	extended family/relative
mana	supernatural origins
Papālangi	white/European
tapu	customary prohibition

T. P. Fadgen, *Mental Health Public Policy in Global Context*,
https://doi.org/10.1007/978-981-15-6479-6

Index

T. P. Fadgen, *Mental Health Public Policy in Global Context*,
https://doi.org/10.1007/978-981-15-6479-6

The manufacturer's authorised representative in the EU is Springer Nature Customer Service Centre GmbH, Europaplatz 3, 69115 Heidelberg, Germany. If you have any concerns regarding our products, please contact ProductSafety@springernature.com

Printed and bound by CPI Group (UK) Ltd, Croydon, CR0 4YY
30/09/2026
02225325-0005